IMAGES
of Rail

Portland's Interurban Railway

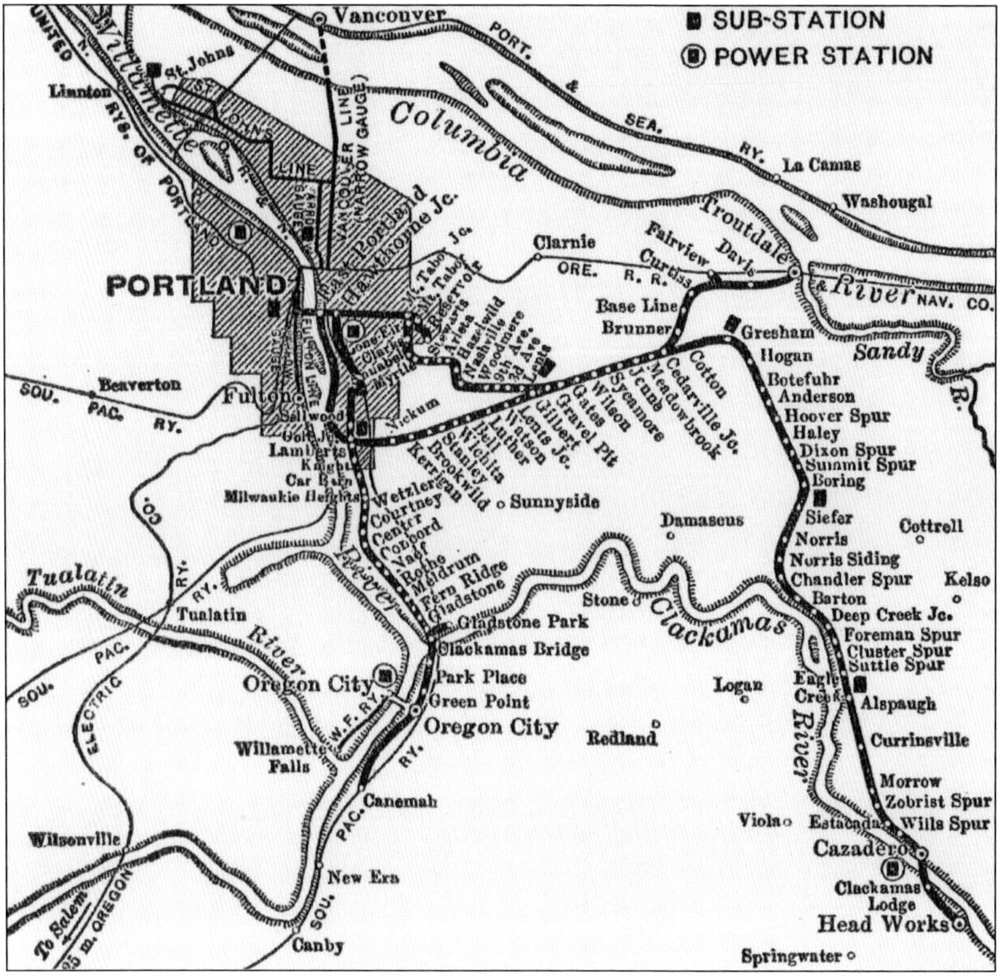

This 1909 *Electric Railway Journal* map shows the Portland Railway, Light & Power Company's interurban lines to Oregon City and Estacada, as well as the branches to Gladstone Park, Troutdale, and Mount Scott. Also illustrated are the Bull Run Line, which was still part of Mount Hood Railway & Power, and the interurban-like, narrow-gauge city division lines to St. Johns and Vancouver. (Author's collection.)

On the Cover: Service on the Estacada Line began with a single mixed train in 1904. The only city along the line was Gresham, with a population of 150. Things changed after the Oregon Water Power & Railway Company built the town of Estacada. Within months, seven trains operated daily, and, as can be seen on this postcard photograph taken in front of the Hotel Estacada, Sunday ridership increased dramatically. (Courtesy Mark Moore.)

IMAGES
of Rail

PORTLAND'S INTERURBAN RAILWAY

Richard Thompson

ARCADIA
PUBLISHING

ISBN 978-0-7385-9617-4

Published by Arcadia Publishing
Charleston, South Carolina

Printed in the United States of America

Library of Congress Control Number: 2012940882

For all general information, please contact Arcadia Publishing:
Telephone 843-853-2070
Fax 843-853-0044
E-mail sales@arcadiapublishing.com
For customer service and orders:
Toll-Free 1-888-313-2665

Visit us on the Internet at www.arcadiapublishing.com

Dedicated to my uncle Stuart Bradley Webb (1920–2004), who fostered my love for streetcars.

Contents

ACKNOWLEDGMENTS

As always, when researching electric railways, I am grateful to my late friends, and fellow trolley enthusiasts, William K. "Bill" Hayes, G. Charles "Chuck" Bukowsky, and John T. Labbe, for their encouragement over the 30 years spent gathering the materials used in my books. This volume would not have been possible without their assistance.

I also wish to thank Roy Bonn, Eileen Fitzsimons, Norm Gholston, Kenn Lantz, Mark Moore, Steve Morgan, Don Nelson, Jerry Risberg, and James West for graciously sharing images from their collections.

I am very grateful to my partner, Jan Hofmann, and my friend Tracy Brown for diligently proofreading the manuscript through its inevitable permutations and for helping select images.

Unless otherwise noted, all images in this book are from the author's collection. Original photographers are cited wherever possible. Detailed car rosters can be found on the author's website, vintagetrolleys.com.

INTRODUCTION

During the first decades of the 20th century, the nation witnessed the rise and fall of the electric interurban railway, a transportation phenomenon that was to play a vital role in the period between the time in which intercity travelers depended on steam railroads and one in which rubber-tired transit reigned supreme. Although initially thought to hold unlimited potential, this interurban era was cut short by the advent of affordable automobiles.

In Oregon, as elsewhere, the time of the interurban began with a surge in railway building. Portland became the hub of an electric rail network as the Oregon Electric Railway and the Southern Pacific Railroad built competing lines through the Willamette Valley to Eugene (122 miles away) and Corvallis (88 miles distant). However, this book is not about the long-distance interurbans. That history is set forth in the author's previous Arcadia work, *Willamette Valley Railways*, in the Images of Rail series. This volume tells the story of the locally developed Portland interurbans that led the way.

Suburban electric railways were preceded during the 1880s by steam "dummy" railroads, so called because they utilized railroad coaches pulled by small locomotives enclosed in wooden bodies resembling streetcars. Pioneering narrow-gauge railroads and steam dummy lines established the first links to outlying communities. Interestingly, none of them had a downtown terminus, even after bridges were built. The Morrison Street Bridge crossed the Willamette River in 1887, followed in 1888 by the Steel Bridge, and the Madison Street Bridge in 1891, but those spans would be used by horsecars or trolleys.

Steam-driven streetcars were an Industrial Age solution to the challenge horsecars faced in trying to reach distant suburbs. Their design was also much better adapted to city running than were large railroad locomotives. Even so, it was not enough for everyone; many considered the smoke, steam, and whirling machinery a nuisance, as well as a danger to passing horses. The eastside city of Albina passed an ordinance banning their use through town. Expense, in addition to this civic opposition, caused the companies operating railways into the countryside to turn to steam dummy locomotives only as a temporary expedient.

As the move toward electrification got under way, two affiliated Portland companies, the Metropolitan Railway and the East Side Railway, ordered trolleys designed for use in a more railroad-like environment. These vehicles may not have looked like later rolling stock, but they were the first rudimentary interurbans and catapulted Oregon into the forefront of a new age.

Streetcars had run between cities before the East Side Railway began building its line from Portland to Oregon City. The Newark and Granville Street Railway in Ohio, which began on December 28, 1889, is sometimes credited with being the first interurban in the country, but it was a seven-mile streetcar line that became part of an interurban network later. There were also two intercity electrics in Washington State in 1891, however, the Fidalgo & Anacortes Railway ceased operating after a couple of days, and the Tacoma & Steilacoom Railway started as a city line through the woods. The Oregon system would prove to be unique.

The East Side Railway completed the first true interurban line in the United States on February 16, 1893. It was the first to use electricity generated by hydroelectric power and the first to operate in a manner similar to that of a mainline steam railroad. The 14-mile route between Portland and Oregon City operated cars at speed, largely outside city limits, over mostly private rights-of-way. The railway hauled freight and carried mail and express packages. Its rolling stock evolved into heavier, longer, railroad-style cars that bore little resemblance to streetcars. Most passengers boarded at waiting stations instead of street corners.

In 1903, successor Oregon Water Power & Railway Company added the longest line, a 35-mile run eastward to Estacada. Further extensions were added after the Portland Railway, Light & Power Company (PRL&P) consolidated interurban and city lines in 1906. The Troutdale branch opened in 1907. In 1913, PRL&P electrified the 30-mile Bull Run Line begun by the Mount Hood Railway.

PRL&P also converted several former steam dummy routes into electric operations that initially resembled interurban lines. This was particularly true of rolling stock. Some of the narrow-gauge, interurban-style cars on the St. Johns and Vancouver lines were too long for the tracks running into downtown Portland until the right-of-way was modified. The Mount Scott Line to Lents used actual interurban cars at first because it was an interurban branch that inherited standard-gauge equipment from the Oregon City and Estacada lines. These lines began to evolve into suburban streetcar operations during the 1910s as veteran cars were replaced by ones similar in appearance to city trolleys.

The major railroads, driven by ambitions to rival steam railroads, created electric interurban networks south and west of Portland. The region east of the Willamette River, lacking large population centers, was left to Portland's street railway company. PRL&P would carve its own, albeit smaller-scale, empire from the groundwork begun by predecessor companies whose grandiose dreams had included interurban routes to Salem, Eugene, Mount Hood, Eastern Oregon, and the state of Washington. These lines, operated later on by the Portland Electric Power Company and finally by the Portland Traction Company, experienced little change until the 1930s.

The interurban character of the Oregon City and Springwater Divisions began to fade during the last years of passenger service, when secondhand metal-bodied streetcars made their appearance. The replacement of traditional wooden rolling stock with more modern suburban trolleys began in 1940. The final batch of used cars arrived from Los Angeles in 1953.

Service reductions were made on the Oregon City and Gresham lines, yet the interurban ticket office and waiting room in Portland remained at the center of it all until access across the Hawthorne Bridge was cut in 1956. Two years later, on January 25, 1958, America's first true interurban became one of the last to be abandoned.

Revival began in September 1986, when the Tri-County Metropolitan Transportation District of Oregon (Tri-Met) returned electric railway transit to the Portland area after an absence of nearly 30 years. As new light-rail lines are added to a growing Metropolitan Area Express (MAX) system, their tracks often follow in the footsteps of the historic interurban lines.

One

Steam Interurbans

THE DUMMY LINES

The time of the electric interurban railway had not yet arrived when the first Portland area railroad companies laid tracks to outlying communities north, south, and east of town. Since these suburbs were beyond the reach of horse-drawn streetcars, and conversion to electric trolleys was not yet feasible, most initial efforts relied on small locomotives housed in streetcar-like wooden bodies designed to be less frightening to passing horses. These mechanized "dummy" streetcars were the predecessors of today's light-rail vehicles.

Willamette Bridge Railway introduced the first steam dummies on July 9, 1888. Their Mount Tabor Steam Line reached Southeast Sixty-ninth and Belmont Streets on June 7, 1889. From September 1892 until July 1894, an extension to Russellville (Southeast 102nd and Stark) was operated by the Portland, Mount Tabor & Eastern Railway. The Mount Tabor Line was converted to electric operation in 1896.

The Portland & Vancouver Railway inaugurated dummy service to the Columbia River on September 15, 1888. Before bridges were built, the route was from the Stark Street Ferry to the Columbia Ferry. The line was electrified in June 1893.

On June 21, 1889, the Mount Tabor Street Railway Company commenced operation on a steam railroad to Southeast Fifty-fifth Street and Hawthorne Avenue. On June 18, 1892, the Portland, Chicago & Mount Scott Railroad added an extension to Lents. Electrification began in 1891 and was completed to Lents in June 1901.

The Willamette Bridge Railway's steam service to St. Johns opened on November 1, 1889, in conjunction with the first trolley in Portland. The St. Johns Line was electrified in 1903.

On November 5, 1890, the City & West Portland Park Motor Company opened a steam dummy line from South Portland to the development of West Portland Park near Southwest Barbur Boulevard. The railway failed in the Panic of 1893, before a planned city trolley division could begin using a unique counterbalance assist system on Hamilton Street.

In time, these electric railway forerunners were either abandoned or absorbed into the city streetcar system. The 1890s would mark the beginning of the electric interurban era.

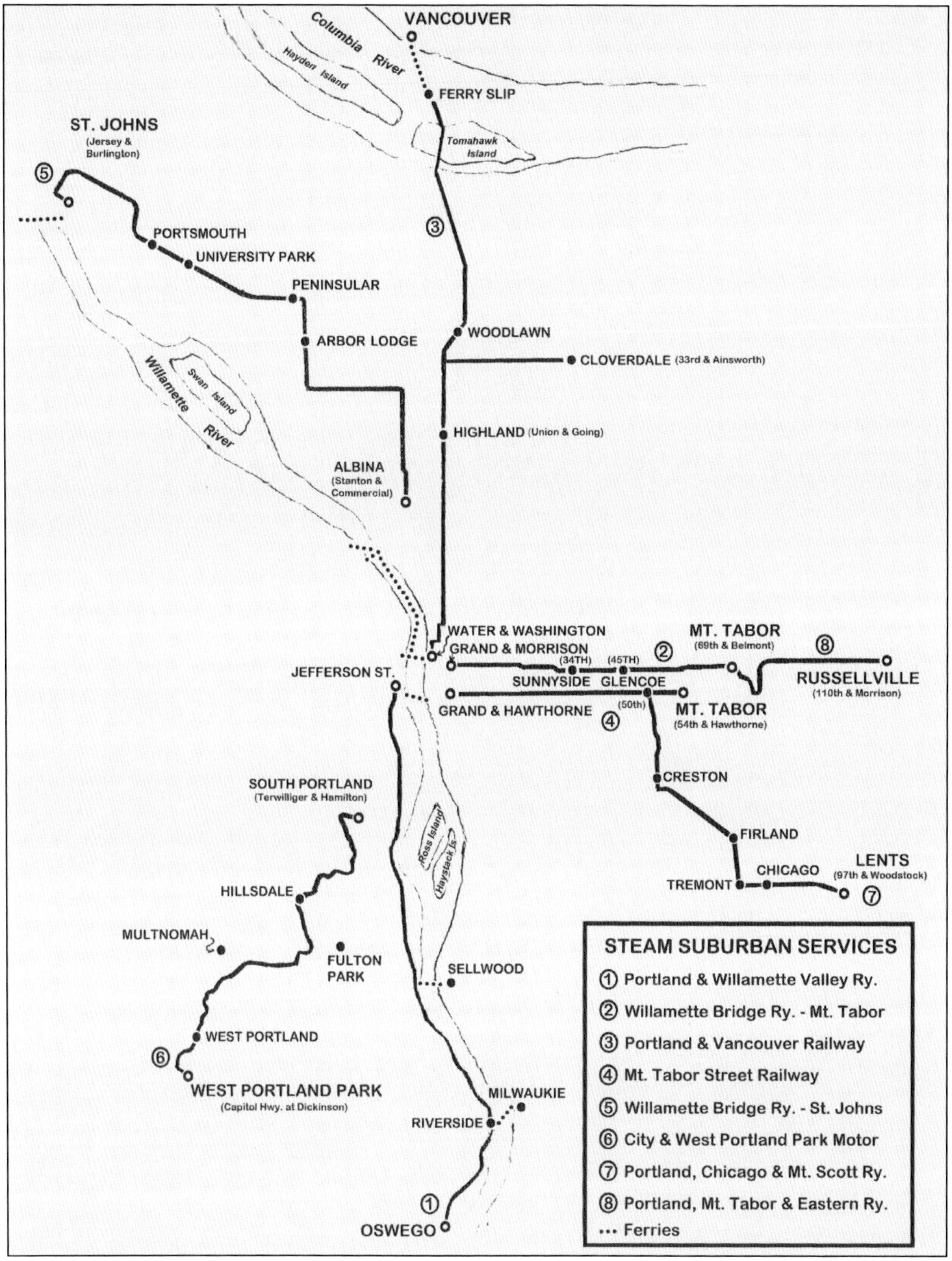

This map showing Portland area steam suburban services during 1888–1893 is based on a drawing done by rail historian David L. Stearns. These railways were the steam-powered forerunners of the electric interurban railways, and most of them went on to become interurban-like streetcar lines. All but the first of these (the narrow-gauge Portland & Willamette Valley Railway) were operated with steam dummy locomotives.

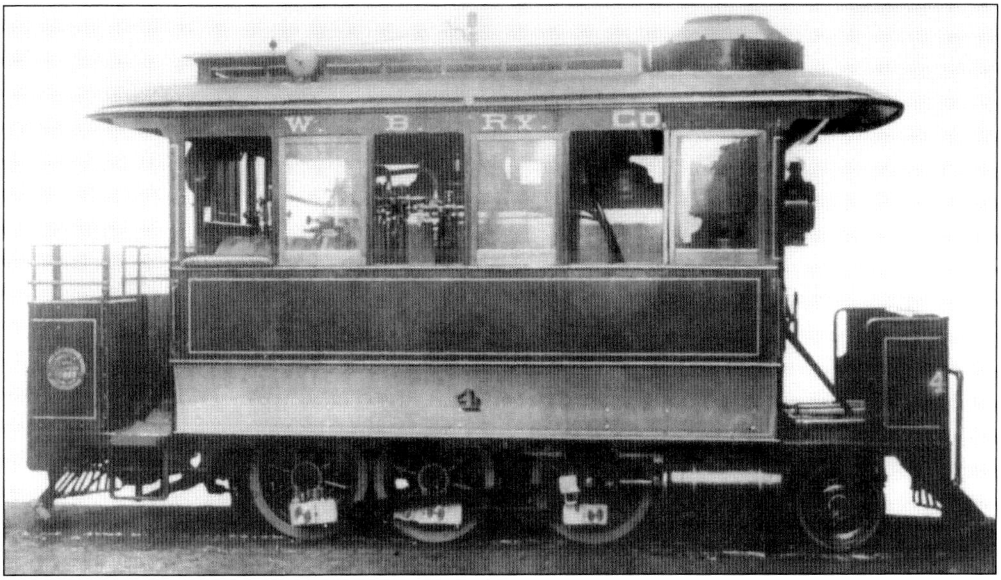

Trains on Portland's first suburban railways were usually pulled by small steam locomotives, known as "dummies" because they were enclosed in wooden bodies resembling streetcars. No. 4, seen in this photograph at the Baldwin Locomotive Works in March 1890, was the heaviest dummy yet ordered by the Willamette Bridge Railway. The 2-6-0 engine was a 25-ton "monster" capable of pulling any number of passenger cars up the slopes alongside Mount Tabor.

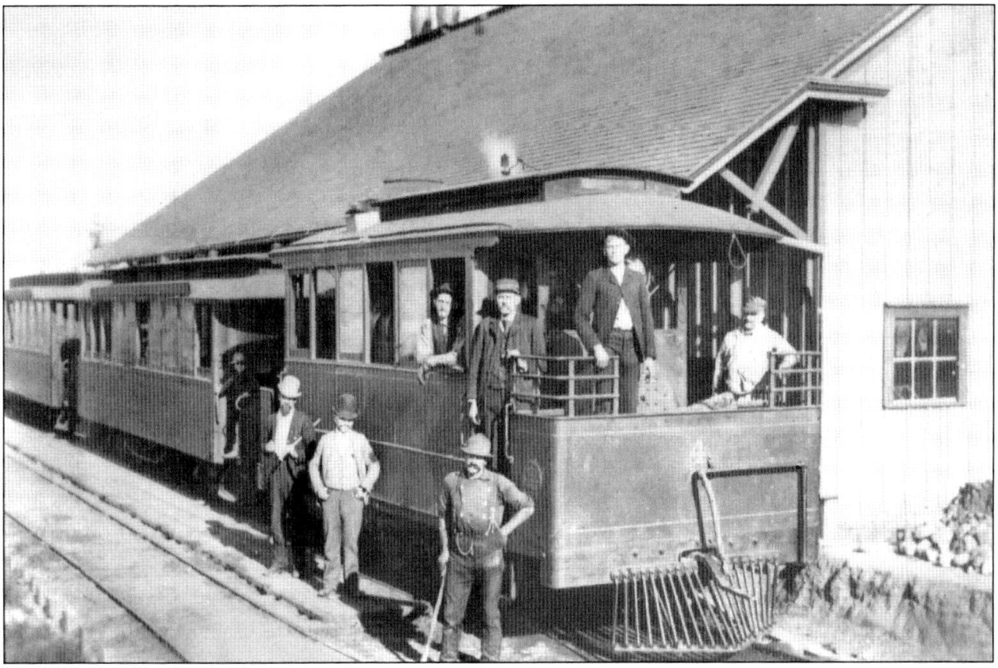

In 1889, the Mount Tabor Line was extended eastward from Sunnyside to this site atop Mount Tabor at present-day Southeast Sixty-ninth Avenue and Belmont Street. Motor No. 4 and two trailers are seen next to the locomotive shed. Shown are, from left to right, the following: (on the ground) two unidentified men and Daniel Hooker; (in train) Pete Kerney (in window), conductor Charles Shaw, unidentified, and engineer Ben Speake. (Courtesy Jerry Risberg.)

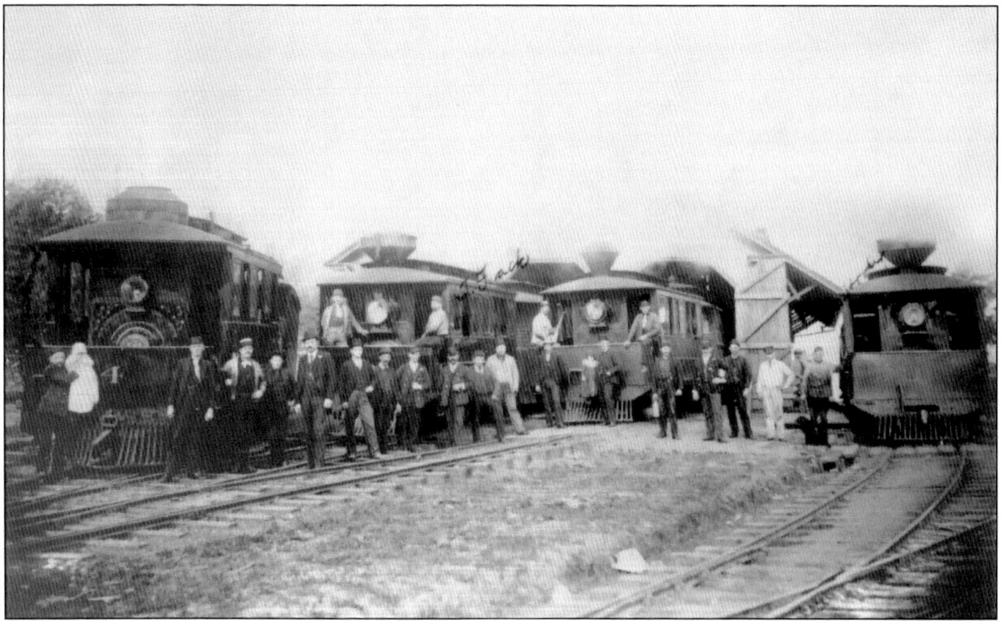

City & Suburban Railway steam motor crews, including manager Homer Campbell (fifth from left), pose at the Mount Tabor locomotive shed in the summer of 1892. The C&S had taken over from Willamette Bridge Railway the previous September. On the left are dummies Nos. 4, 2, and 3, and on the right is No. 1 of the Portland, Mount Tabor & Eastern, which C&S operated under contract.

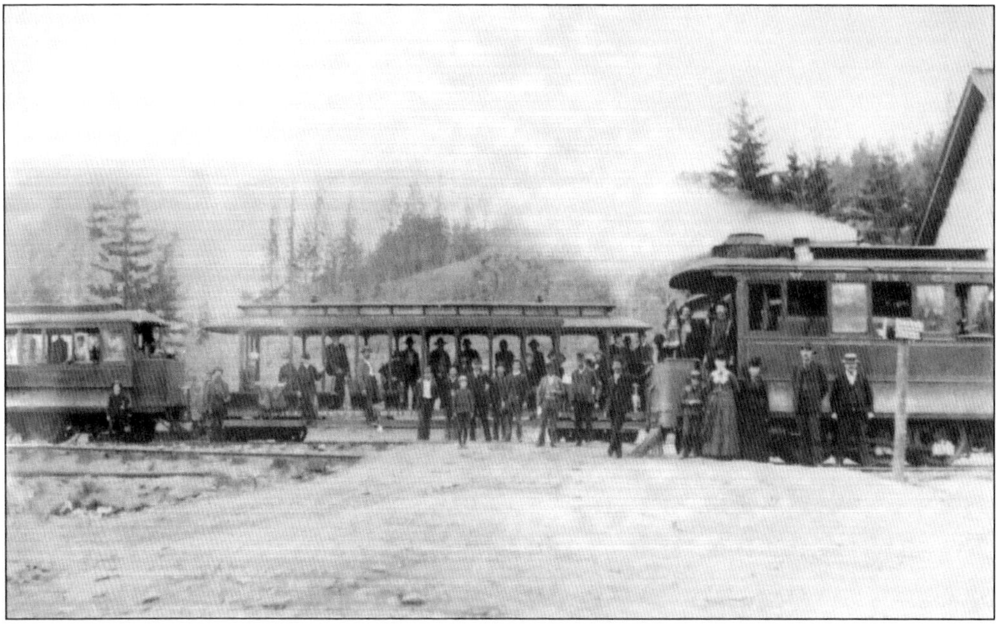

Two trains are seen at the Mount Tabor terminal around 1893. The locomotive and coach on the left is ready to depart for Russellville on the Portland, Mount Tabor & Eastern Railway, while the Mount Tabor Line train at right has arrived from East Portland. The Willamette Bridge Railway had become the City & Suburban Railway in 1891, but rolling stock was not relettered for several years.

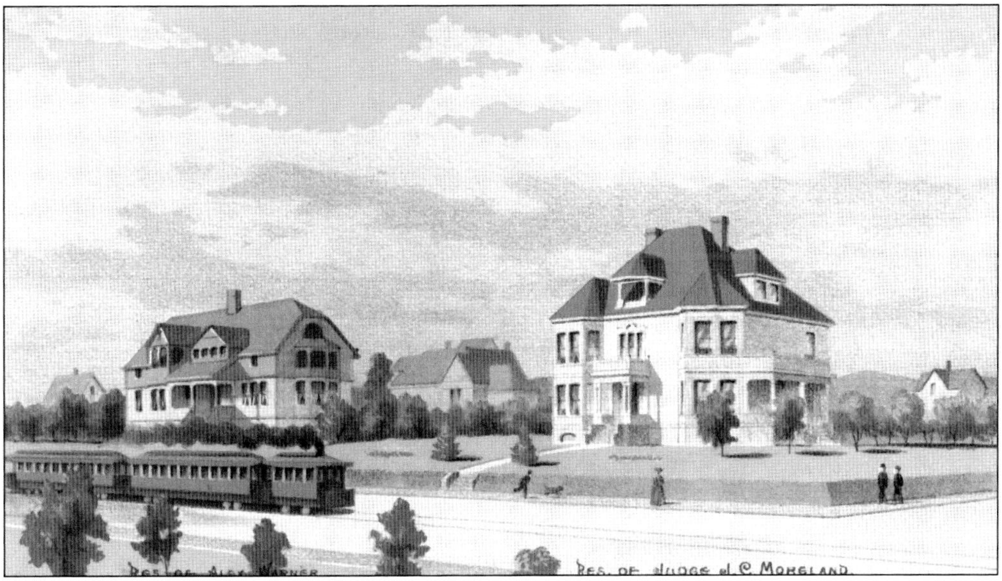

This 1890s Clayton and Oliver Company color advertisement promoting the "charming residences on the beautiful western slope of Mount Tabor" depicts a two-coach steam dummy train passing the residences of Alex Warner and Judge J.C. Moreland. The new train was an integral part of a development that already included a schoolhouse and lots with choice young fruit trees. (Courtesy Norm Gholston.)

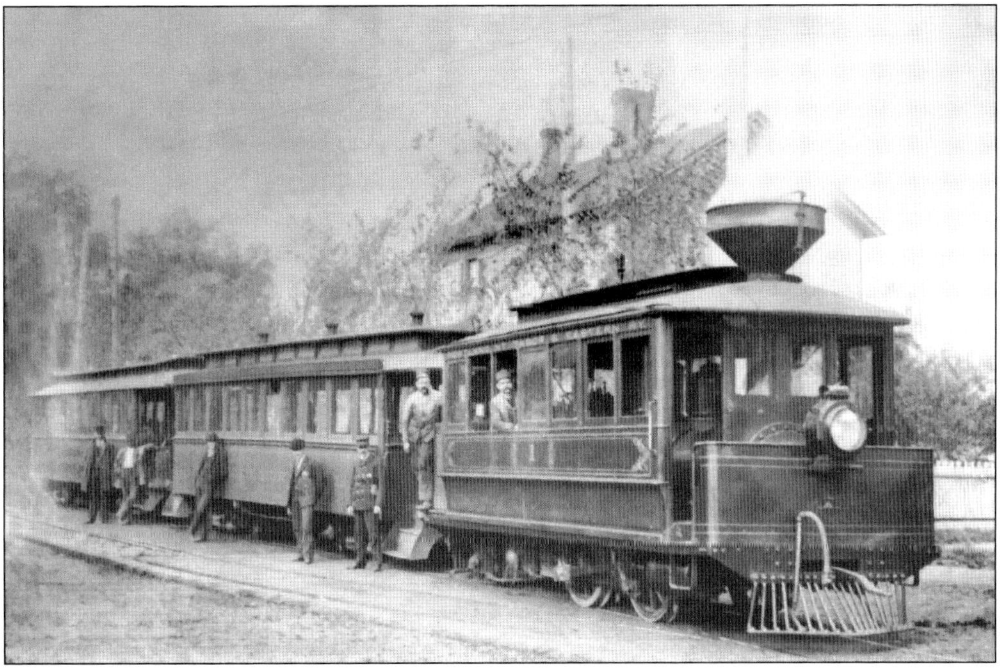

From 1892 to 1894, the Portland, Mount Tabor & Eastern Railway ran from Mount Tabor to Southeast 102nd Avenue and Stark Street in Russellville, the farthest east any interurban traveled for many years. After the company went bankrupt, locomotive No. 1 was transferred to the Mount Tabor Line. It is seen here with two coaches at the East Portland terminus on Southeast Morrison Street at Southeast Sixth Avenue.

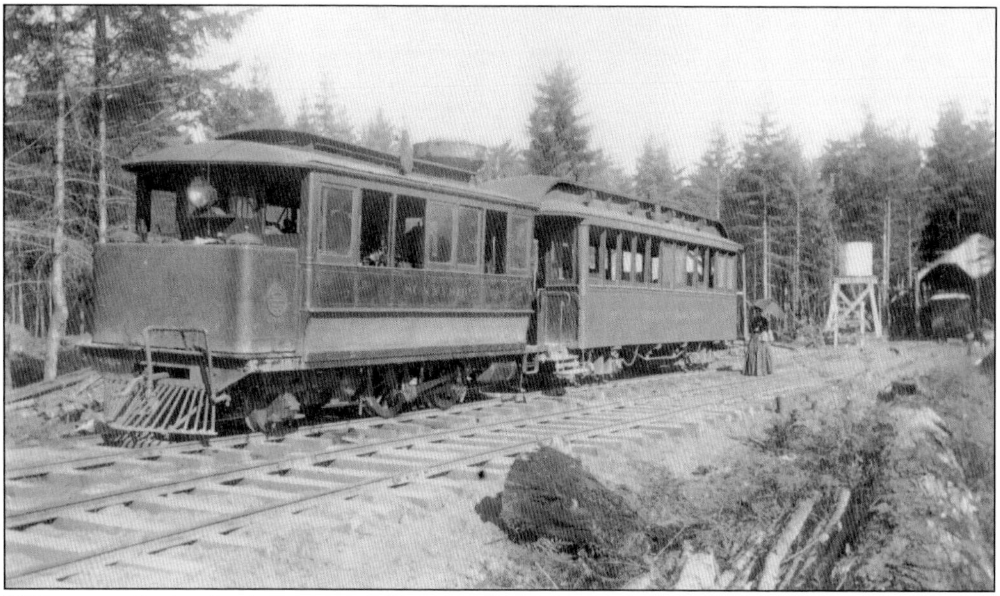

Willamette Bridge Railway engine No. 2 and coach No. 10, seen here at the Mount Tabor locomotive shed, was the first train on the partially completed St. Johns Line. On November 1, 1889, Willamette Bridge Railway president Homer Campbell and a dozen friends rode the first trolley on the Pacific Coast. Partway along, they transferred to this dummy train for the trip up to Smith's Farm, a mile from St. Johns.

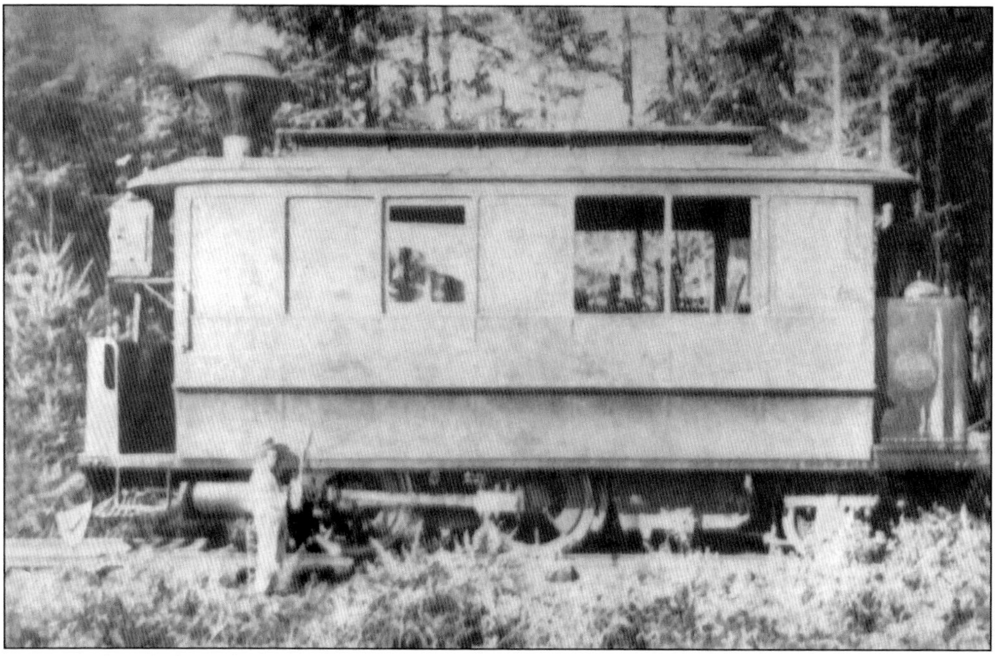

A young boy helps oil a St. Johns Line steam dummy locomotive (either No. 2 or 3) in this charming 1890s snapshot. The Portland Peninsula was predominantly rural at this time, and the line that traversed it would be the last steam railway built in Portland. By the time the St. Johns Line opened, Portland had more steam dummy engines than all the rest of the Pacific Northwest combined.

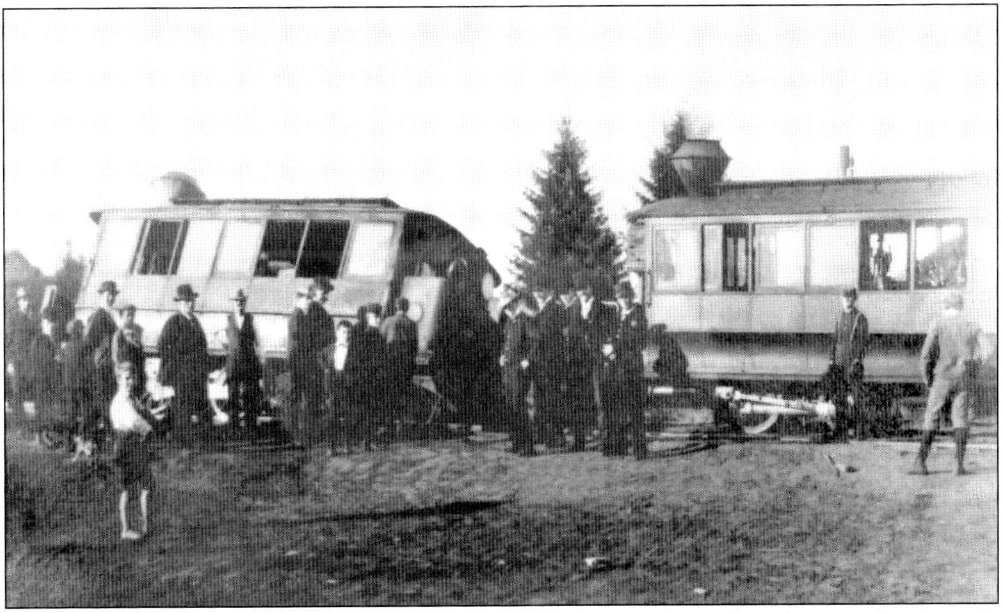

Things did not always go smoothly on suburban steam motor lines, but, fortunately, the only thing injured in this accident was the schedule. While crews worked to clear up a derailment on the St. Johns Line, and policemen posed, one of the locomotive firemen joined the onlookers to take this picture of Willamette Bridge Railway steam dummy engines No. 2 and No. 3.

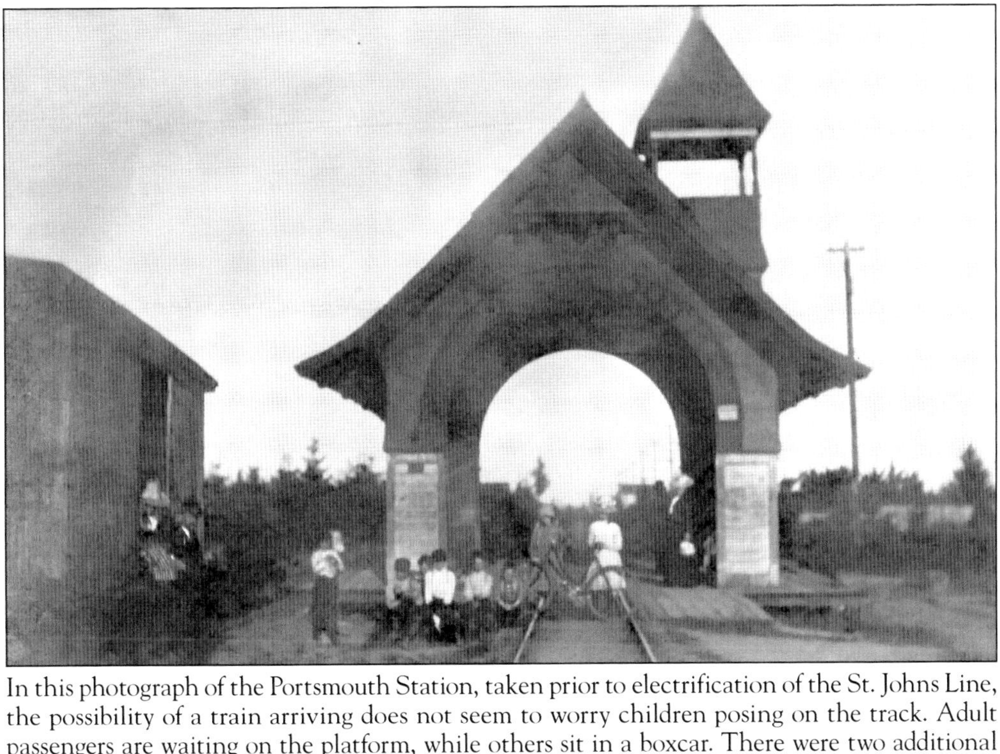

In this photograph of the Portsmouth Station, taken prior to electrification of the St. Johns Line, the possibility of a train arriving does not seem to worry children posing on the track. Adult passengers are waiting on the platform, while others sit in a boxcar. There were two additional locomotive sheds on the Willamette Bridge system: at North Stanton and Commercial Streets in Albina, and on Mount Tabor. (Courtesy Don Nelson.)

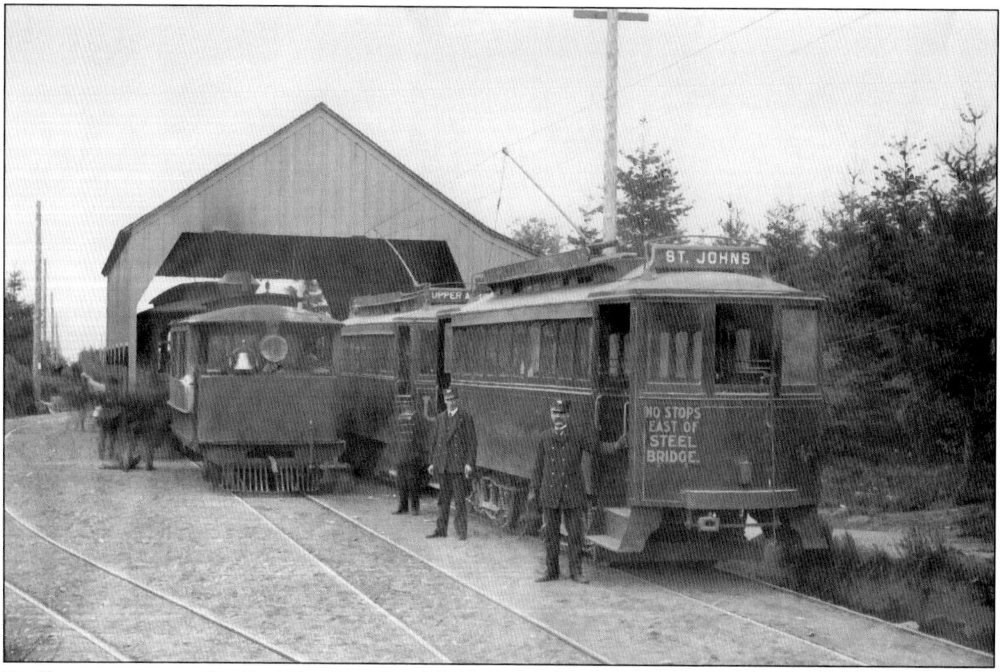

Trolleys met trains for St. Johns at the Albina transfer station during the steam dummy years. The original transfer point had been at North Goldsmith (now Interstate) and Russell Streets, but after the City & Suburban Railway took over in September 1891, the transfer station was moved to North Moore and Killingsworth Streets. The shed seen in the above photograph remained in use until two years after electrification in 1903.

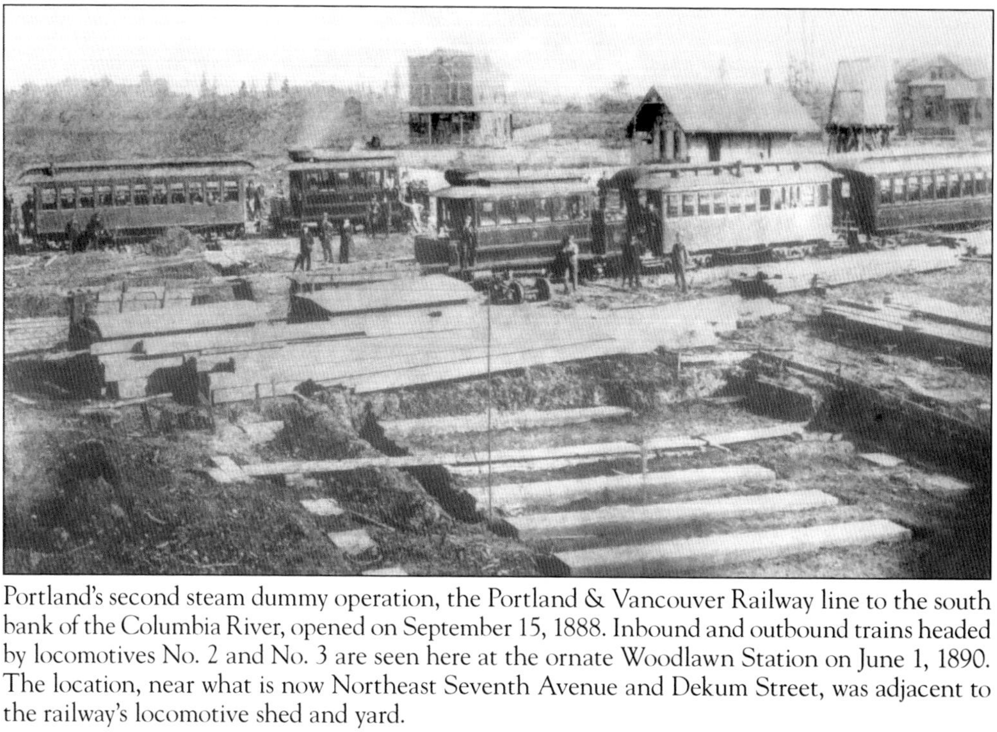

Portland's second steam dummy operation, the Portland & Vancouver Railway line to the south bank of the Columbia River, opened on September 15, 1888. Inbound and outbound trains headed by locomotives No. 2 and No. 3 are seen here at the ornate Woodlawn Station on June 1, 1890. The location, near what is now Northeast Seventh Avenue and Dekum Street, was adjacent to the railway's locomotive shed and yard.

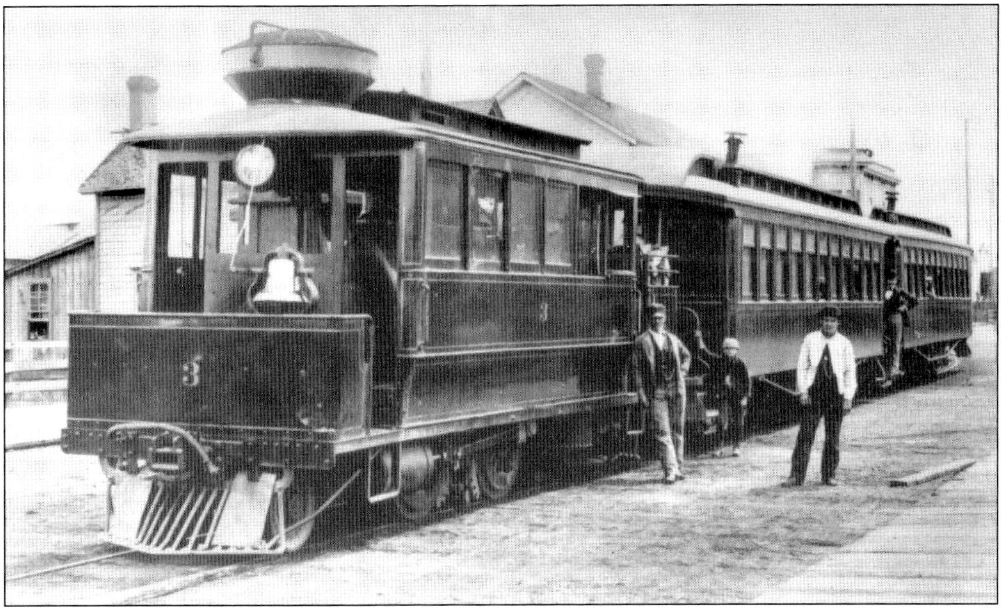

Before bridges crossed the Willamette and Columbia Rivers, Portland & Vancouver Railway passengers caught ferries at each end of the line. In a photograph taken around 1892, motor No. 3 is waiting at the East Portland terminus for Vancouver-bound passengers from the Stark Street Ferry. The railway ticket office and station were nearby on Southeast Water and Washington Streets.

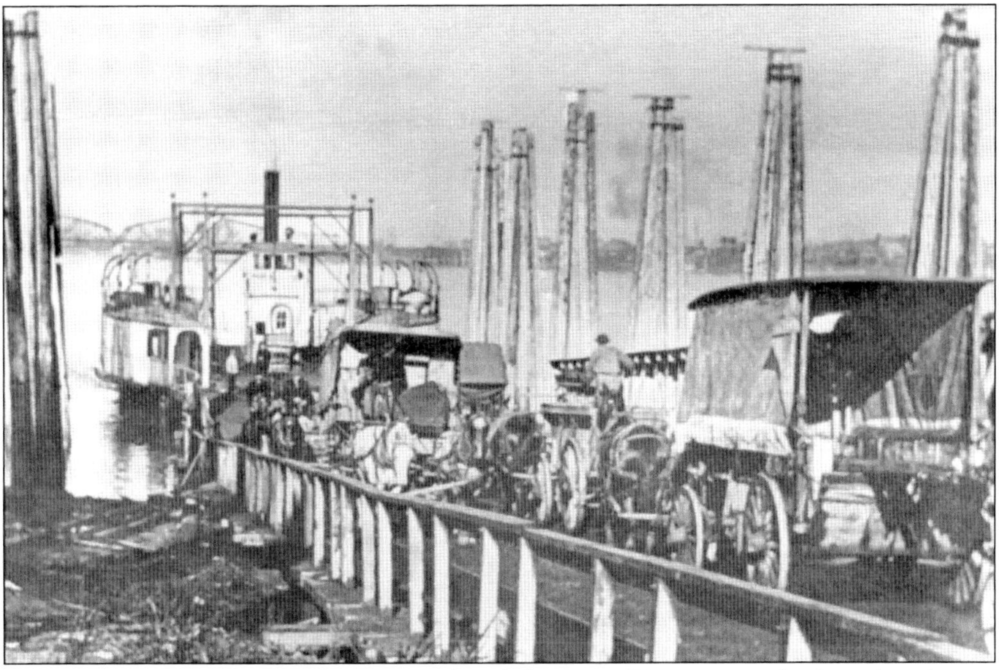

Passengers and cargo are seen lining up to board the *City of Vancouver* at the ferry slip adjacent to the Portland & Vancouver Railway depot on Tomahawk Island. The side-wheeler was built at the St. Johns Boat Yard in 1909. In the background is the Columbia River Railroad Bridge, the first span across the Columbia. Ferry service was discontinued on January 2, 1917, following completion of the Interstate Bridge.

PORTLAND AND VANCOUVER

RAILWAY CO.

The Popular Route for Tourists to

VIEW MOUNT HOOD

And the Snow-Capped Ranges,

— AND THE —

MAGNIFICENT SCENERY OF THE COLUMBIA RIVER.

QUICK TIME. PULLMAN CARS. BALDWIN MOTORS.

LEAVE EAST PORTLAND	ARRIVE VANCOUVER	LEAVE VANCOUVER	ARRIVE EAST PORTLAND
6 35 A M	7 20 A M	LEAVE WOODLAWN 6:15	6 29 A M
8 00 A M	8 45 A M	6 30 A M	7 35 A M
9 20 A M	10 10 A M	8 15 A M	9 10 A M
10 50 A M	11 40 A M	9 40 A M	10 35 A M
12 10 P M	12 55 P M	11 10 A M	12 04 P M
1 15 P M	2 00 P M	LEAVE WOODLAWN 12:45	1 03 P M
1 55 P M	2 40 P M	12 25 P M	1 13 P M
2 35 P M	3 20 P M	1 30 P M	2 27 P M
3 15 P M	4 00 P M	2 10 P M	3 07 P M
3 55 P M	4 40 P M	2 50 P M	3 47 P M
4 35 P M	ARRIVE WOODLAWN 4:53	3 30 P M	4 27 P M
5 15 P M	6 00 P M	4 10 P M	5 07 P M
6 20 P M	7 05 P M	5 30 P M	6 17 P M
9 30 P M	ARRIVE WOODLAWN 9:13	6 35 P M	7 27 P M

On Wednesdays and Saturdays train will leave East Portland at 11:30 P. M., connecting with ferry leaving Vancouver at 11:45 P. M.

TRAINS CONNECT WITH STEAMER FOR LA CAMAS AND WAY POINTS.

SPECIAL RATES MADE FOR PICNICS AND EXCURSIONS.

Tickets for sale at Ticket Office, L Street Depot, East Portland, Stark St. Ferry and on Transfer Boat at Vancouver.

FRANK DEKUM, Pres. H. H. HOLMES, Acting Supt.
H. B. DYER, Auditor.

In this 1891 timetable from the R.L. Polk & Company city directory, the Portland & Vancouver Railway promoted the magnificent Columbia River scenery to prospective tourists. Connections could be made for steamboats heading farther upriver to Camas, Washington (then known as La Camas) and beyond. Listed here are 14 daily trains in each direction, including extra trains from Woodlawn. With steam dummy locomotives attaining speeds of 30 miles an hour, the eight-mile trip from East Portland to the Columbia River Landing took only one-half hour, in spite of the 13 stops on the line. The fare was 25¢.

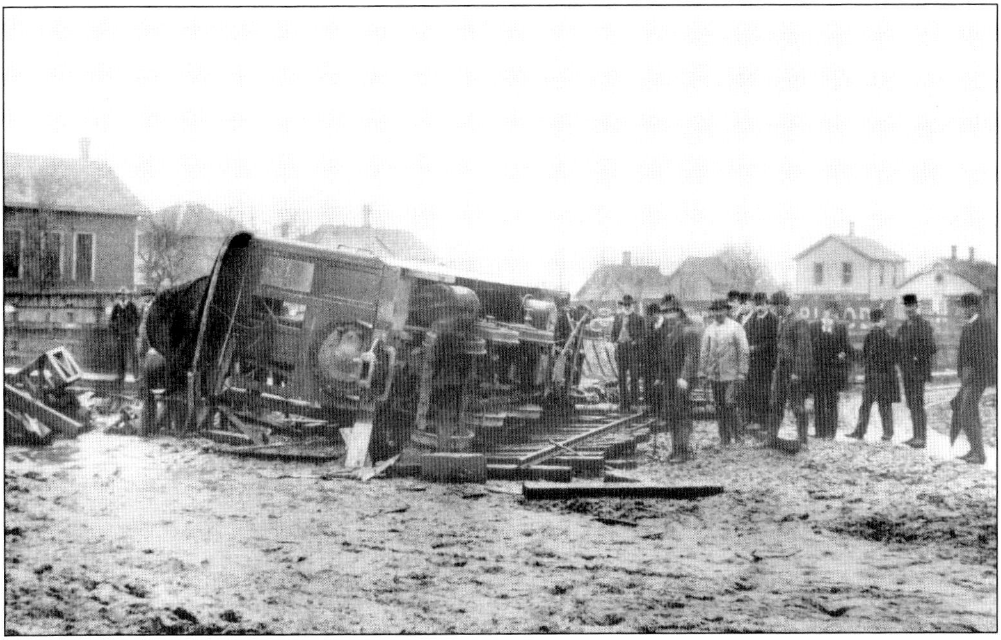

A fatal wreck on the Portland & Vancouver Railway occurred at Northeast Union Avenue and Couch Street on April 4, 1893, just two weeks before the line was converted to electric streetcar operation. A sticky throttle caused the locomotive to approach a curve at excessive speed and tip over. Sadly, 30-year-old engineer John Hans was pinned beneath the locomotive and severely scalded, later dying.

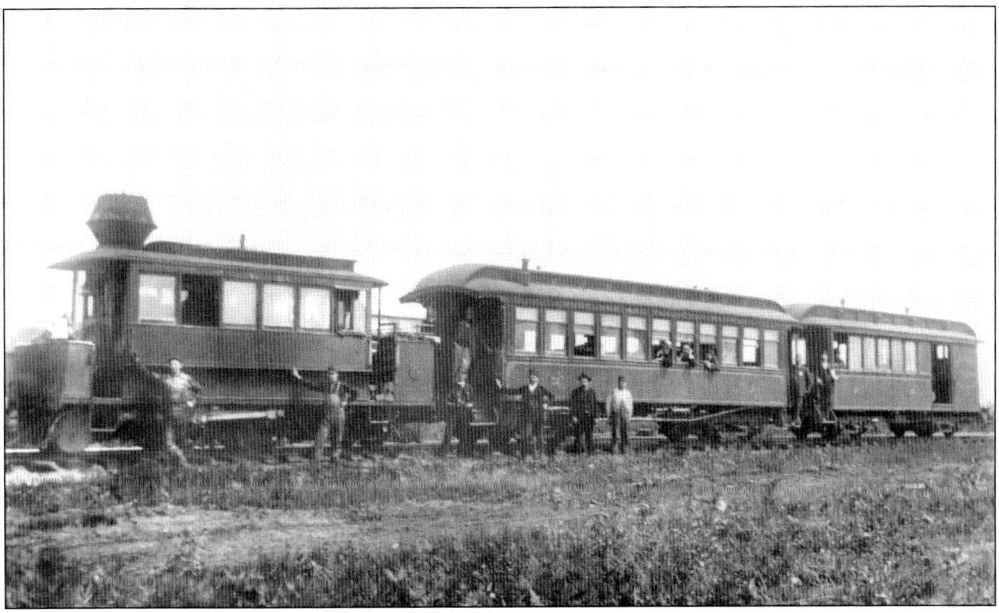

The Portland & Vancouver Railway Company was the first to convert to electric operation. Pictured here at Highland Station on June 24, 1893, is the last steam dummy train to make the run. There were nearly as many employees aboard for the occasion as passengers, including two engine crewmen, four conductors, a policeman, and an official (on the platform) who is thought to be the railway's president, Frank Dekum.

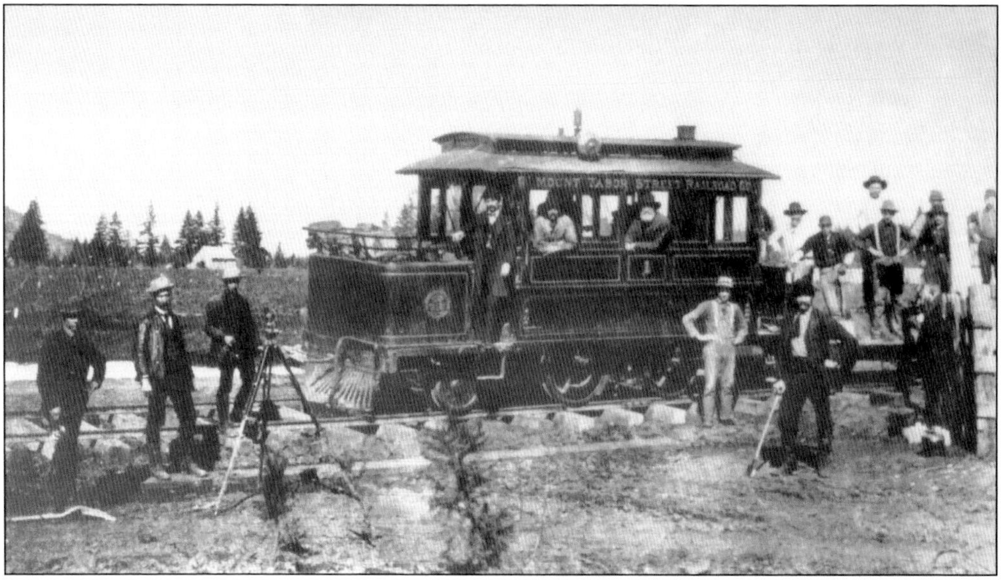

On June 21, 1889, the Mount Tabor Street Railroad launched Portland's third steam motor service. Their Hawthorne Avenue Line ran east on Hawthorne from Grand Avenue in East Portland to Southeast Fifty-fifth Avenue in South Mount Tabor. This 1892 photograph of locomotive No. 1 was taken on Southeast Fifty-second Avenue and Powell Boulevard during the surveying for the Portland, Chicago & Mount Scott Railway.

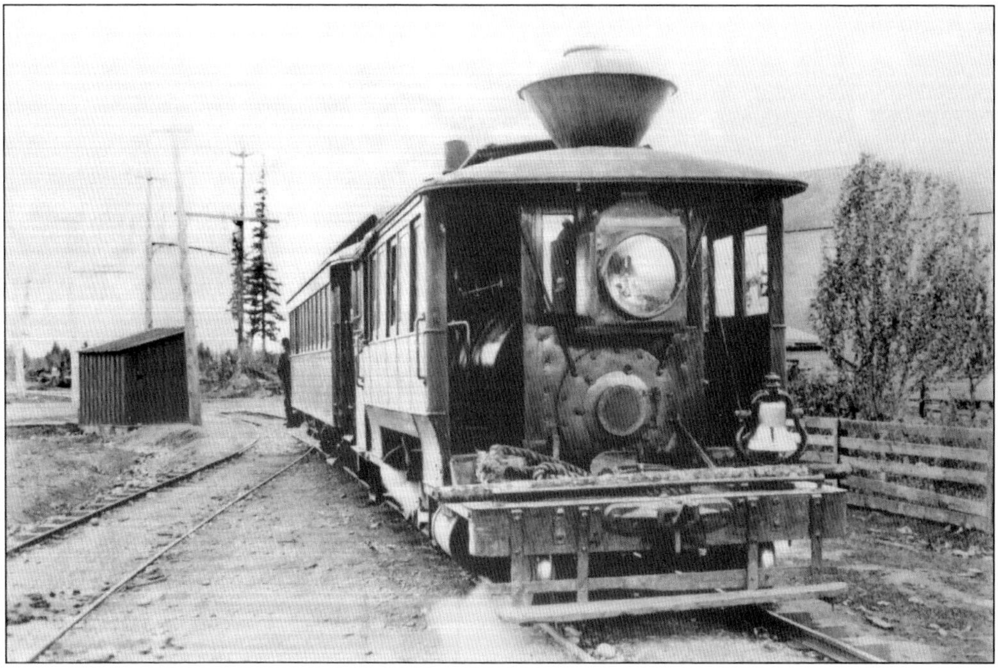

The Portland, Chicago & Mount Scott Railroad completed an extension from Hawthorne Avenue to Lents on June 18, 1892 (Chicago was a housing development along the way). When the line was electrified by the Oregon Water Power & Railway in 1901, its locomotive was transferred to the new Springwater Division to inaugurate service to Gresham. This train is departing Lents Junction, near Southeast 102nd Avenue and Foster Road, for Gresham.

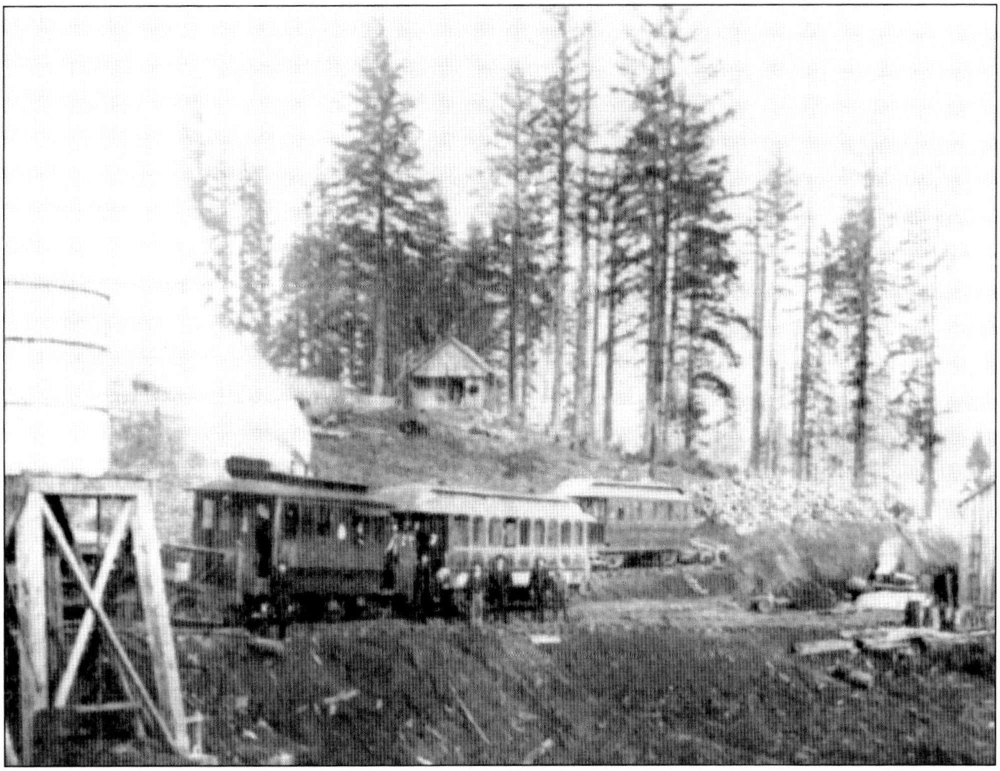

The City & West Portland Park Motor Company began operation to the West Portland Park development on November 5, 1890. The winding route ran from present-day Southwest Hamilton Street and Barbur Boulevard in South Portland, through Hillsdale and Multnomah, to a point near Southwest Barbur and Luradel Street. The coaches in this photograph were later electrified and are thought to have seen service in Forest Grove.

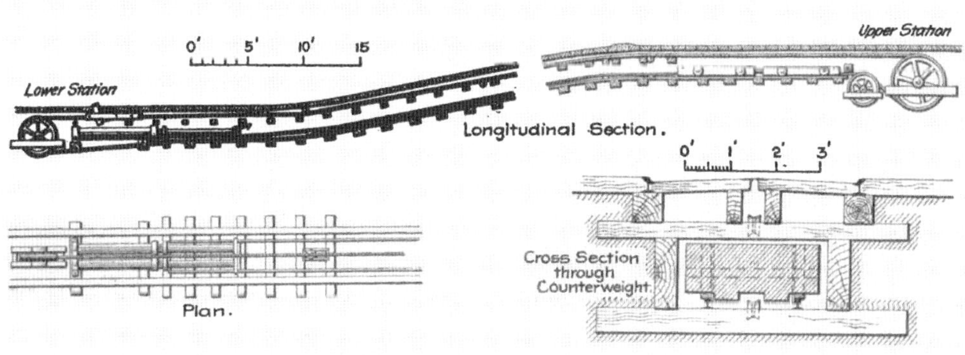

FIG. 2.—KUHLMANN'S COUNTERBALANCE SYSTEM OF OPERATING ELECTRIC CARS ON STEEP GRADES.

Among the challenges faced by the City & West Portland Park Motor Company in constructing its line was the 14-percent grade on Hamilton Street. As a solution, trolleys were to be assisted by small counterbalancing cars moving in the opposite direction beneath the tracks. Unfortunately, the company failed and its City Division trolley line never opened. Neighbors eventually petitioned for removal of this clever Kuhlmann counterbalance system. (*Electrical Engineer,* July 12, 1893.)

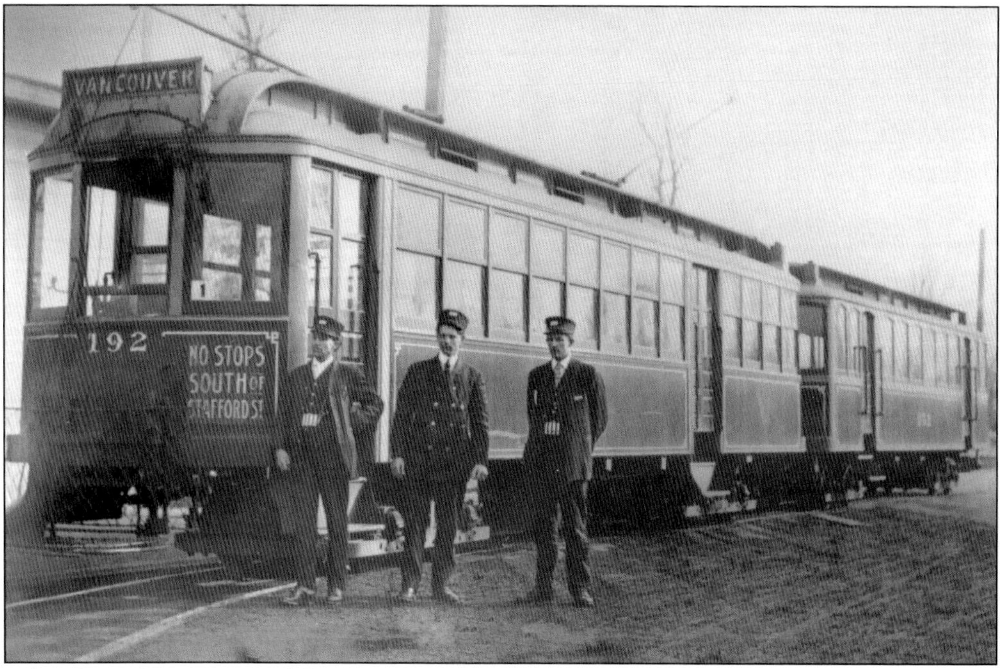

After electrification, several former steam dummy lines exhibited many of the characteristics of interurban railways, even as regular streetcars began to supplement original rolling stock in the 1910s. One example was the narrow-gauge Vancouver Line. Train No. 1, consisting of combine No. 192 and trailer No. 352, is seen here at Hayden Island Station around 1913. The motor, originally Portland Consolidated Railway 601, had been built for the Vancouver Line in 1905.

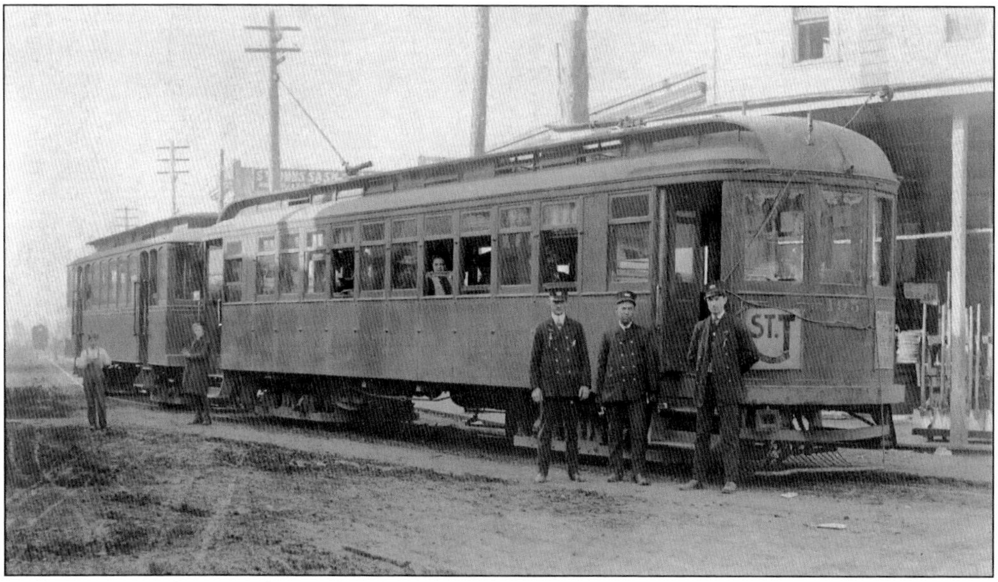

In this c. 1905 photograph, Portland Consolidated Railway No. 195 and trailer No. 352 wait at the terminus in front of St. Johns Hardware on North Jersey and Philadelphia Streets. No. 195 was one of the narrow-gauge "St. Johns" convertible cars built by the City & Suburban Railway to replace the steam dummies in 1903. These cars were too big to enter Portland until bridge and track modifications were made. (Courtesy Mark Moore.)

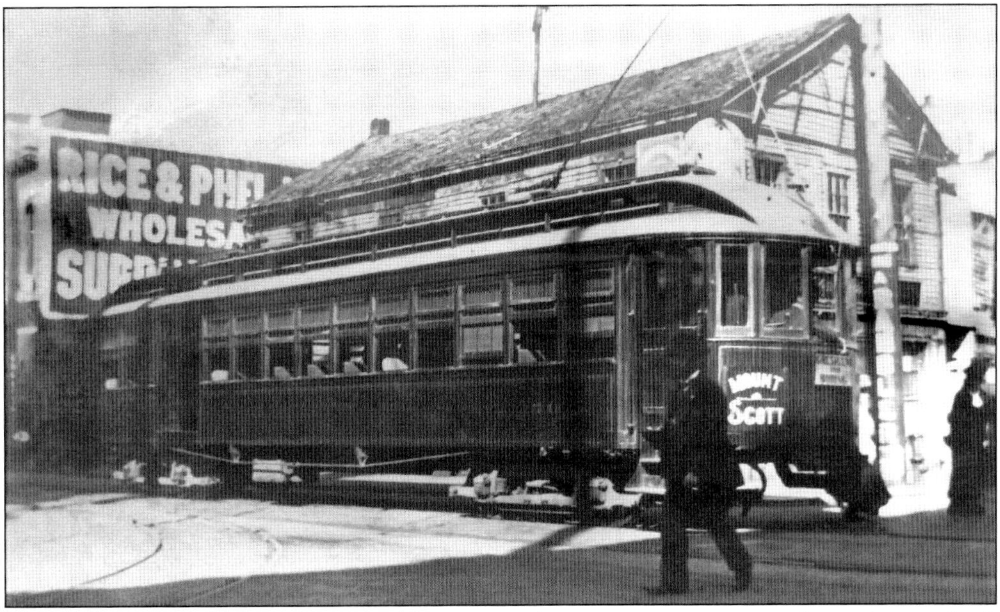

During the early 1900s, as they evolved from steam dummy routes to streetcar lines, the standard-gauge Hawthorne and Mount Scott Lines used equipment inherited from the interurban divisions. Oregon Water Power & Railway combine No. 50 is seen here around 1903 at Southwest First and Washington Streets on the Mount Scott Line. The dash sign "Gresham and Boring" refers to the transfer point at Lents Junction. (Courtesy Don Nelson.)

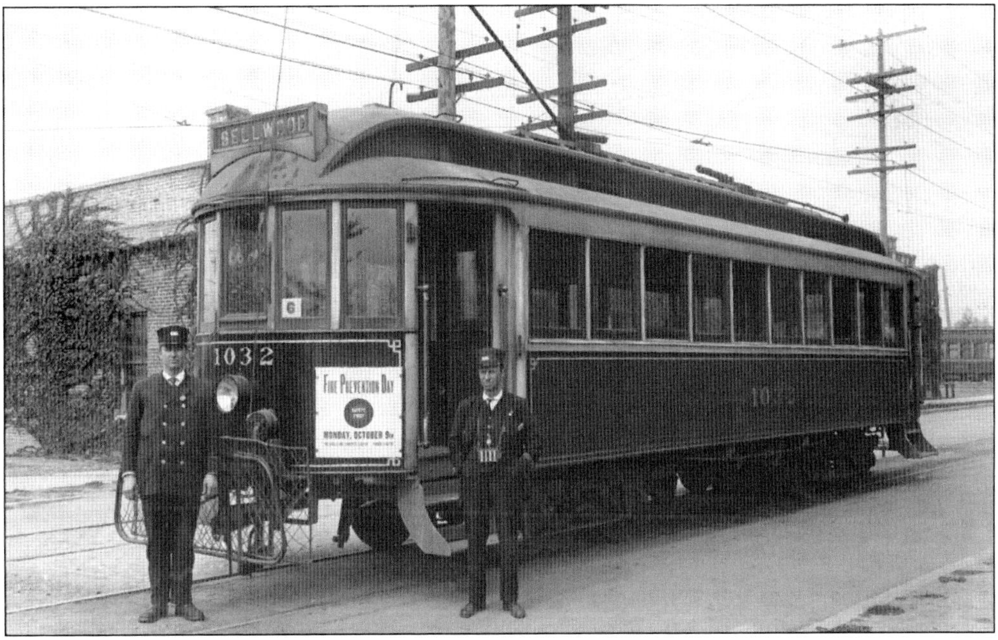

Although never a steam dummy line, the Sellwood Line was another standard-gauge streetcar line that initially used interurban cars. It became a streetcar line in 1903 when the interurbans stopped running through Sellwood. By the time this 1911 photograph was taken next to the Sellwood carbarn on Southeast Thirteenth Avenue, PRL&P had deemed the No. 1032 outmoded and relegated it to Sellwood Line duty. (Courtesy Mark Moore.)

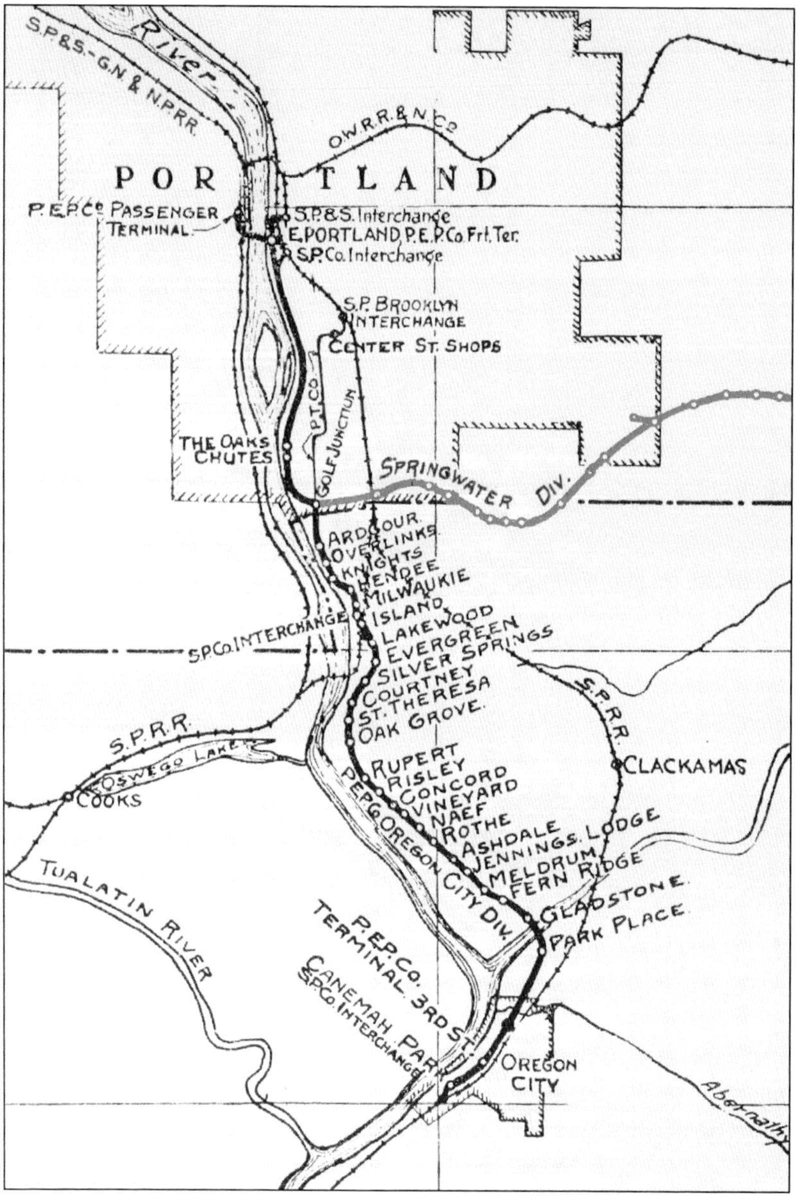

This map shows the historic Oregon City Line in 1946, at the close of the Portland Electric Power Company (PEPCO) years. On the map, 32 stations can be identified, including two stops in Oregon City and three on the river route between downtown Portland and Golf Junction. The branch to Gladstone Park is long gone, but the extension to Canemah Park is still evident, albeit for freight trains only. The 14.6-mile route, opened by the East Side Railway in 1893, became the Portland City & Oregon in 1901, the Oregon Water Power & Railway in 1902, and then became part of the sprawling Portland Railway, Light & Power system in 1906. Philadelphia ownership remained basically the same as the railway went through a number of later name changes; PEPCO in 1924, Pacific Northwest Public Service Company in 1930, then back to PEPCO in 1933. In 1946, a California holding company reorganized the railway as the Portland Railroad & Terminal Division. After the city bus lines were removed in 1952, the interurban operation was known simply as the Portland Traction Company.

Two

The First True Interurban

The Oregon City Line

Steam dummies, narrow-gauge railroads, and suburban streetcars provided the first public transit to outlying settlements. When electric interurban railways arrived on the scene, they expanded upon that concept in undeveloped territory south and east of Portland.

George W. Brown incorporated the East Side Railway on May 15, 1891, with the intent of building to Eugene. He first purchased the Mount Tabor Street Railway, which was constructing a steam motor line toward Mount Tabor.

George and James Steel headed the rival Metropolitan Railway, which launched the second trolley line in Portland on January 1, 1890. Their six-mile Fulton Line was planned as the initial leg of a west side route to Oregon City; however, the Steel brothers concluded an alliance with the East Side Railway instead, purchasing that company on May 15, 1892.

The East Side Railway began operation to Brooklyn on November 2, 1891. Local subsidies funded extensions to Sellwood on June 7, 1892, and Milwaukie on August 13, where citizens had donated land for a carbarn. On September 11, the track reached Oak Grove, and a month later it was nearing the Clackamas River. Service to Oregon City commenced on February 16, 1893. Until 1901, a one-half-mile branch also ran up Dartmouth Street to the Gladstone Chautauqua grounds.

The East Side Railway would not exist for long; the 1893 depression and a fatal accident in which a car fell from the Madison Street Bridge resulted in bankruptcy. A receiver foreclosed on January 7, 1901, forming the Portland City & Oregon Railway, which extended the mainline from Oregon City to Canemah in 1901 and built a picnic ground there.

Accidents, labor unrest, and high operating costs preceded acquisition by the Oregon Water Power & Railway (OWP) on June 5, 1902. Then, on May 2, 1908, after extensions had been made to Gresham, Estacada, and Troutdale, new owner Portland Railway, Light & Power ceased operating the OWP as a separate company. By this time, Portland's streetcars and its interurban railway were controlled by banking interests in Philadelphia and New York.

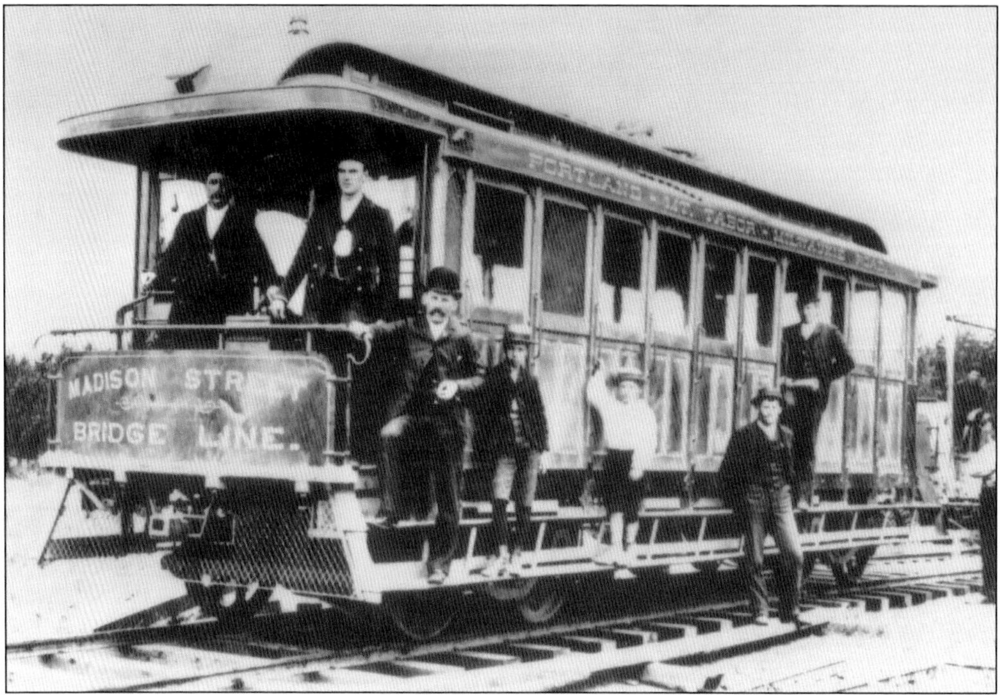

This oldest known East Side Railway photograph shows the *Alva* on the Madison Street Bridge Line in 1891, around the time initial operation commenced along Southeast Eleventh Avenue and Milwaukie Road to Brooklyn. Like boats, the first interurbans were given women's names. But the *Alva*, built locally by Vulcan Manufacturing in 1890, is thought to have been inspired by a visit from a man—the Spanish Duke of Alba.

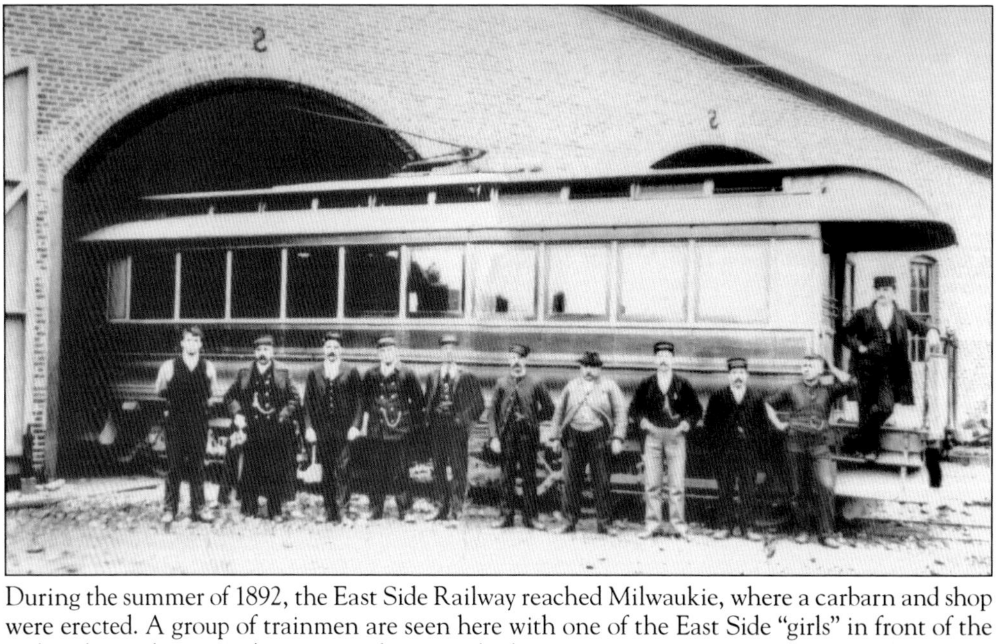

During the summer of 1892, the East Side Railway reached Milwaukie, where a carbarn and shop were erected. A group of trainmen are seen here with one of the East Side "girls" in front of the Milwaukie carbarn. Within a year, the roster had grown to 16 motor cars and 10 trailers. After this barn was replaced in 1910, it became a boxing venue and then Mullan's Garage.

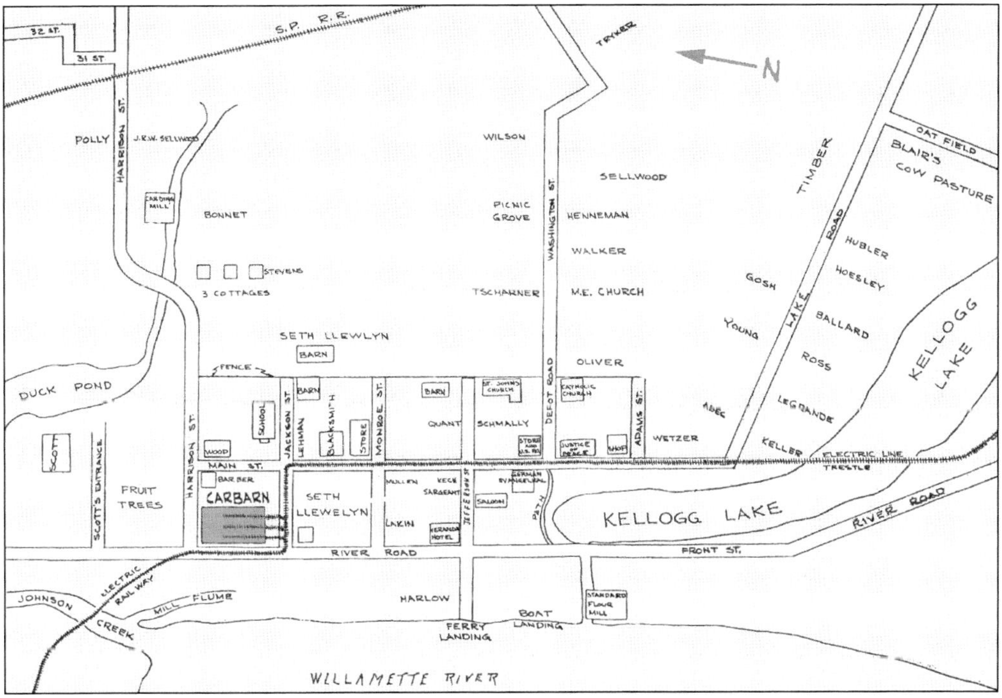

In December 1892, the East Side Railway completed a 100-by-200-foot brick carbarn and shop on Southeast Jackson Street in Milwaukie. In 1901, an addition to the east side of the building doubled its size. The interurban line originally crossed Kellogg Lake on a trestle. It was moved from Main Street to private right-of-way next to the river in 1930 during the construction of McLoughlin Boulevard.

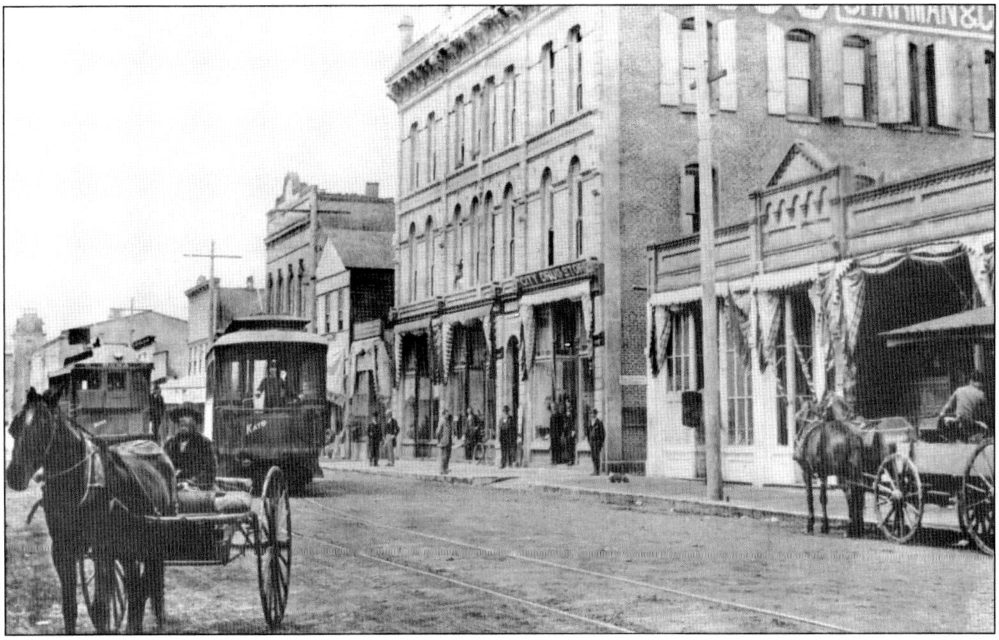

The *Bona* and *Kate*, trolleys on the nation's first interurban, are passing each other on Main Street in Oregon City during the early 1890s. The *Bona*, on the left, was built in Portland by the Columbia Car & Tool Works in 1891. The older *Kate* was the product of a national car builder.

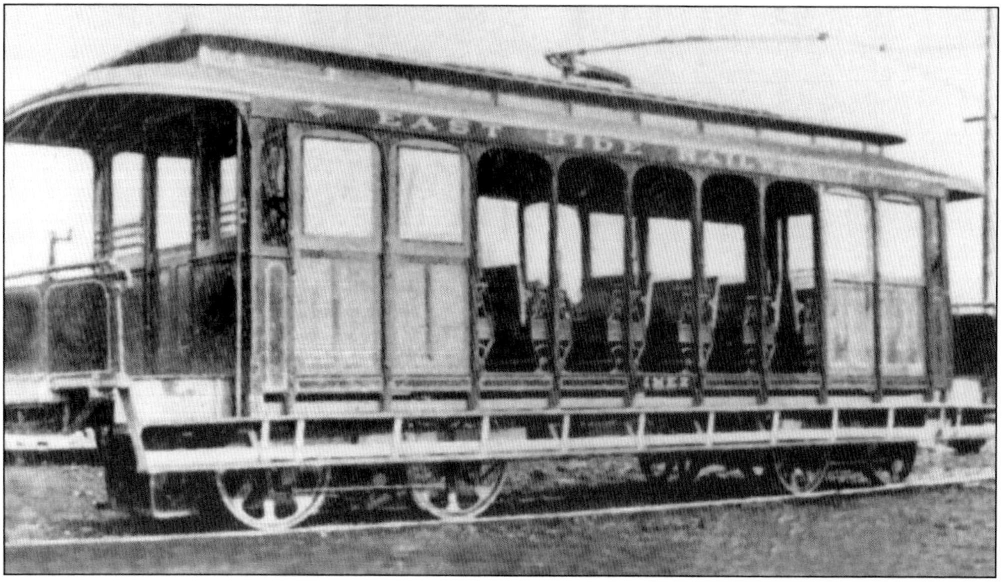

This picture from the May 1893 *Street Railway Journal* illustrates how the removal of side panels converted the *Inez* into an open streetcar. Unfortunately, the *Inez* came to an untimely end on the foggy morning of November 1, 1893, when it skidded on icy rails and plunged through the open draw of the Madison Street Bridge into the Willamette River. Seven died in what was Portland's worst streetcar accident.

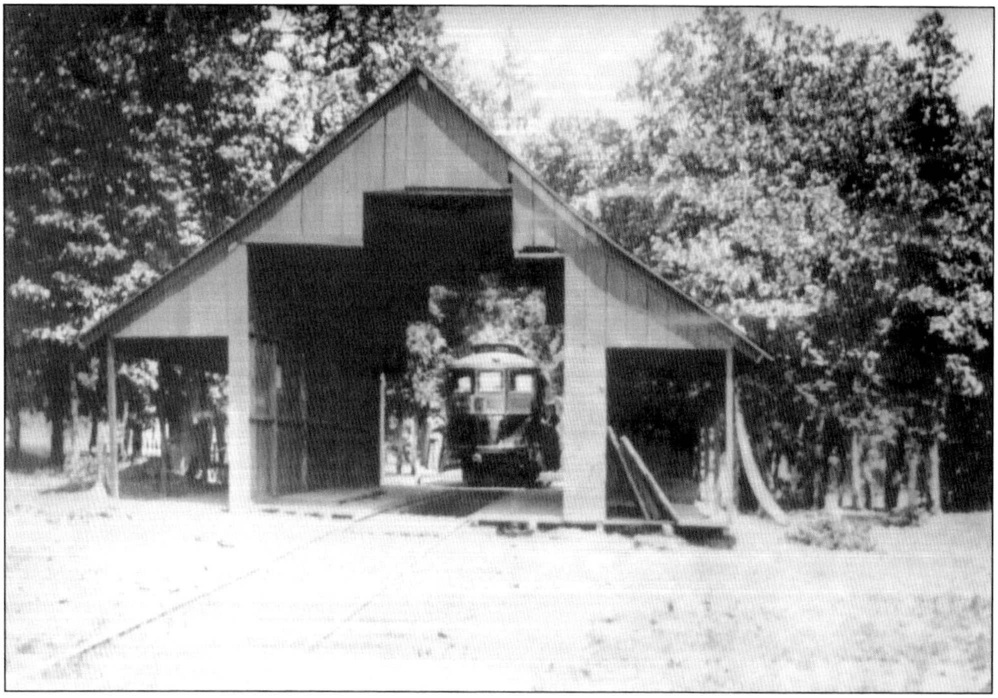

Soon after completion of the Oregon City Line in 1893, a one-half-mile branch line was built from Gladstone to the Chautauqua Park, and a station-carbarn was constructed nearby. One car was kept here and used for shuttle service between Oregon City and the park. The route was discontinued in 1901, as the Portland City & Oregon Railway struggled to control expenses.

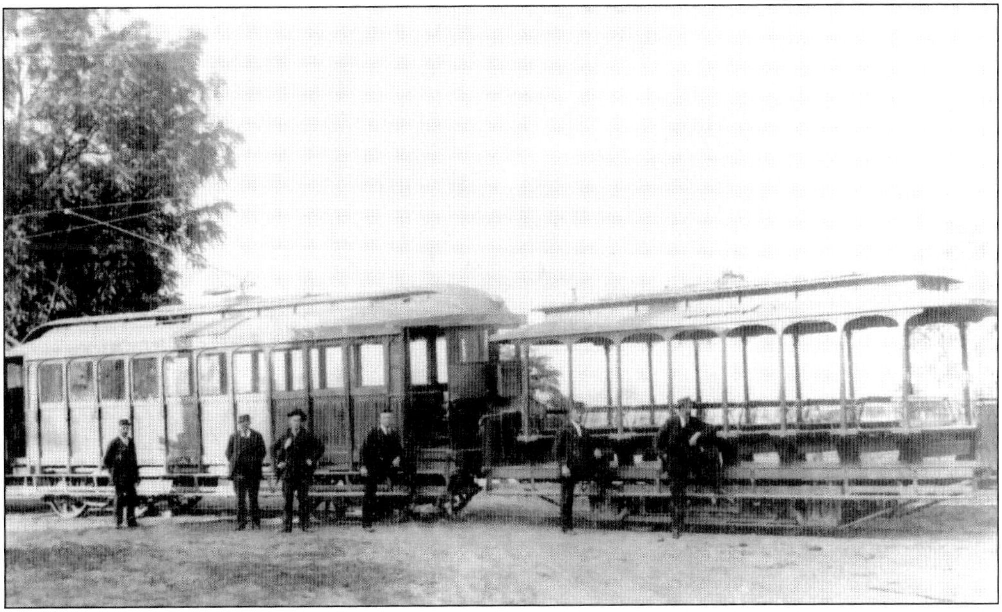

The *Alva* and an open four-wheel trailer await Oregon City passengers in this late-1890s photograph, taken during the period that the Steel Brothers were guiding the East Side Railway through receivership. The 10 removable side panels that made *Alva* a "summer and winter" convertible car are clearly visible, as are the bay window–like "portable vestibules" that partly enclosed platforms.

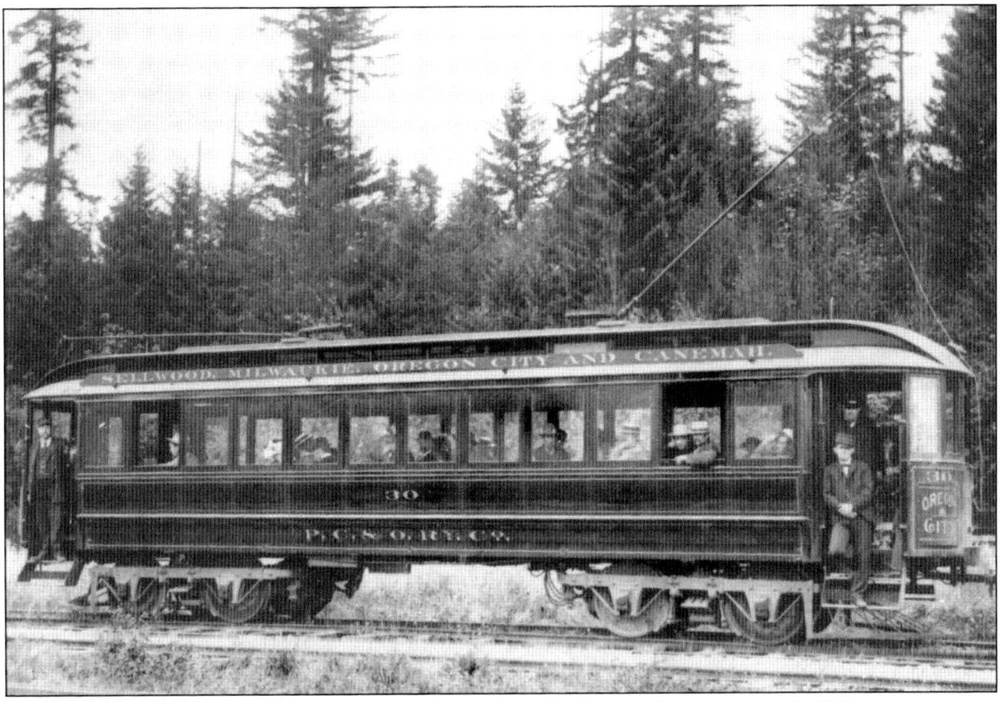

In 1901, the Portland City & Oregon Railway launched an ambitious car-rebuilding program at the Milwaukie carbarn. As the original East Side Railway cars were modernized, their names were replaced with numbers. First out of the shop was No. 30, seen here on the Oregon City Line with a letter board reading "Sellwood, Milwaukie, Oregon City and Canemah."

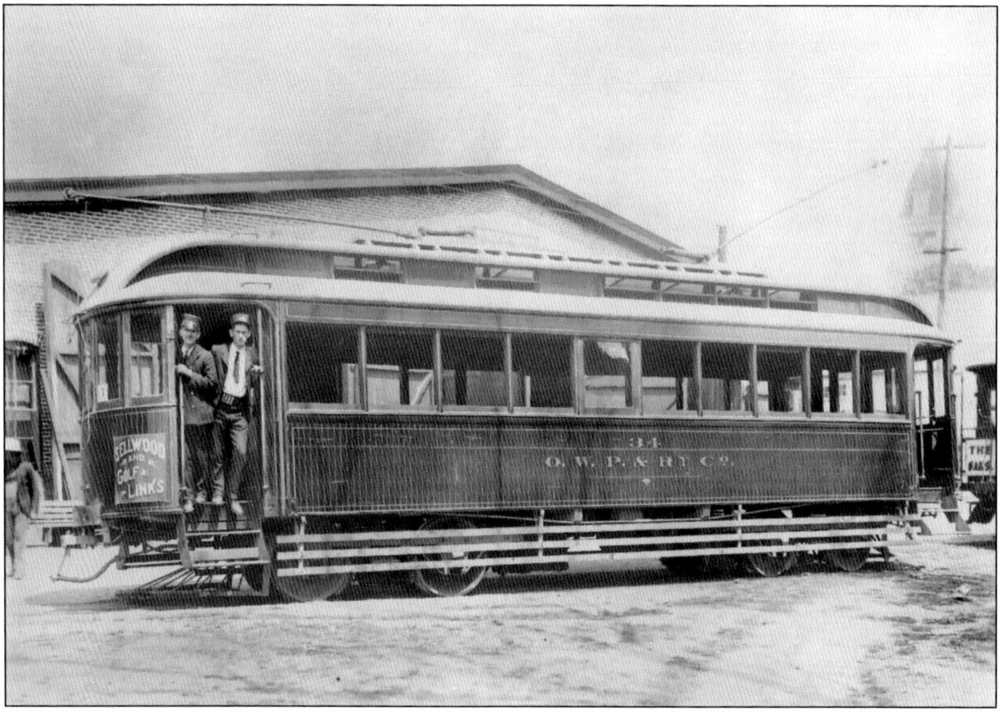

No. 34 was one of four interurbans ordered by the Portland City & Oregon Railway in 1901 from the W.L. Holman Car Company in San Francisco. It is seen here ready for service to "Sellwood and Golf Links." In 1904, successor OWP rerouted mainline interurbans over a new river route, leaving Sellwood cars on their own. The golf links became today's Waverly Country Club. (Courtesy Mark Moore.)

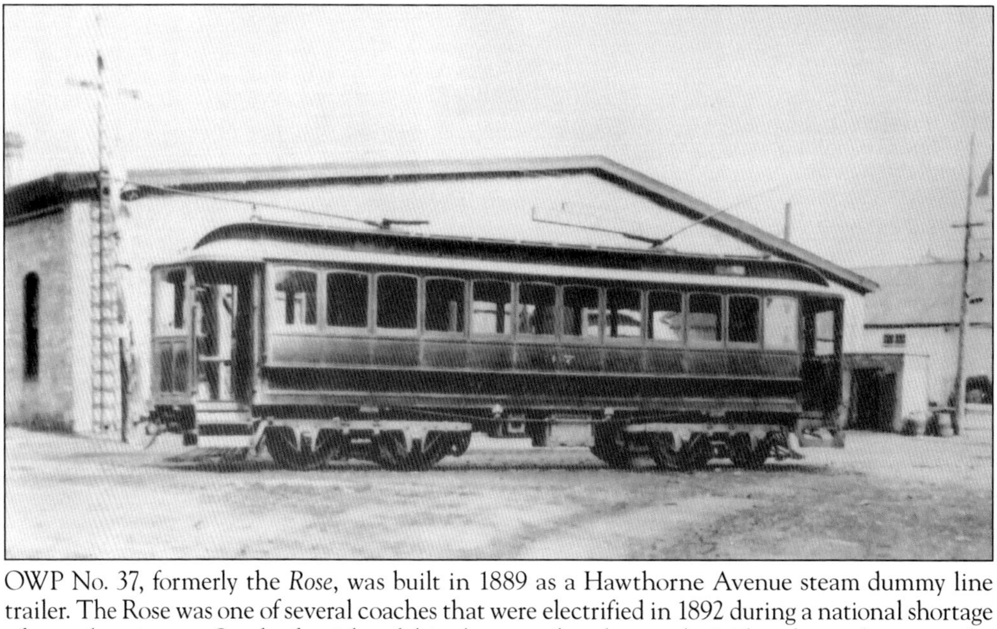

OWP No. 37, formerly the *Rose*, was built in 1889 as a Hawthorne Avenue steam dummy line trailer. The Rose was one of several coaches that were electrified in 1892 during a national shortage of new electric cars. On the far right of this photograph, taken at the Milwaukie carbarn, are the 1901 extension and the tower of the public school on Jackson Street.

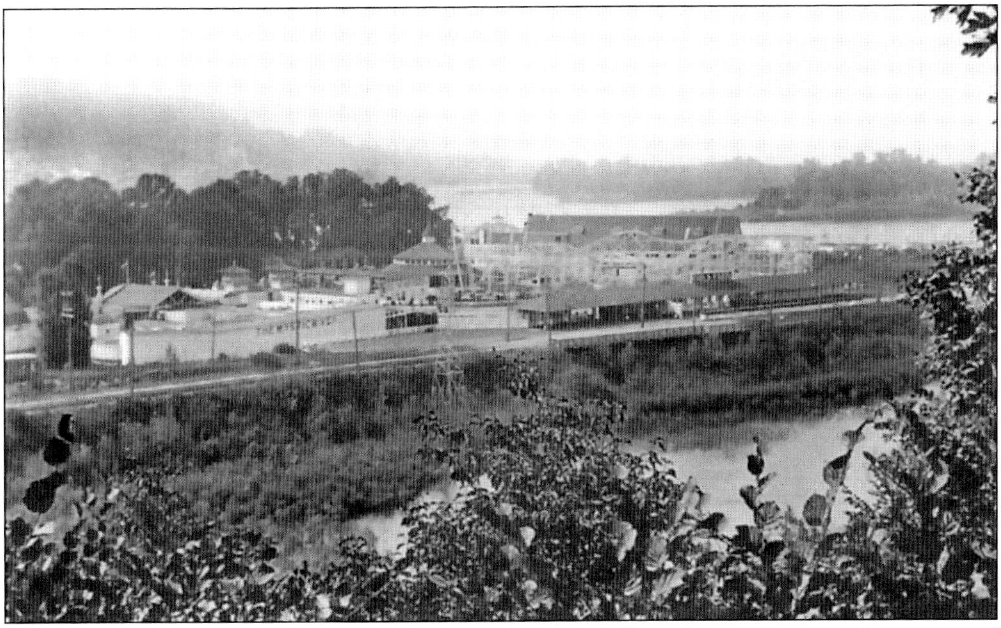

OWP opened The Oaks on the Willamette River below Sellwood on May 30, 1905, as a way to increase ridership on the Oregon City and Estacada Lines. One of the 10 oldest amusement parks in the country, it is the only one still in operation in the Portland area. An early interurban car can be seen approaching the station on the left-hand side of this stereopticon photograph. (Courtesy Mark Moore.)

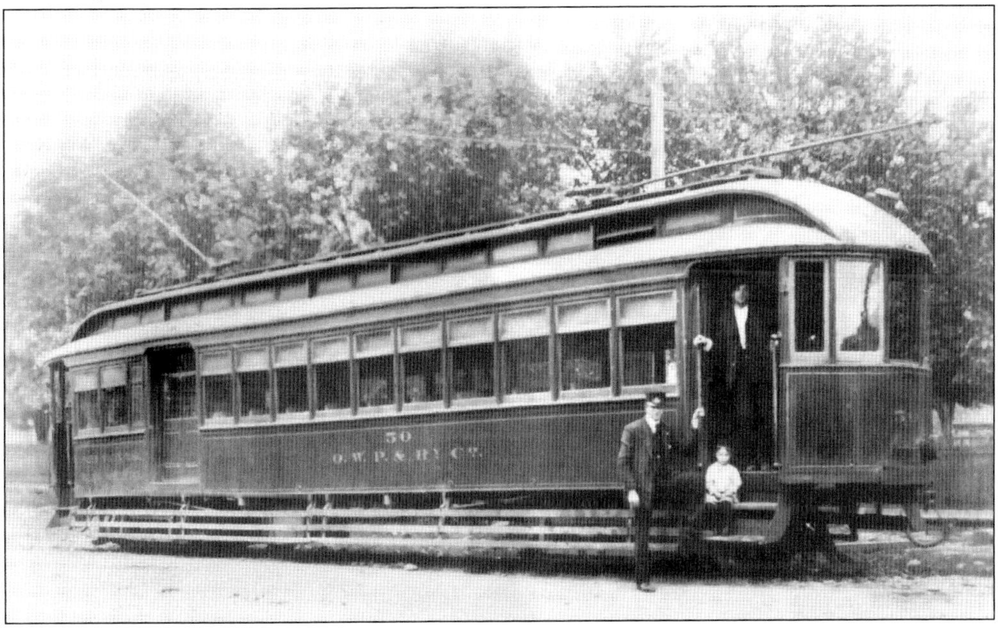

Motorman Albert A. Reck (on platform) and conductor Guy A. Seavey pose with a young passenger on car No. 50 at Milwaukie in 1910. Four such "combines" were ordered from the W.L. Holman Company in 1893 to carry mail, express freight, and passengers. In later years, the freight section was used as a smoking compartment. As can be seen, PRL&P left the OWP name and number on some interurbans for several years.

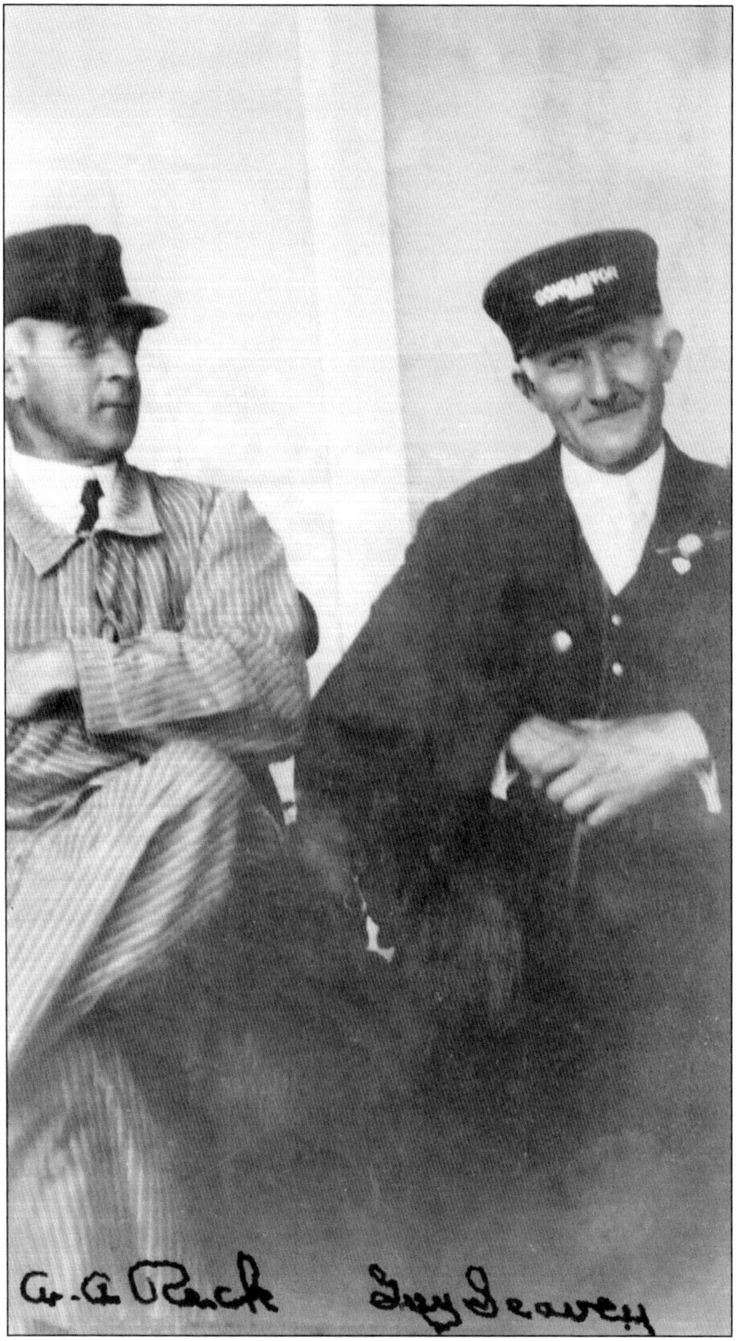

Albert A. Reck, Portland's most written about interurban trainman, posed for this portrait with friend and workmate Guy A. Seavey around 1920. Reck (left) is dressed as what was known as a "motoneer" (a motorman-engineer), and Seavey is wearing his conductor's uniform. Both men were longtime railway employees; Seavey was said to have been the oldest conductor, while Reck became the senior motorman. Reck signed on with the Oregon Water Power & Railway Company on December 17, 1906, and retired from the Portland Traction Company 48 years later at 77 years of age. He was known to passengers and employees as "The Wreck." (Courtesy Mark Moore.)

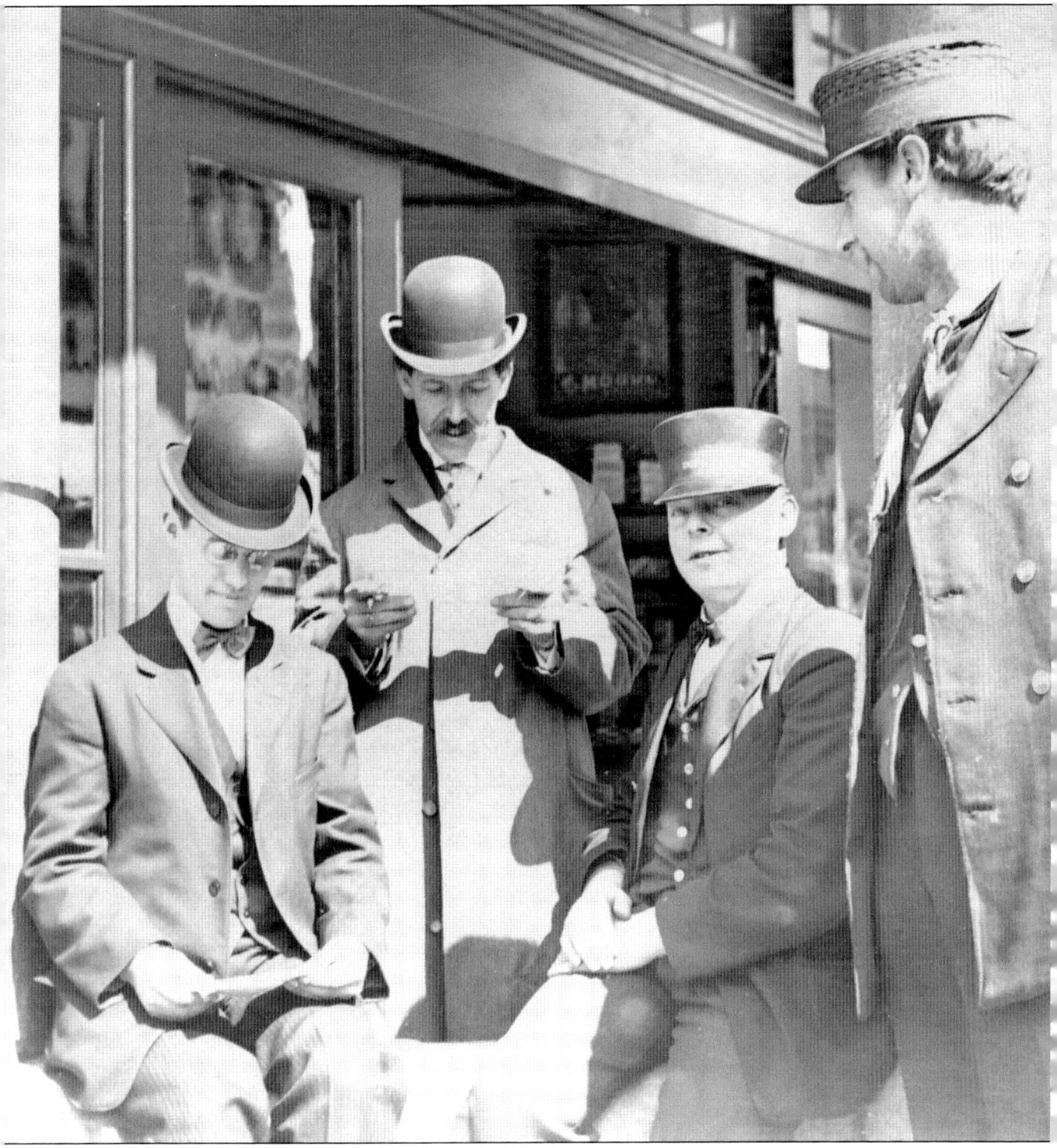

Motorman Albert A. Reck took this c. 1914 photograph showing, from left to right, assistant PRL&P paymaster ? Swinray, interurban division superintendent Julius J. Miller, inspector Charles Shipley (inspectors were what are now called supervisors), and motorman Tony Copple. They appear to be examining checks, and it is interesting to consider that at this boom time for electric railway building employees worked six to seven days a week for 11¢ an hour. Note the classic advertisement for Egyptian Mogul cigarettes in the background. (Photograph Albert A. Reck; courtesy Mark Moore.)

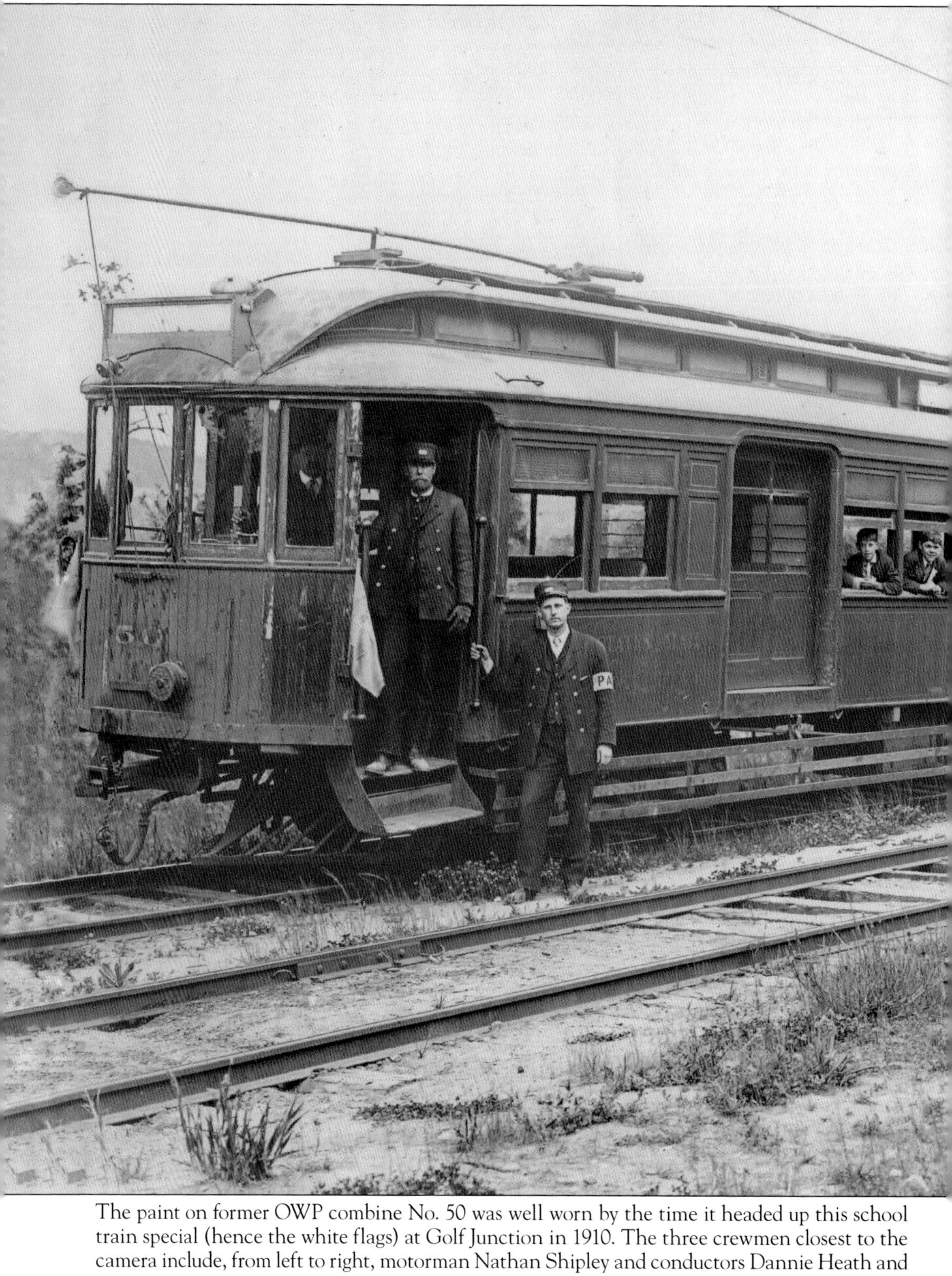

The paint on former OWP combine No. 50 was well worn by the time it headed up this school train special (hence the white flags) at Golf Junction in 1910. The three crewmen closest to the camera include, from left to right, motorman Nathan Shipley and conductors Dannie Heath and

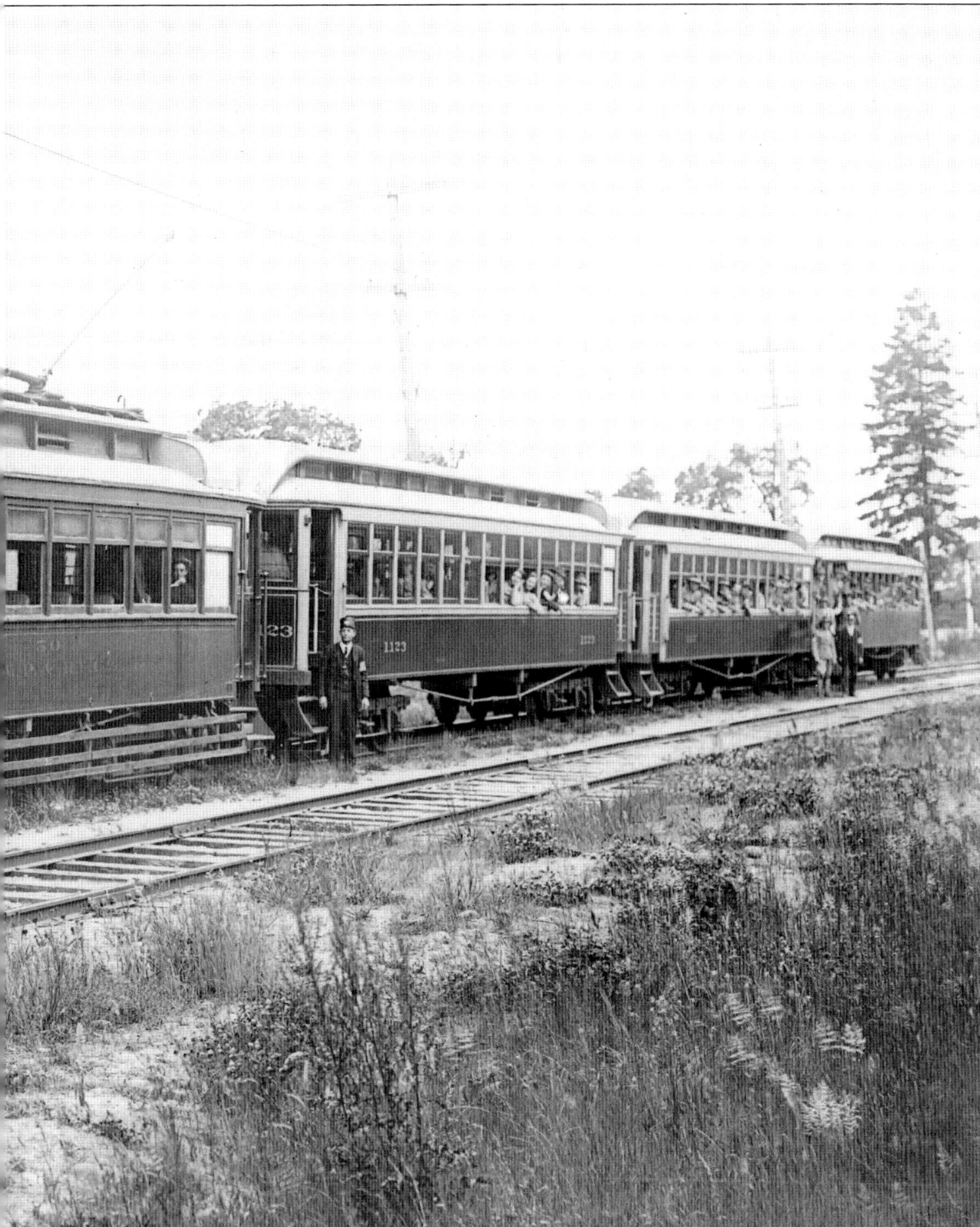

William Cochran. The first two closed trailers, Nos. 1123 and 1121, are looking more handsome since they were rebuilt by the Portland Railway, Light & Power Company just three years before. All of the cars in this photograph were retired in 1936.

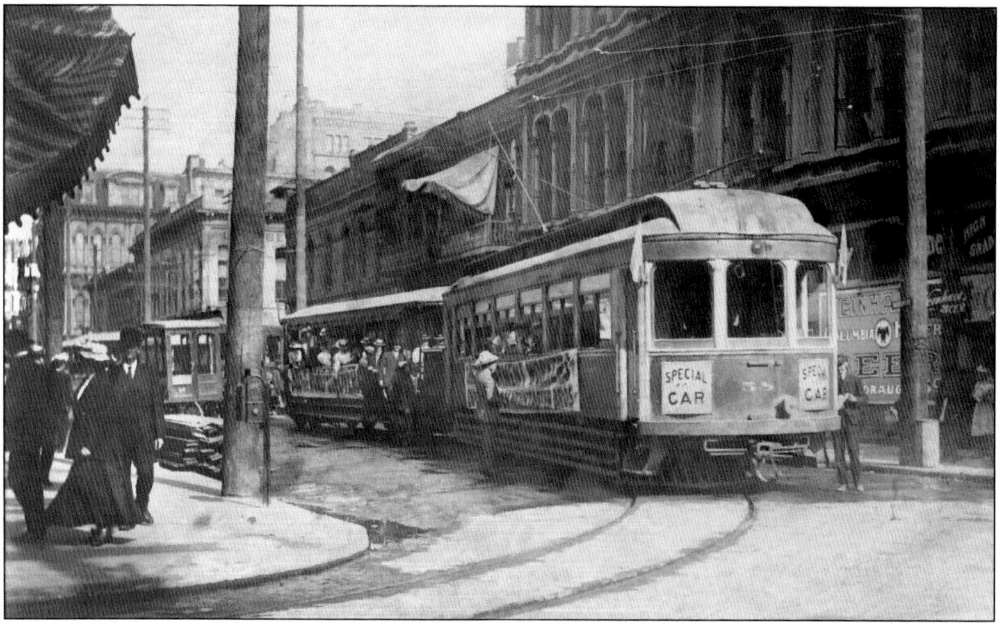

An Oregon City car waits in the background while a two-car Boss of the Road excursion train to Estacada, headed by OWP No. 58, loads on Southwest First and Alder Streets in downtown Portland on July 20, 1907. It looks like the gentleman standing in the street has supplied bottles of beer from the public house on the corner to several happy passengers on the first car. (Courtesy Jerry Risberg.)

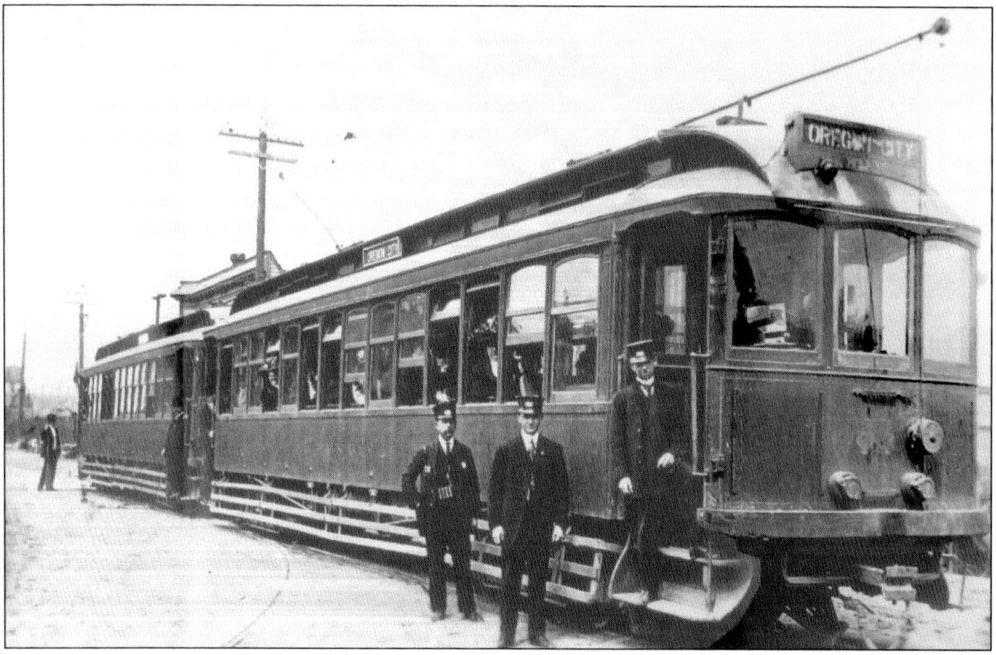

In this c. 1905 photograph, two conductors and a motorman are ready to depart with a two-car special headed by OWP No. 63. The passengers are departing Water Street in East Portland for what will probably be an excursion to The Oaks or Canemah Park. Not yet aboard at the rear of the train is a gentleman holding what looks like a paddle. Note the arc street lamp.

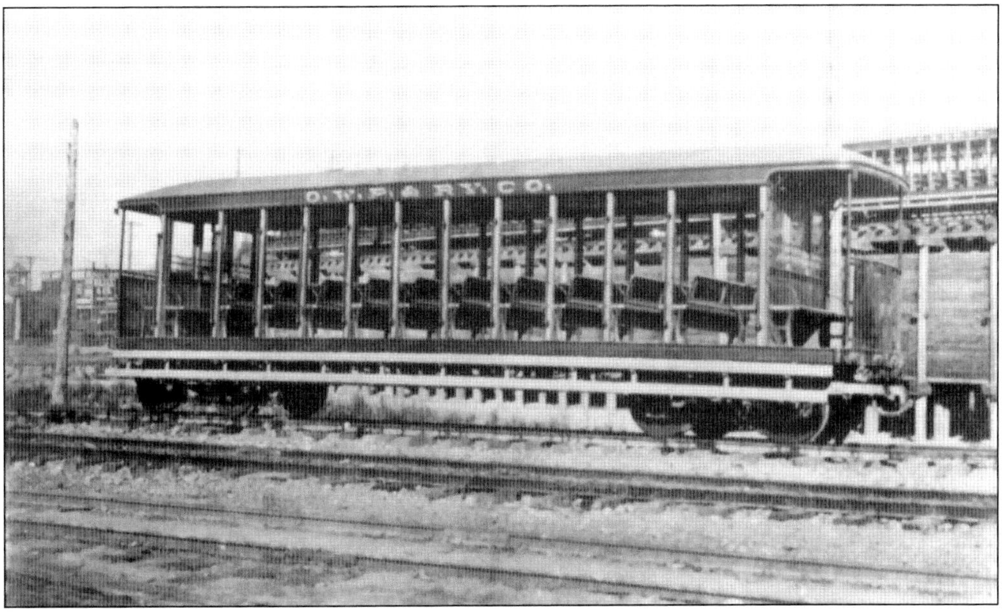

No. 75, one of 21 open trailers built by OWP in 1904–1905, is seen here stored in the East Portland Yard. In the background at far left is the dispatcher's tower/crossing guard post next to the Southern Pacific Railroad tracks on Southeast First Avenue and Hawthorne Boulevard. The attendant signaled clearance for streetcars to cross the railroad tracks (see page 108).

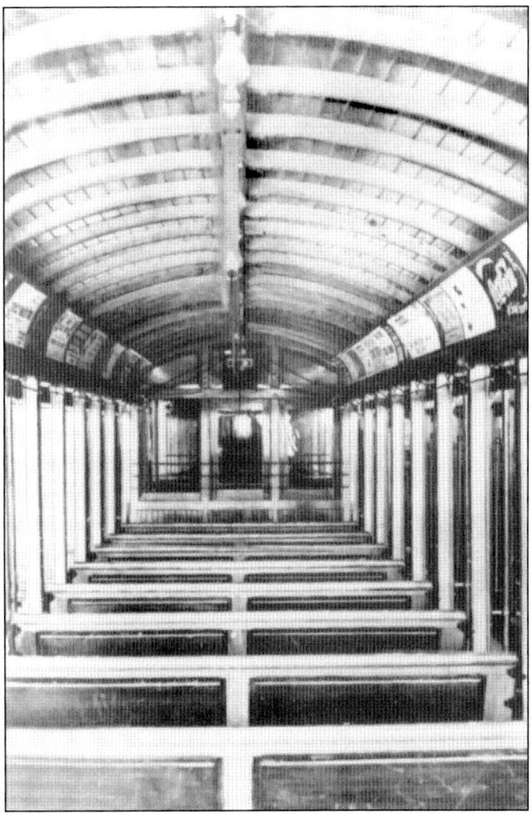

This interior view of an open 75-class trailer shows the wooden cross-bench seating. There were 10 benches that could be faced in either direction, and four fixed seats mounted on the bulkheads at each end of the car. When this series was scrapped in 1934, two roofs were saved for use at Oaks Amusement Park as a miniature railway station and an entrance marquee at the skating rink.

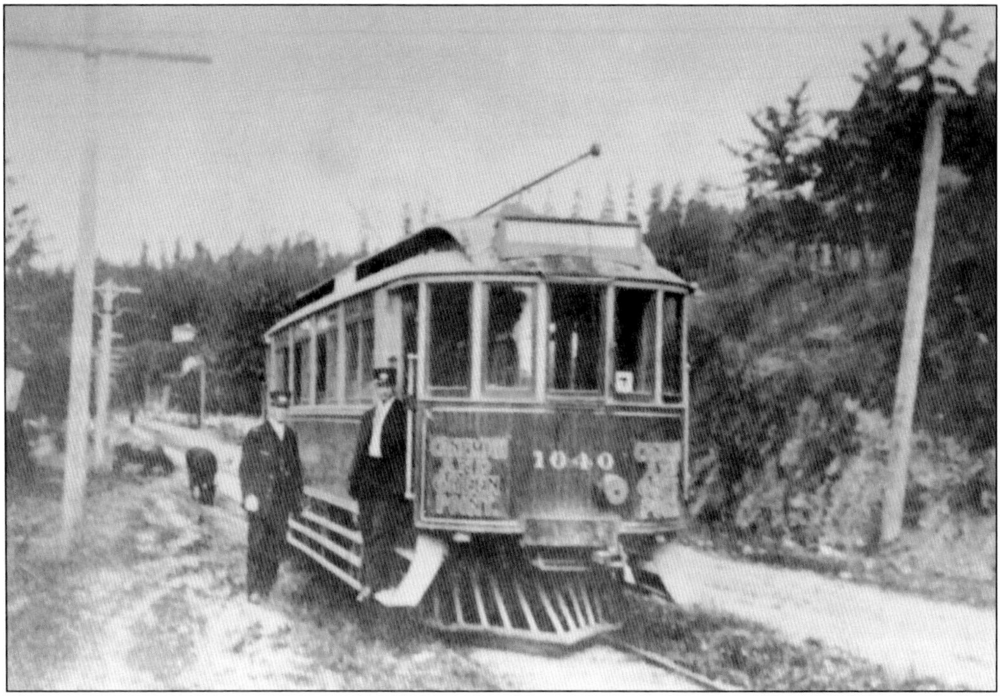

Note the cows wandering onto the track behind No. 1040, seen in Green Point and Canemah shuttle service on the Oregon City Line around 1901. This is one of the reasons early interurbans had wooden pilots, or cowcatchers. The car was one of three ordered by the East Side Railway from the Laclede Car Company in St. Louis. By 1907, PRL&P had sent it to Salem for use as a city streetcar.

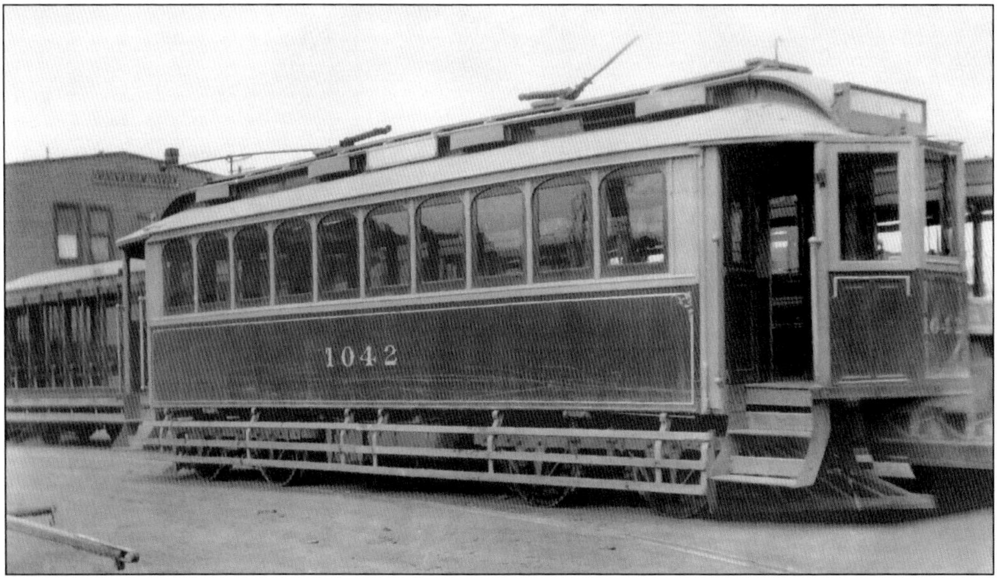

No. 1042 had been extensively rebuilt when this picture was taken next to the Central Hotel in East Portland. The ornate window braces betray its origin as the East Side Railway's *Alva*, but the patented Heacock and Lovejoy convertible side panels are long gone. *Alva* was built in Portland in 1890 by the Vulcan Car Company before it became the Columbia Car & Tool Company. (Courtesy Mark Moore.)

No. 1049, seen here at the Sellwood carbarn in 1930, was a handsome combine built by the W.L. Holman Company in San Francisco in 1903. During a 1908 rebuilding, its baggage and express section was converted into a smoking compartment. For six years after retirement in 1931, the car survived as a "wrecker"—a work car used to retrieve disabled trolleys along the line. (Photograph Fred L. Blaisdell.)

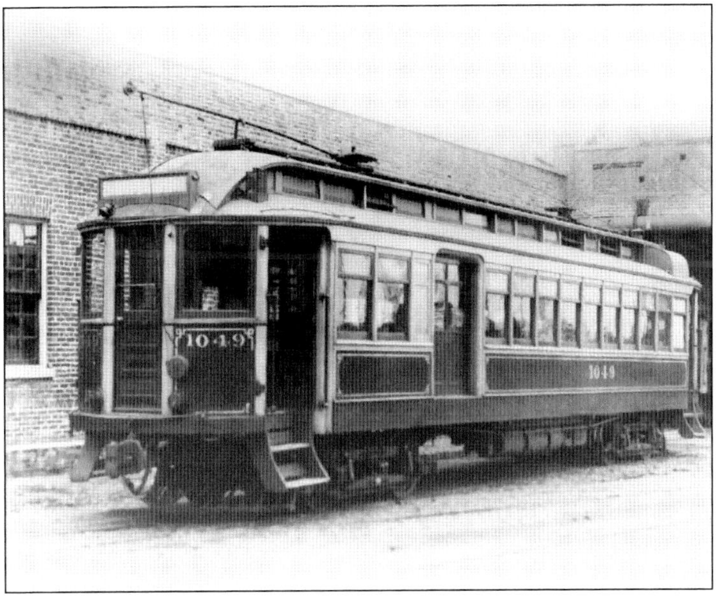

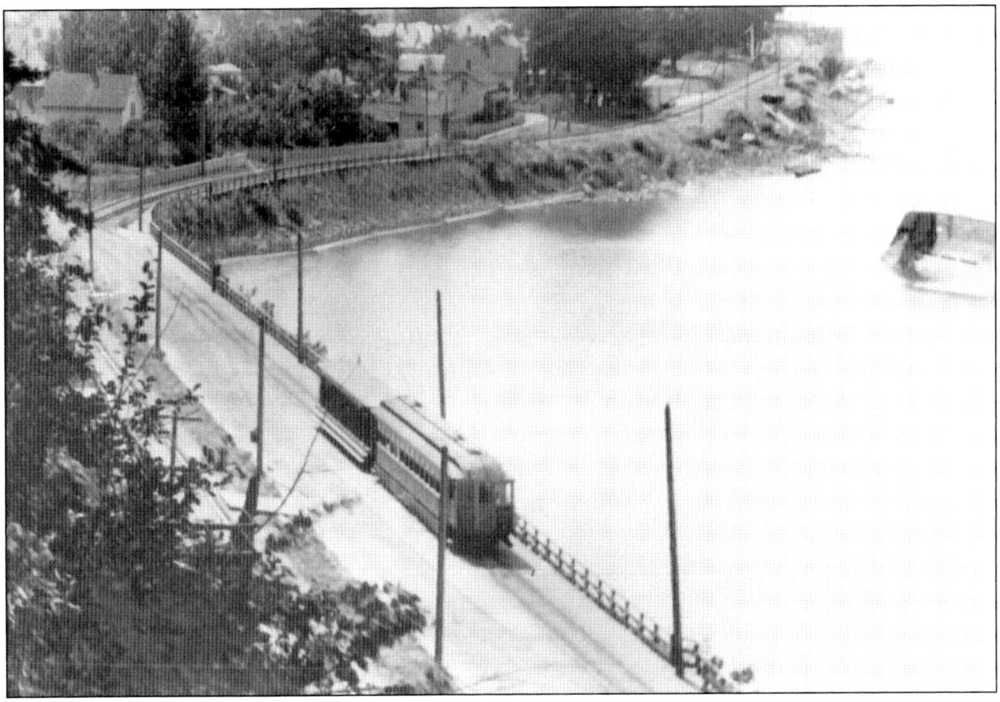

In this c. 1915 photograph, an interurban and open trailer depart the Canemah end of the Oregon City Line. In the background is the Southern Pacific Railroad crossing. The Portland City & Oregon Railway Company overcame opposition from the SP in extending its line here in 1901. Its plans to build all the way to Salem were never realized; however, a popular park was built on the bluff overlooking the Willamette River.

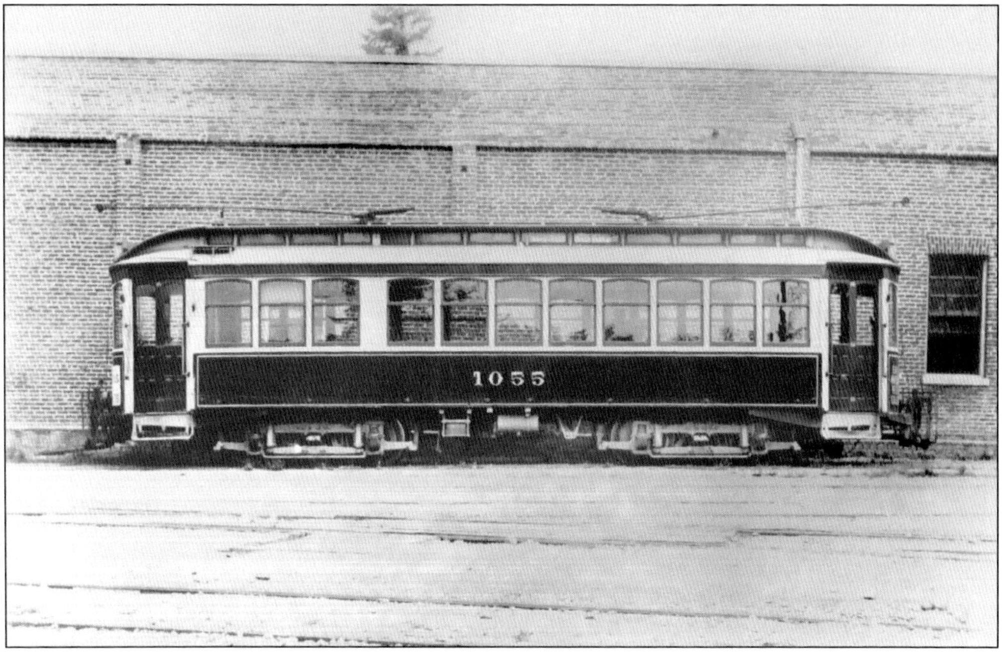

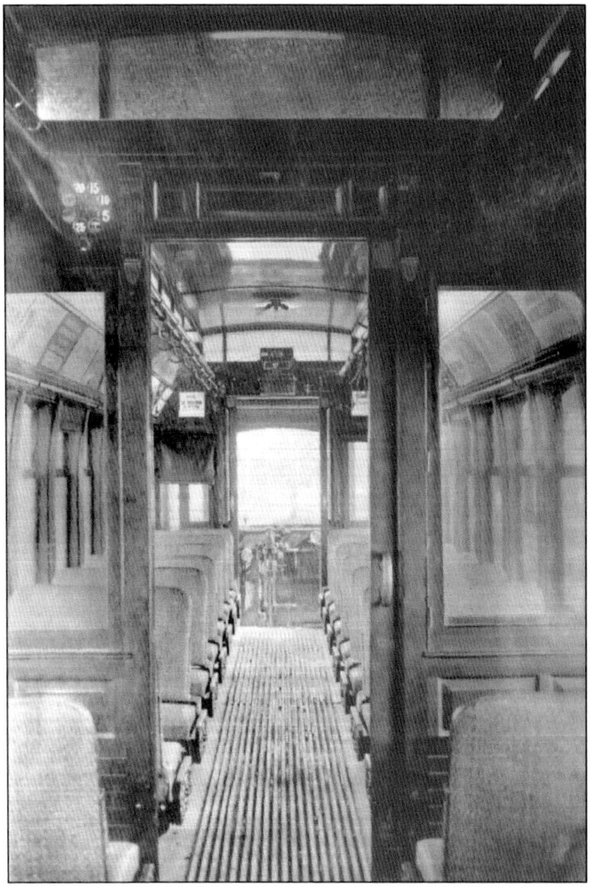

PRLP No. 1055, seen here alongside the Sellwood carbarn, was a two-compartment Brill semi-convertible. The smaller section was for smokers, a practice copied from steam railroad tradition. Long before it was retired in 1939, car No. 1055 had been assigned to the standard-gauge city lines or Oak Grove tripper service.

This well-lit scene reveals a number of details inside OWP No. 56 (sister to No. 1055 above). Notice the sliding doors between the two compartments, Hale & Kilburn rattan seats, standee straps, advertising cards, and the Ohmer fare register (a mechanical device that kept a record of money collected by the conductor). The windows could be slid into wall pockets to create a partly open car.

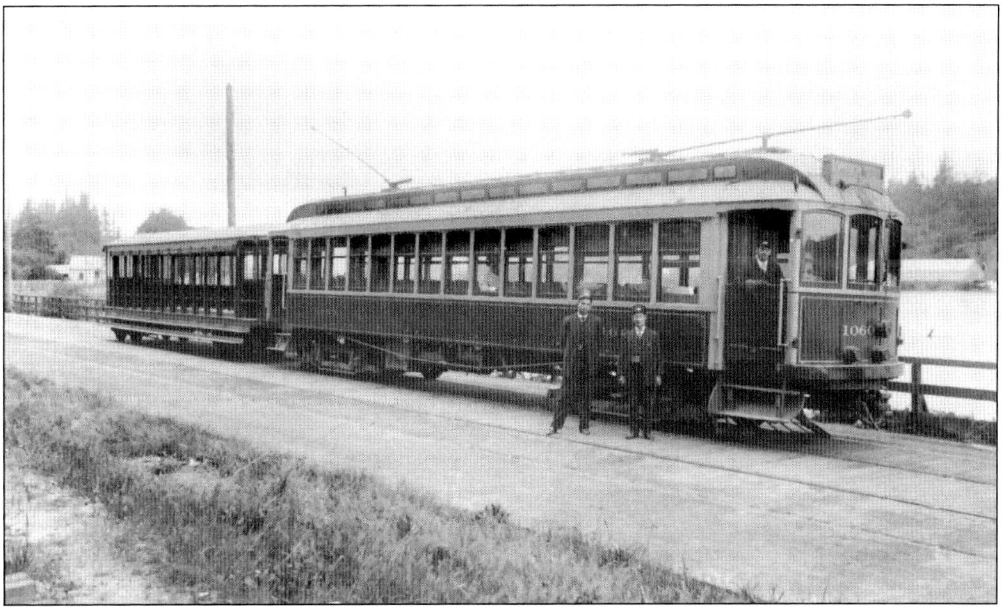

Only one passenger is aboard interurban No. 1060 and an open 1200 series trailer as they get ready to return from Canemah in June 1909. In 1925, car No. 1060 was involved in an accident at Arata Road on the Troutdale Line in which three automobile passengers died. Their car may have been trying to beat the train to the crossing, since motorman Albert A. Reck was absolved of responsibility.

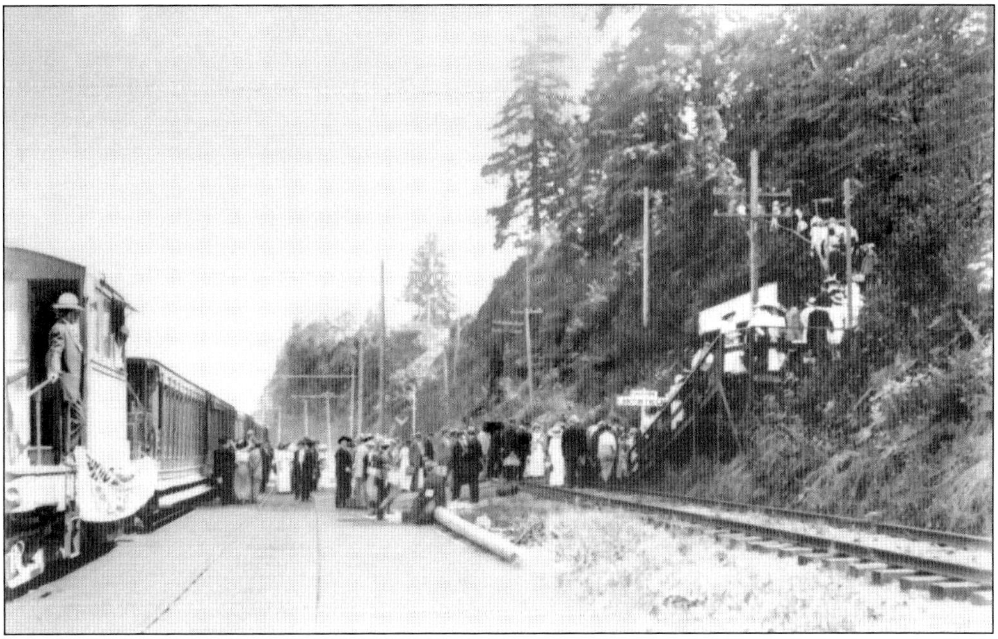

It was not unusual for electric freight locomotives to haul long special trains, as can be seen in this August 1913 photograph. At least five open trailers are evident behind "steeplecab" motor No. 1401 at Canemah. Disembarking International Photo Engraver's Union excursionists are climbing the hill to the picnic grounds. The sign at the bottom of the steps reads "CAUTION LOOK FOR THE CARS."

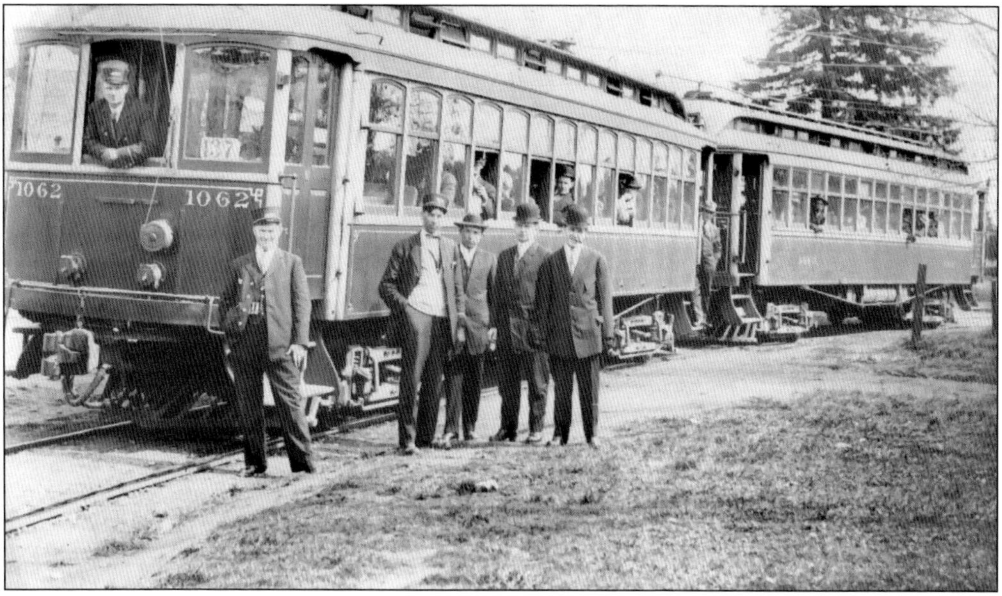

Cigar-chomping company brass pose with the crew of cars No. 1062 and No. 1063 at Golf Junction in 1910. Well-loaded train No. 137 is inbound on the Oregon City Line. No. 1062 caught fire just north of The Oaks on the afternoon of August 7, 1929, but the $500 damage was repaired and the car continued in service until 1936. Note the lack of interconnecting train doors on this series of Brill interurbans.

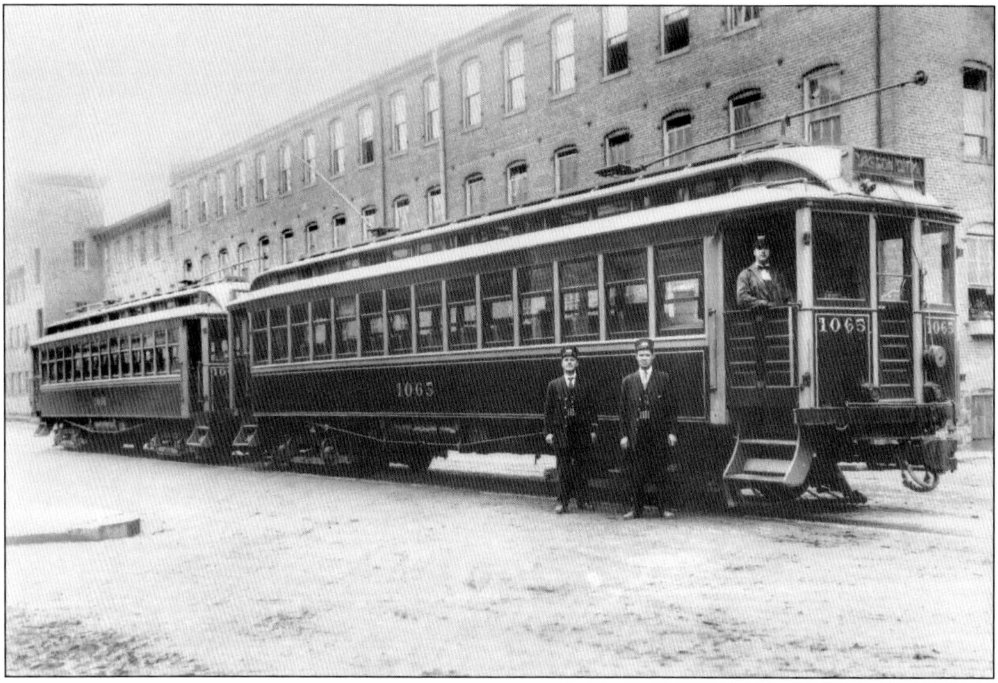

Cars No. 1065 and No. 1066 are seen next to the Oregon City Woolen Mill on Third and Main Streets in this 1912 photograph. For more than 30 years, this mill was known for its brightly colored Native American and novelty blankets. The crew on this train included motorman Joseph B. Simonetti and conductors Charles W. Moore, Nathaniel T. Hart, and Harry W. Simmons (not shown).

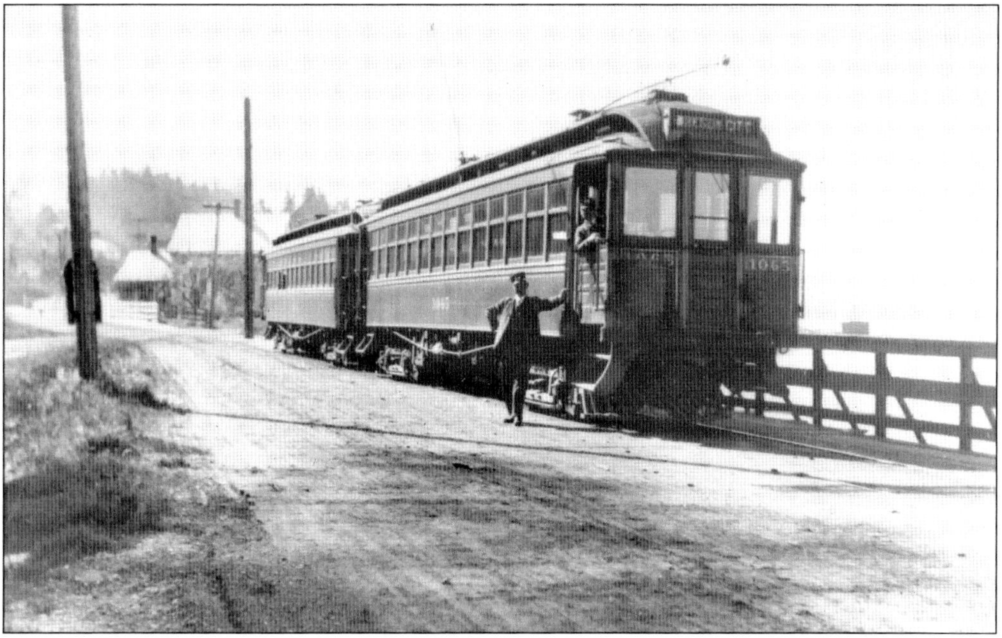

PRL&P No. 1065 and mate are laying over at Canemah in this c. 1913 photograph. They are hemmed in by the Willamette River on the right and the Southern Pacific Railroad mainline on the left. Oregon City local train No. 134 reached Canemah at 1:10 p.m. and departed for Portland 10 minutes later as train No. 135.

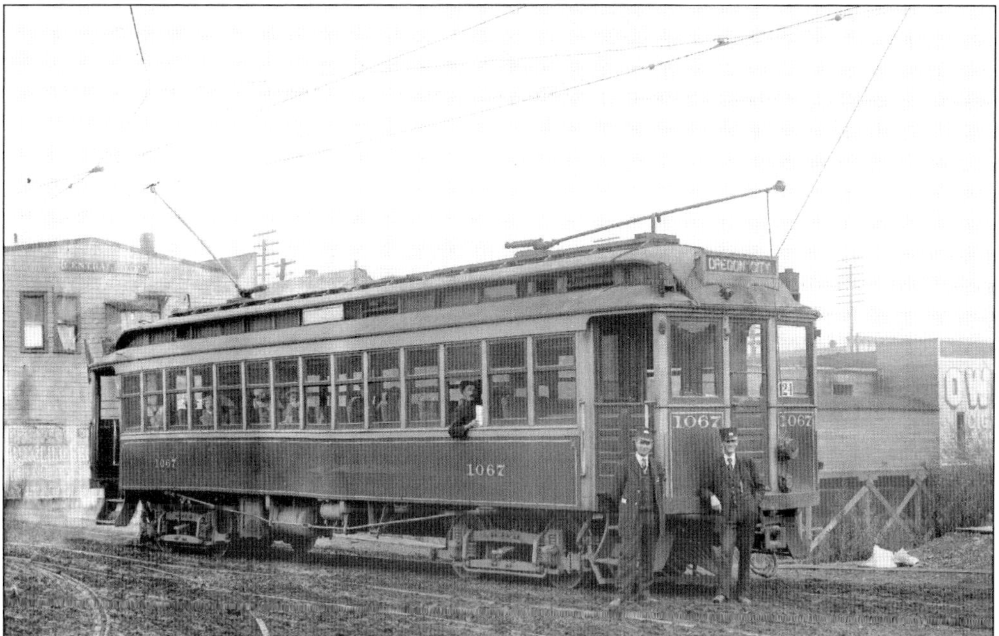

Car No. 1067, seen here on Southeast Water and Hawthorne Streets behind the Central Hotel, was rebuilt by PRL&P in 1907. After being retired in 1946, it survived as a cabin at Cannon Beach. Today, it is the last surviving interurban passenger car built in Oregon. In 1981, the late Mike Parker rescued it for the Oregon Electric Railway Historical Society's collection in Brooks, Oregon.

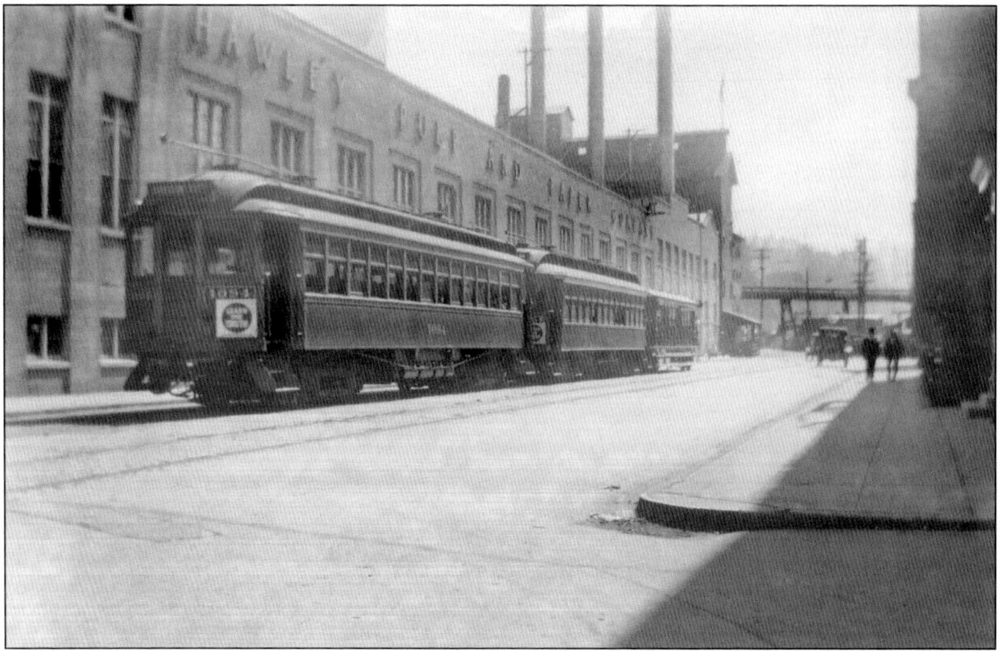

A three-car train, including Nos. 1094, 1064, and an open trailer, is on its way back from Canemah Park as it pauses in front of Hawley Pulp and Paper Company on Main Street in Oregon City on a warm 1910s afternoon. It is still during the PRL&P years, but the pin striping on these cars has already been simplified.

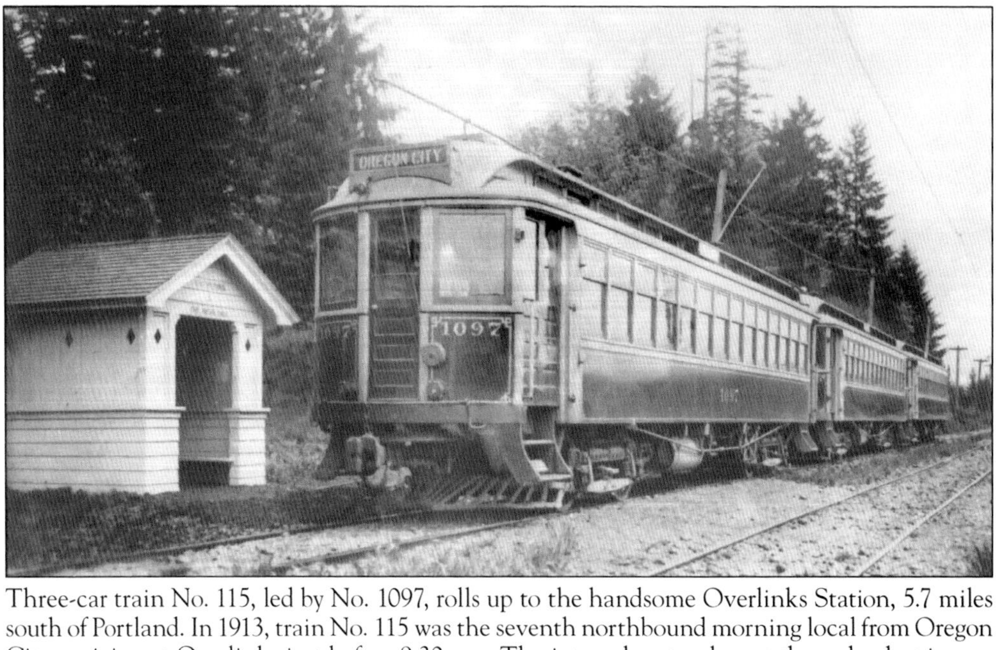

Three-car train No. 115, led by No. 1097, rolls up to the handsome Overlinks Station, 5.7 miles south of Portland. In 1913, train No. 115 was the seventh northbound morning local from Oregon City, arriving at Overlinks just before 9:30 a.m. The interurban tracks cut through what is now Waverley Country Club, making the station name appropriate. Car No. 1097 is reported to have been the last wooden interurban burned for scrap in 1953.

PEPCO car No. 1098 is shown crossing the Clackamas River railway bridge at Gladstone. No. 1098 was the first in its series to be retired, following a wreck in June 1945. This bridge, opened in March 1908, replaced the original structure completed by the East Side Railway in 1893. Its 260-foot length was unusually long for a riveted span.

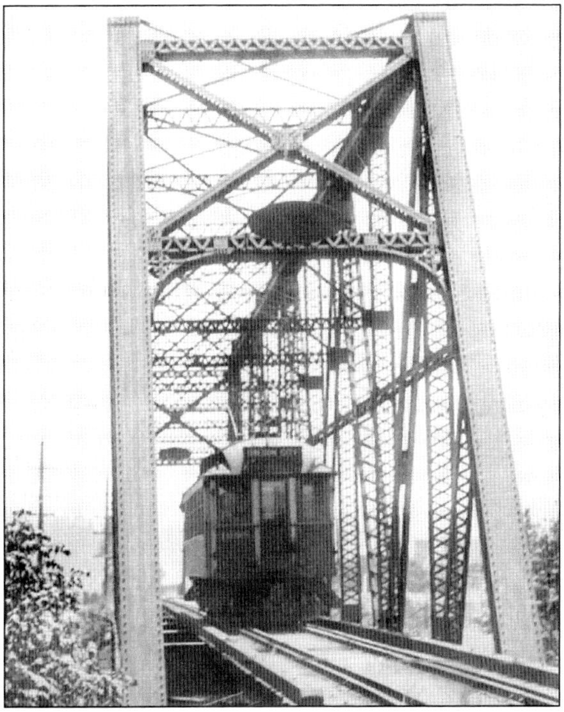

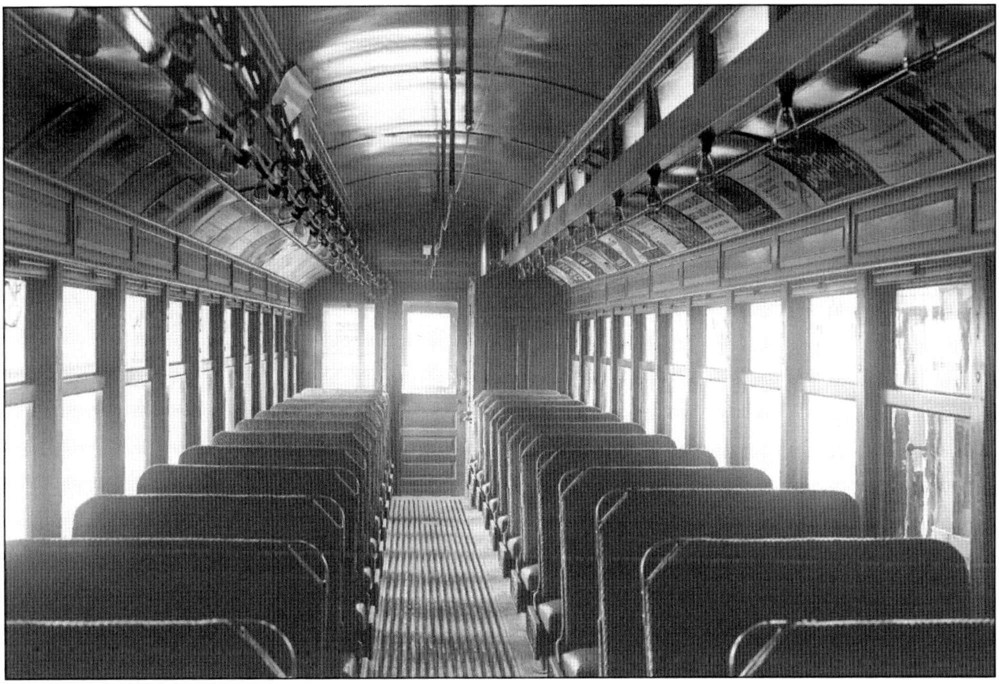

No. 1098 was furnished in a manner typical of Portland's locally built interurbans, including leather walkover seats, exposed light bulbs, clerestory ceilings, fare counter, and advertising cards. In the right background is the lavatory. The late trolley historian Bill Hayes remembered using both the toilet and drinking water facilities on a similar car in 1923, when he was 10 years old. His only comment: "the ice water was warm."

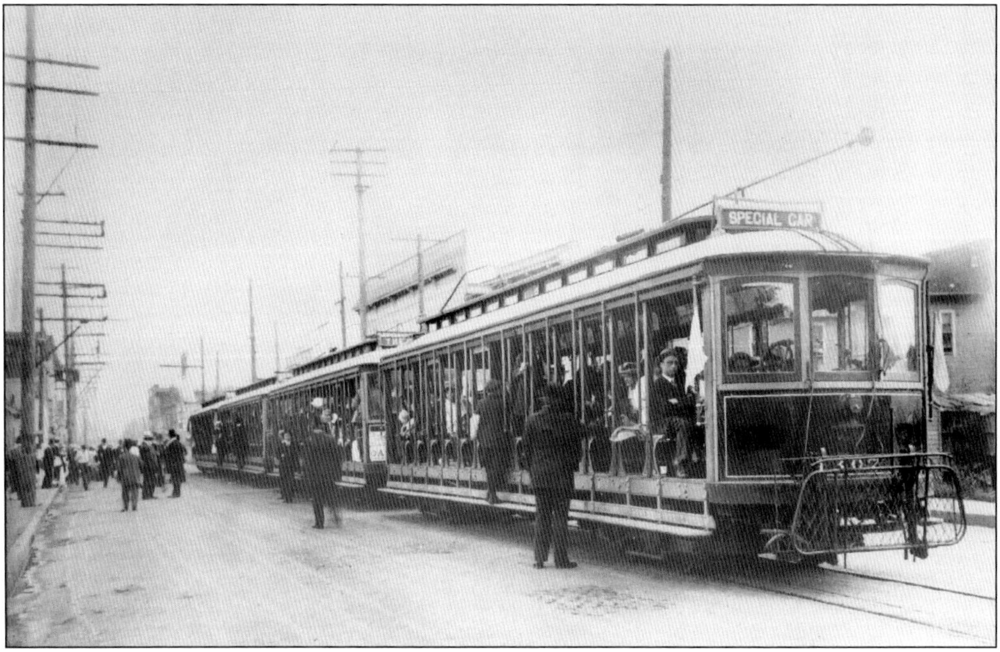

This photograph from the collection of Portland Traction Company superintendent Edward Vonderahe shows four open cars boarding on Southeast Water Street for a policeman's picnic at Oaks Park. The bent trolley pole on lead car No. 1307 is likely the result of reversing without changing poles. The dash sign on the second car advertises a daily band concert at The Oaks. (Photograph Fred L. Blaisdell.)

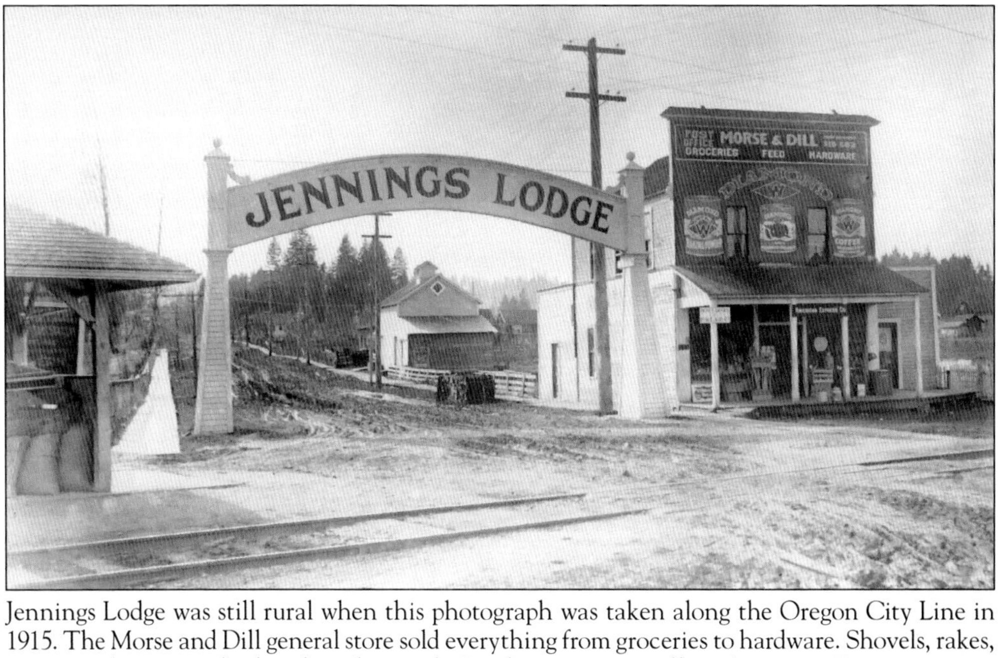

Jennings Lodge was still rural when this photograph was taken along the Oregon City Line in 1915. The Morse and Dill general store sold everything from groceries to hardware. Shovels, rakes, crates, and cans are displayed on the porch. Inside were a post office, American Express agency, and PRL&P ticket office. Ticket offices were also located at Portland, East Portland, Milwaukie, Oak Grove, Gladstone, and Oregon City.

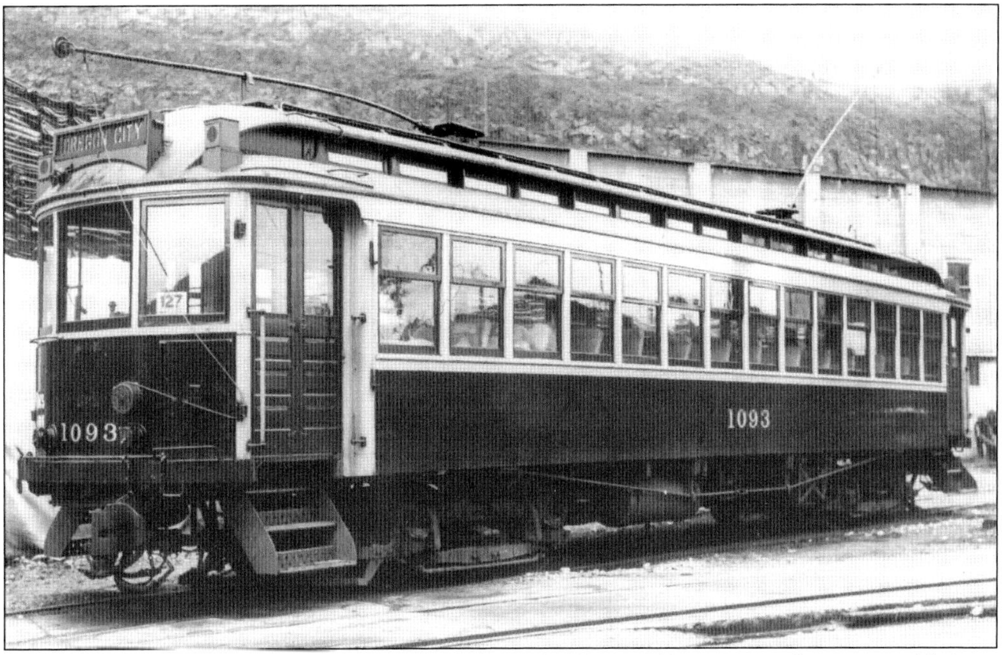

Portland-built interurban No. 1093 is seen here at the Oregon City terminal next to Publisher's Paper Company not long after conversion to one-man operation in the 1930s. It never looked so good again. Except for the lack of train doors and pin striping, it is still close to PRL&P appearance, with red and cream colors and mahogany-stained doors and windows. It is train No. 127 and displays an Oaks Park dash sign.

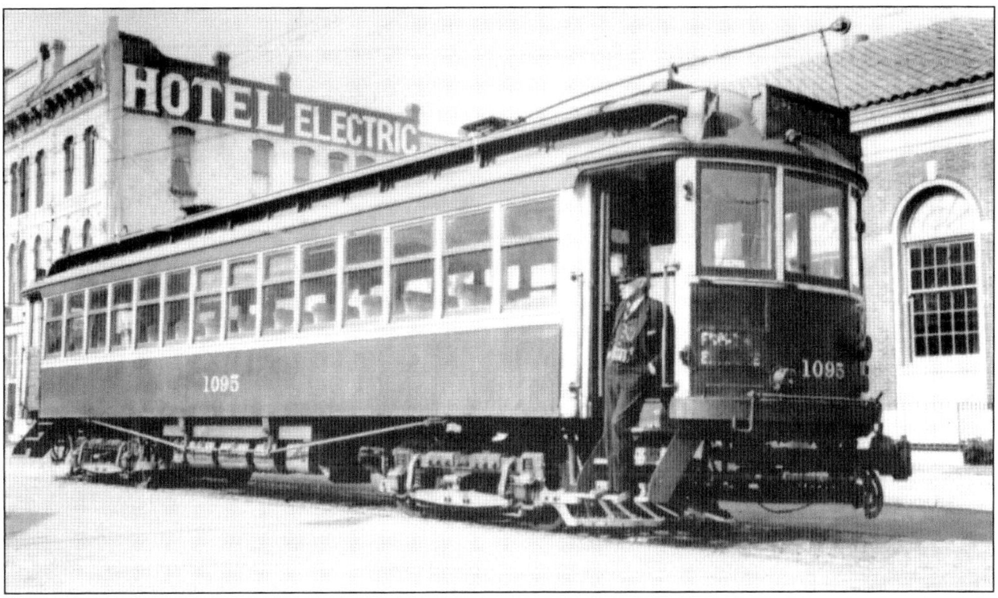

It is the 1940s, and the operator of empty car No. 1095 slouches against the handrail as he lays over at the Oregon City terminus on Main Street. Worn-looking PEPCO No. 1095 is only a couple of years from retirement, when lightweight metal suburban streetcars will supplant the old interurbans. The Hotel Electric makes a fitting background for the nation's first true electric interurban railway.

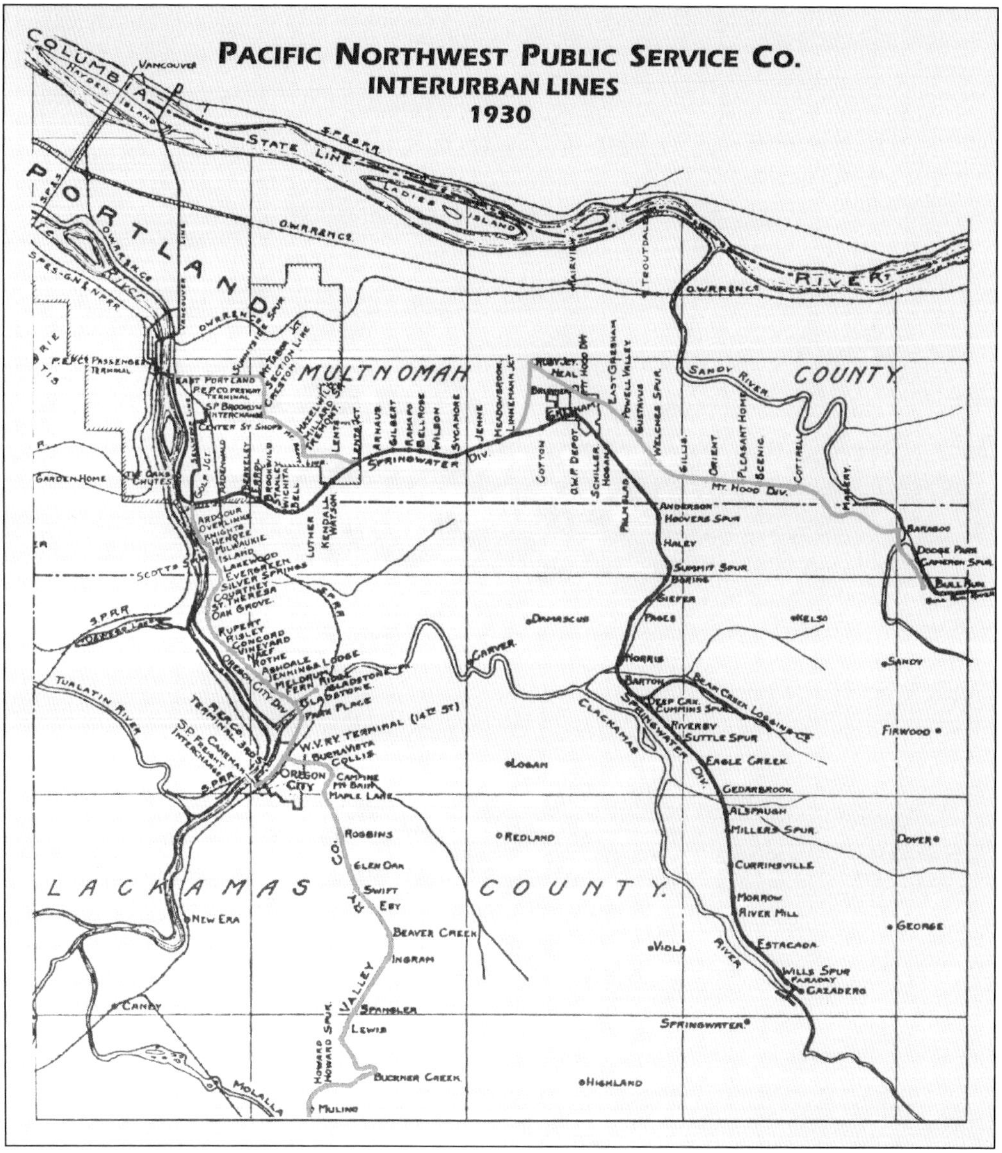

This map highlights the Springwater Division Line to Estacada and Cazadero in 1930, just before the short-lived Pacific Northwest Public Service Company began cutbacks in passenger service. The narrow-gauge line to Vancouver is also illustrated. The Oregon Water Power & Railway Company began construction on the Springwater Division in August 1902 and launched preliminary passenger service to Gresham in January 1903. Until the power plant at Boring went online, trains were hauled by steam locomotives. Service was extended to Boring in October. In June 1904, the longest eastside line was completed to Cazadero, 36 miles from Portland. That August, the river route between Portland and Sellwood was also finished (the previous right-of-way, which can be seen on this map, became the Sellwood Line) and work on the dam at Cazadero began. Further extensions were not used for passenger service. Interurban passenger trains stopped running to Cazadero in 1933, to Boring in 1936, and to Gresham in 1949.

Three

The Longest Run

THE ESTACADA LINE

The first interurbans resembled large streetcars. The East Side Railway's fleet included Brill semiconvertibles from the Metropolitan Railway, Pullman four-wheelers intended for use on the Hawthorne Line, and double truck cars from builders Holman (San Francisco), Brownell (St. Louis), Indianapolis Car, as well as Portland's Columbia Car & Tool Works.

As the experimental 1890s came to a close, standard interurban designs predominated. In 1901, successor Portland City & Oregon Railway (PC&O) started modernizing existing cars while also ordering new ones. The shop in Milwaukie lengthened older rolling stock by splicing cars together, enclosing platforms, adding railroad-style roofs, and installing more powerful motors, effectively creating new cars.

Later cars from the Holman Company rode on trucks (the carriage beneath the car containing the wheels and motors) designed by Portland Railway, Light & Power (PRL&P) vice president Franklin I. Fuller. In 1910, PRL&P began building its own interurbans.

On June 6, 1902, the PC&O became part of the Oregon Water Power & Railway (OWP), which was incorporated to develop hydroelectric power on the Clackamas River. Preliminary passenger service to Gresham, using steam locomotives, started in January 1903. Portland's longest interurban, the 36-mile Springwater Division, was completed to Estacada and Cazadero in 1904 during dam construction.

Estacada trains traveled through deep gorges, along narrow plateaus, and over the highest pile trestle in the world (the 95-foot-high Eagle Creek Trestle) on their way to the forested foothills of the Cascade Mountains. The line was advertised as "the Trout Route" due to good fishing streams along the way. The company built a lodge-like hotel in Estacada. Within months, 52 stations were being served by seven daily trains to Estacada and two "milk trains" to Cazadero.

An ambitious scheme to build into Eastern Oregon did not come to fruition, however, a long extension was added in 1924, the year PRL&P became part of the Portland Electric Power Company. The 23-mile run was used for construction of the Oak Grove Dam, although it never carried passengers.

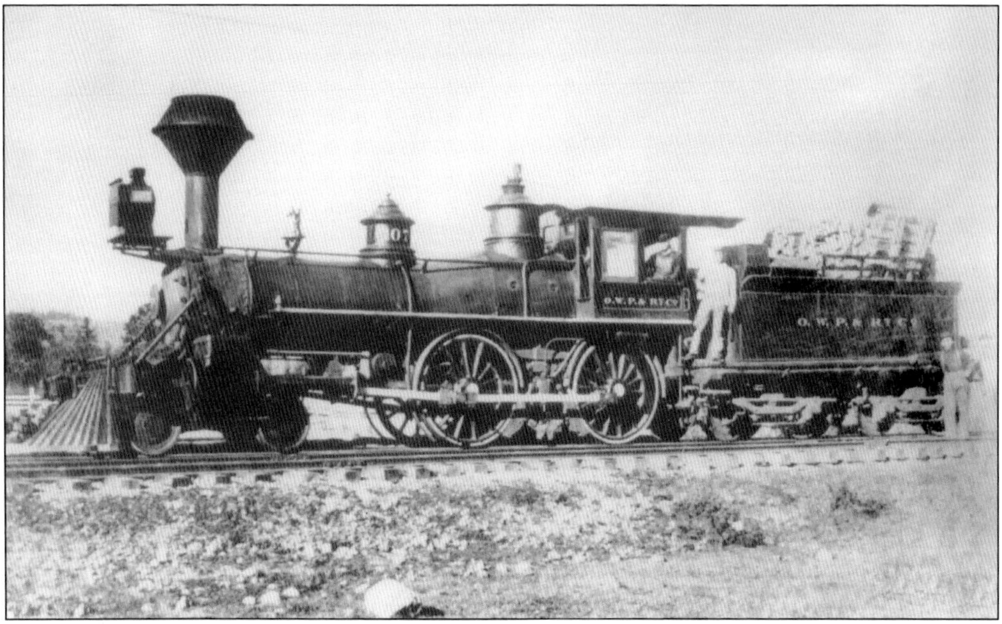

The locomotive acquired by the Oregon Water Power & Railway Company in 1903 looked like something out of the Wild West. The 1882 vintage engine No. 107 replaced the Mount Scott Line steam dummy that had inaugurated passenger service to Gresham. By October, the old Baldwin 4-4-0 was hauling trains to the end of the line at Cazadero. After the line was electrified, OWP's steam locomotives were used on construction trains.

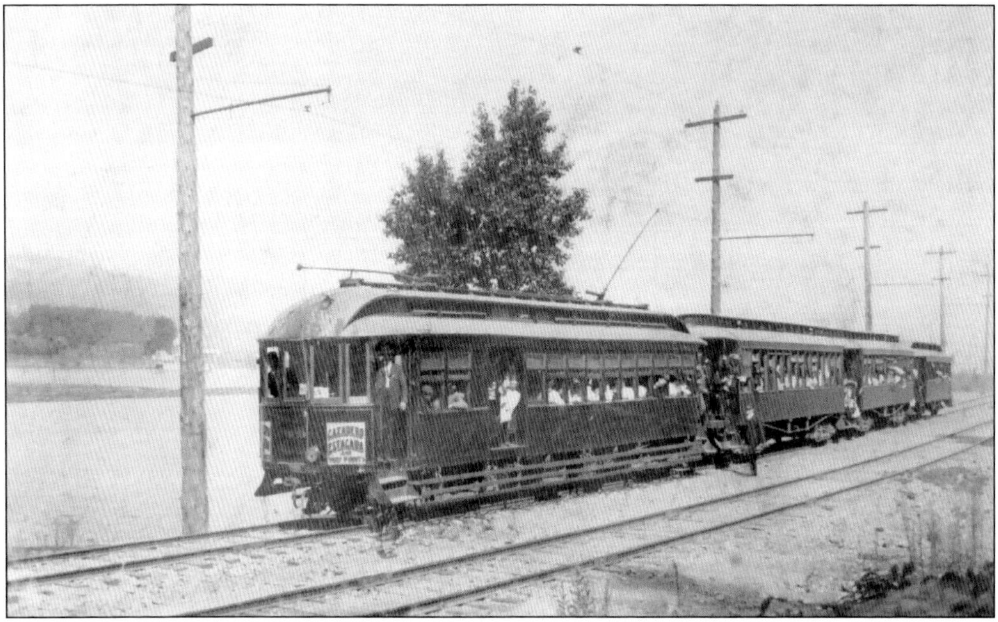

OWP opened its new river route from East Portland to Golf Junction in August 1904, which shaved 25 minutes off travel times to Oregon City and Estacada. Here, while well-loaded Cazadero train No. 26, headed by No. 49, pauses for a photograph along the Willamette River, a conductor hurries forward and young excursionists lean from platforms and freight doors. The dash sign reads "Cazadero Estacada and Way Points." (Photograph Theodore J. Labrecque.)

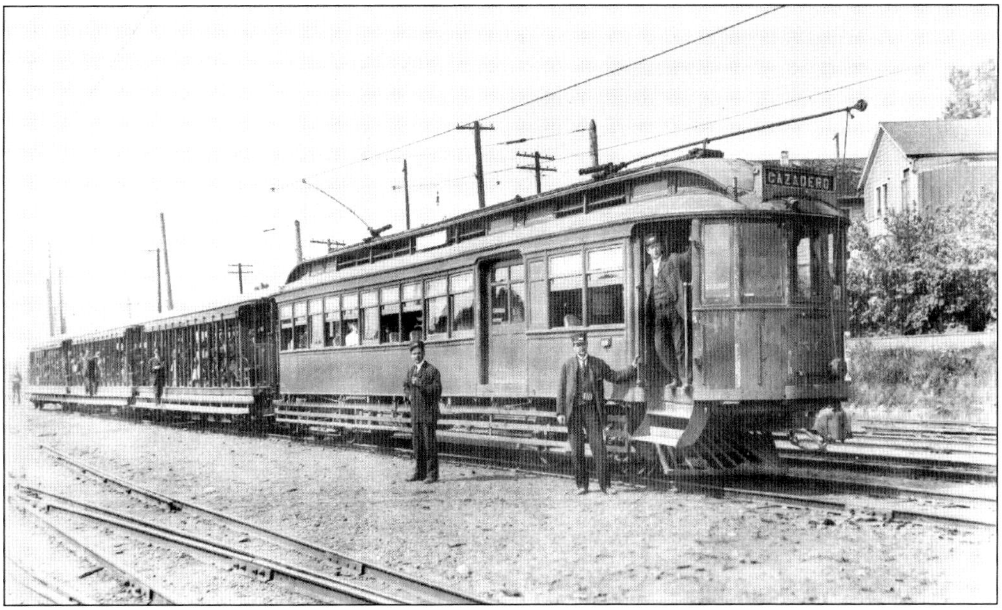

Former OWP combine No. 50 and three open trailers have stopped at the East Portland Yard headlight rack to pick up one of the portable headlights before heading out for late-afternoon duty on the Cazadero Line. The identified crewmen in this c. 1908 photograph are conductor Jim McCowan (standing at foot of platform) and motorman Charles Holmes (in cab doorway). The other conductors are not identified. (Courtesy Mark Moore.)

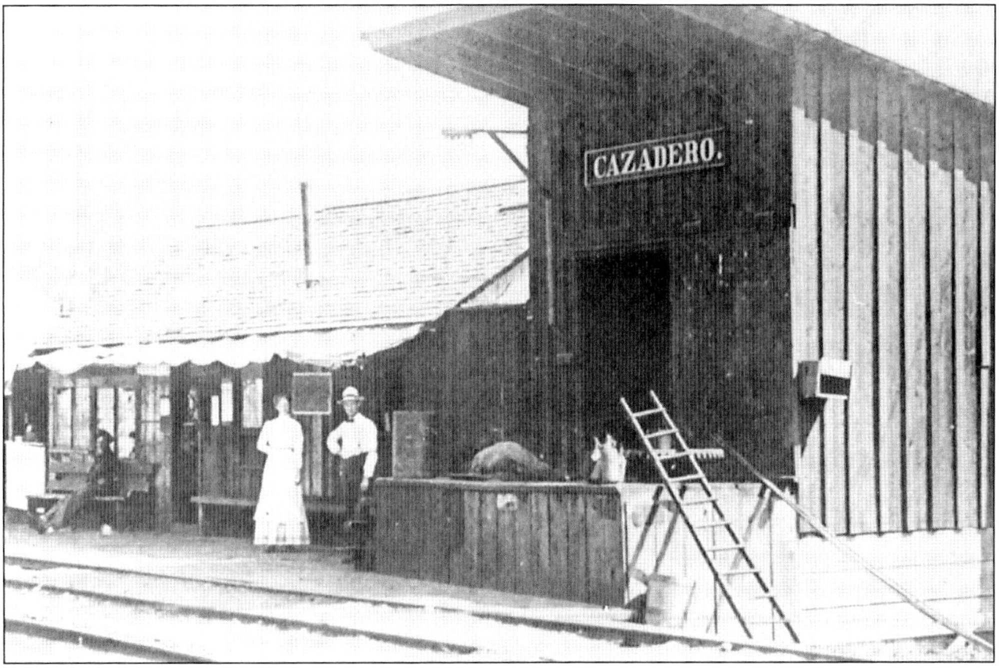

The Springwater Division Line terminated at Cazadero, 36.46 miles from Portland, making it the longest interurban line in Oregon when completed in 1904. The station and freight platform at Cazadero, seen here about 1905, were two miles south of the main stop at Estacada. The name *Cazadero* is said to have been derived from a Native American term for "hunting ground."

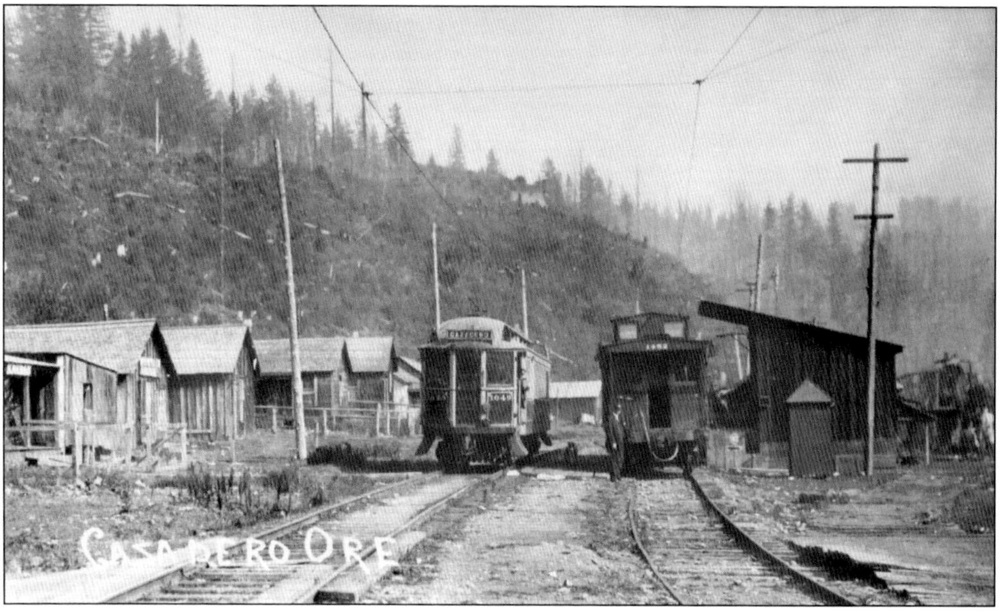

Milk cans are ready to be loaded onto No. 1049, seen at Cazadero Station next to caboose No. 1452. The small buildings next to the tracks include the Mountain House boardinghouse. The single passenger car seems adequate on this apparently quiet day. By the time this photograph was taken, around 1908, train doors had been added to No. 1049 and the caboose built from former box motor No. 103.

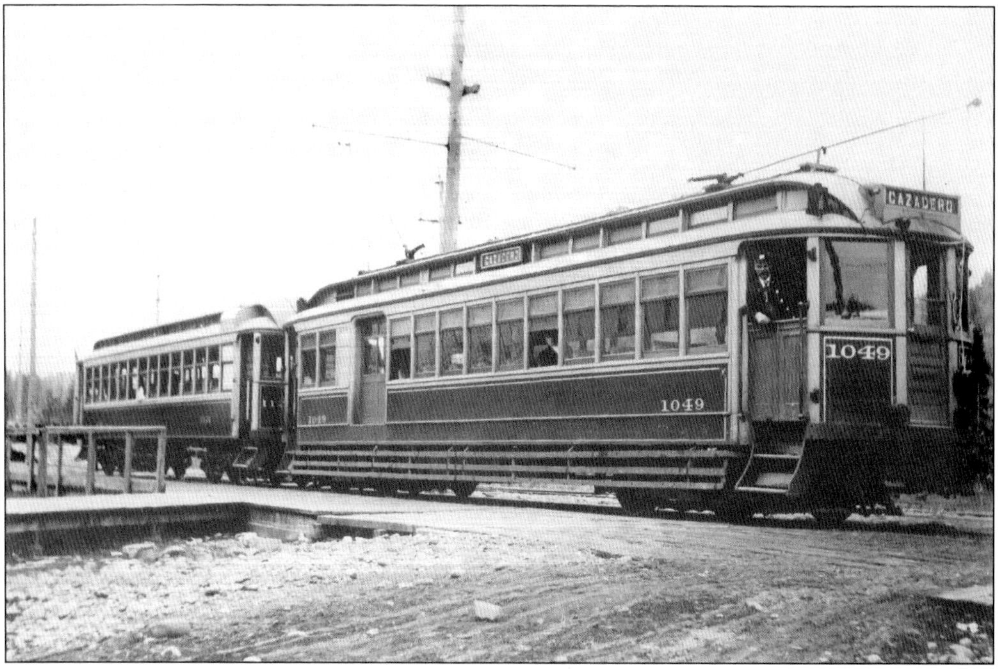

A young woman and the motorman peer from combine (combination freight and passenger car) No. 1049 as it lays over at Estacada around 1910. The second car is toilet-equipped trailer No. 1121. During a 1908 rebuild, PRL&P replaced the original 1903 Holman five-window ends on No. 1049 and added train doors. (Courtesy Mark Moore.)

This 1910 advertisement for the Hotel Estacada promoted its excellent cuisine as well as the good hunting and fishing that could be enjoyed in the area. A meal or stay at this hostelry was often included in the price of an excursion package over the Springwater Division interurban line. The hotel, which was built and owned by the Oregon Water Power & Railway Company, included a bar and dance floor.

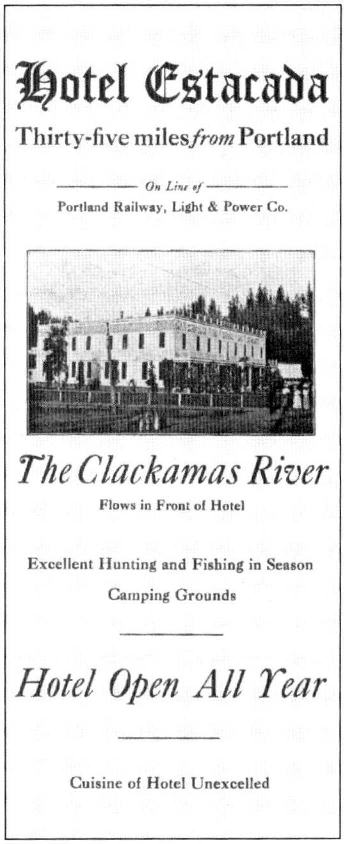

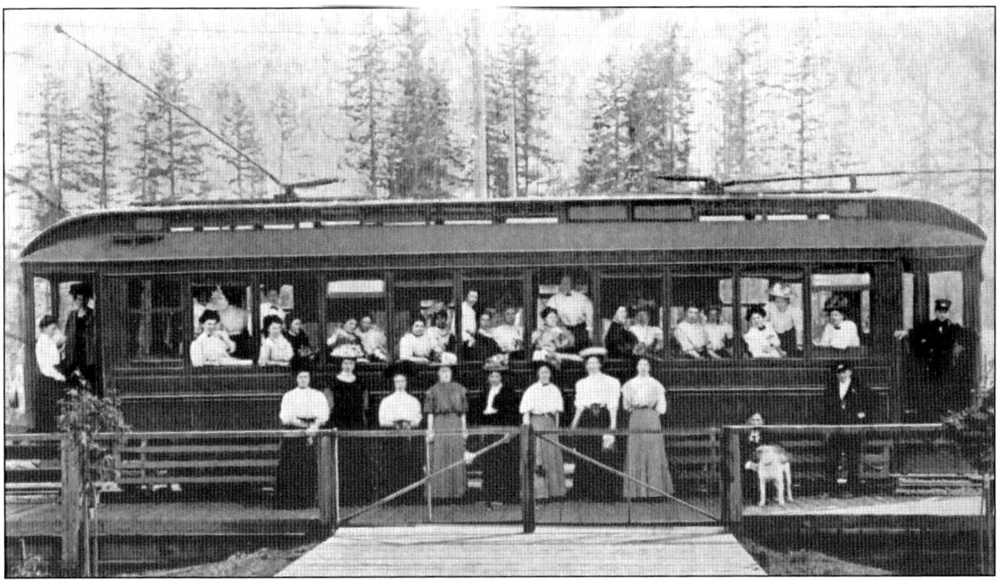

The participants in an interurban schoolteachers' picnic pose for the camera with dog Nero and car No. 1053 or 1054 in front of the Hotel Estacada. The reverse of this postcard explained that a new four-room schoolhouse for elementary and high school grades had been erected in 1906 in a district that was among the most progressive in the county. (Courtesy Jerry Risberg.)

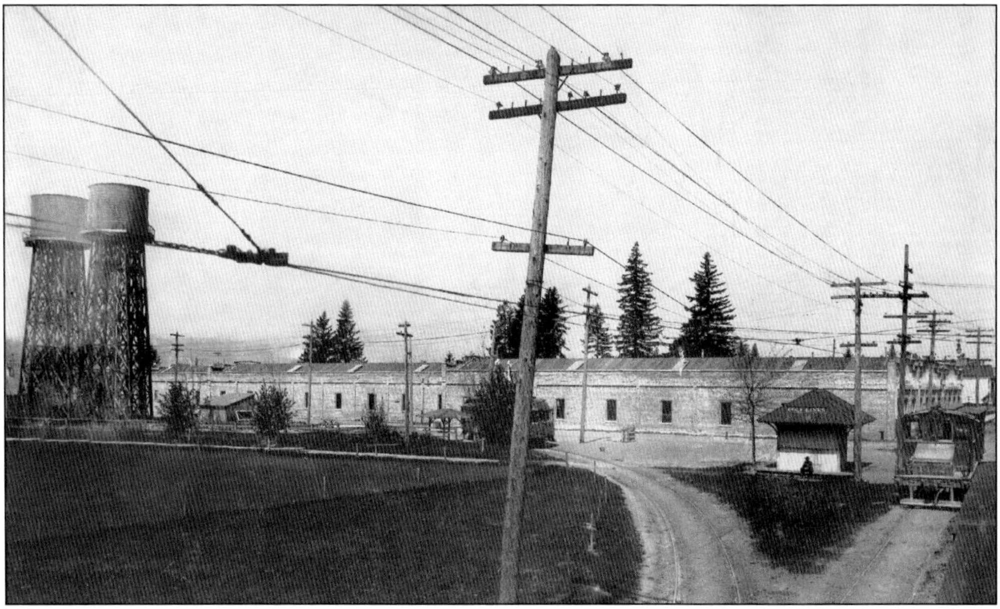

During 1909–1910, a carbarn was erected in Sellwood, and cars formerly housed in Milwaukie were transferred to the new facility. In this south side view of the Sellwood carbarn, one of the former East Side Railway "girls" is taking on its crew at the head of the Oregon City tracks, while steeplecab No. 1402 hauls a freight train down Southeast Thirteenth Avenue past Golf Links Station. (Courtesy Sellwood-Moreland Improvement League.)

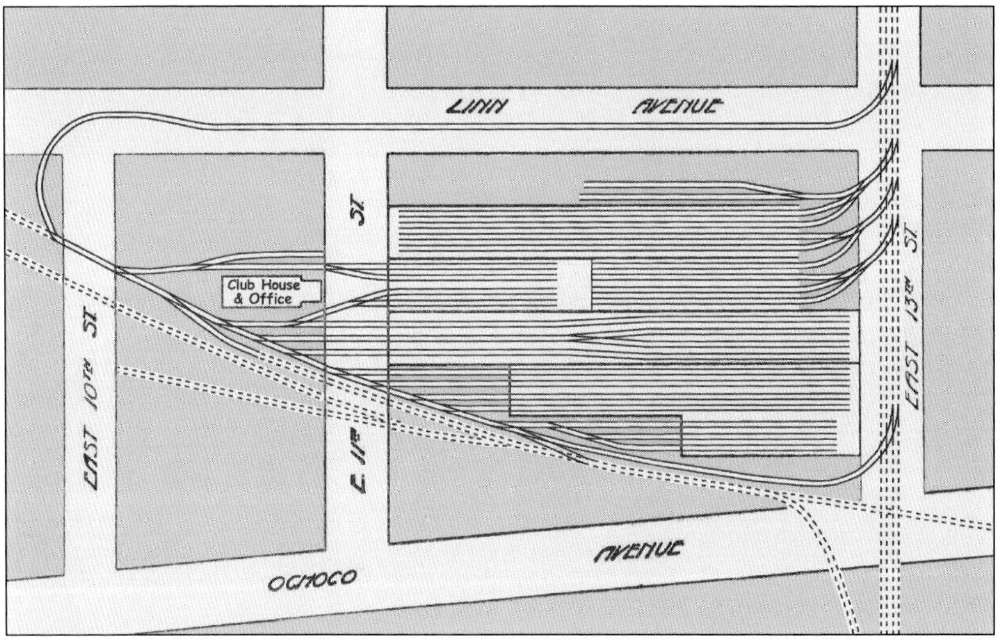

The Sellwood carbarn is displayed in this 1910 plan. On the Eleventh Street side of the carbarn, 14 tracks entered four bays, while eight entered two bays on East Thirteenth Street. Dashed lines represent the tracks from Portland to Estacada or Oregon City, and the Sellwood Line on East Thirteenth Street. The rectangular building at left is the Club House and Office, which is pictured on the next page.

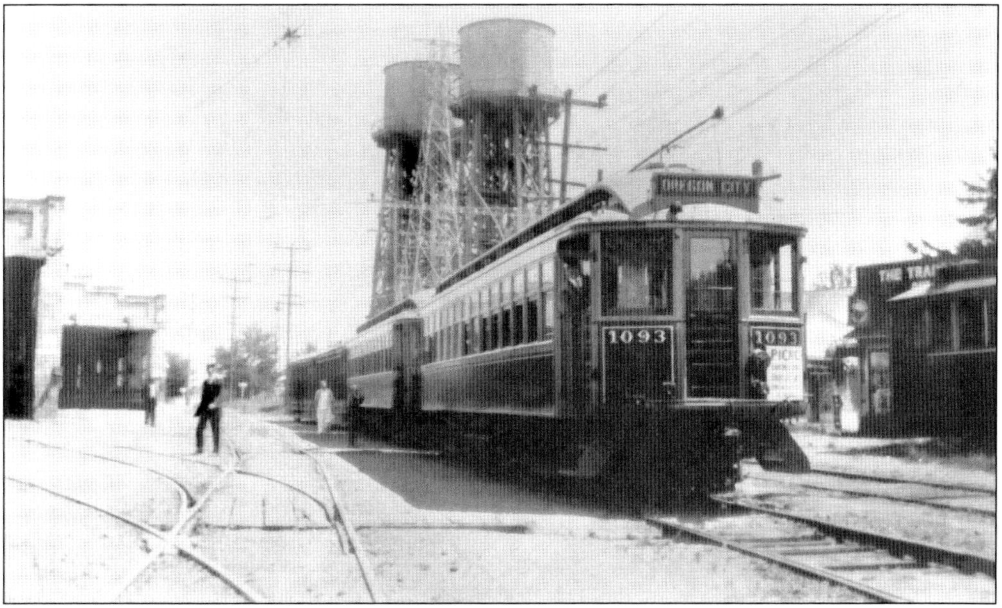

Behind the Oregon City train in this 1928 photograph can be seen, from left to right, Sellwood carbarn bays A and B, the two tall water towers (removed in the 1930s), and a grocery store and lunch room at Southeast Eleventh and Ochoco Streets called the Trainman. The OWP Division was headquartered here until 1940, when the interurbans relocated to the East Portland Yard.

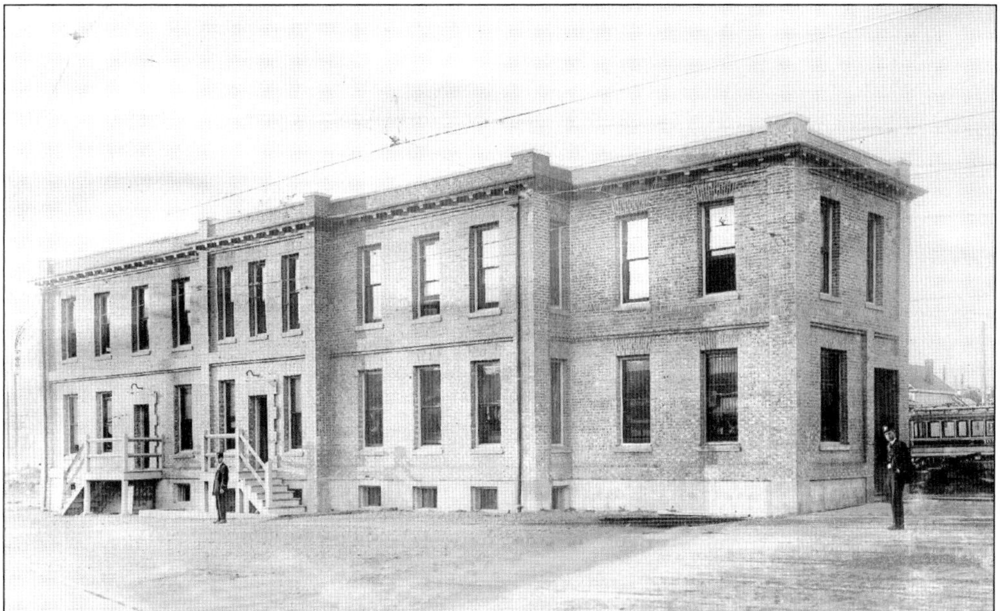

This 1910 construction photograph shows the new clubhouse and office on Southeast Eleventh Street next to the Sellwood carbarn. All carbarns had recreational facilities for employees, but this was the finest. It provided an area in which employees could relax, play pool, and even take a bath. At far right, behind the conductor, is standard-gauge city streetcar No. 1090. (Photograph Fred L. Blaisdell.)

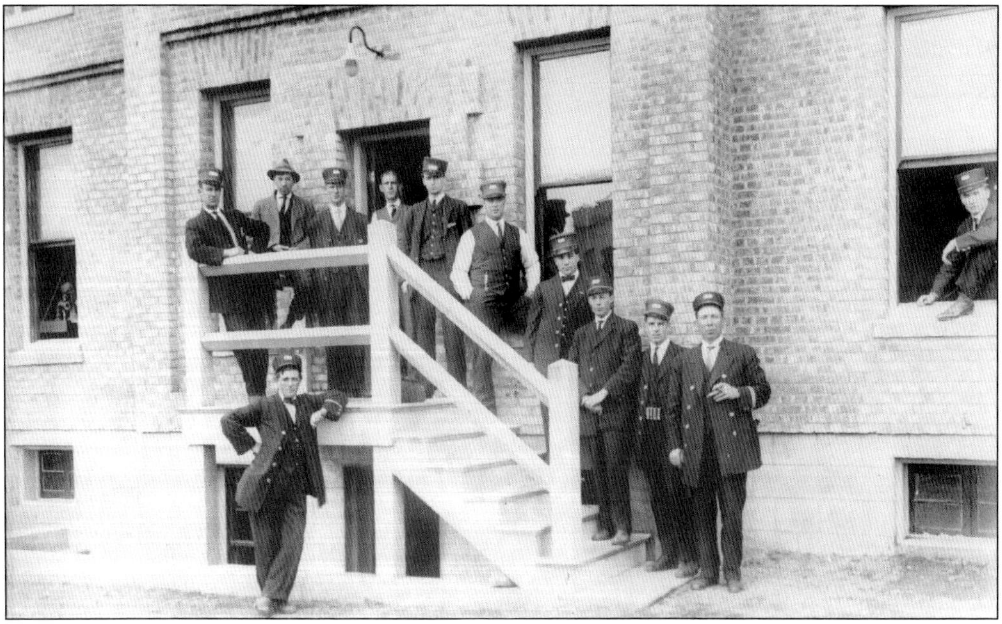

The PRL&P employees in this group photograph at the Sellwood Club House are unidentified, but we can tell something about them. For example, the carman with a cigarette in his hand is a senior motorman (two stripes on his sleeve), and there are two office personnel at the top of the stairs (wearing suits). Note the telephone in the office window at left. (Photograph Fred L. Blaisdell.)

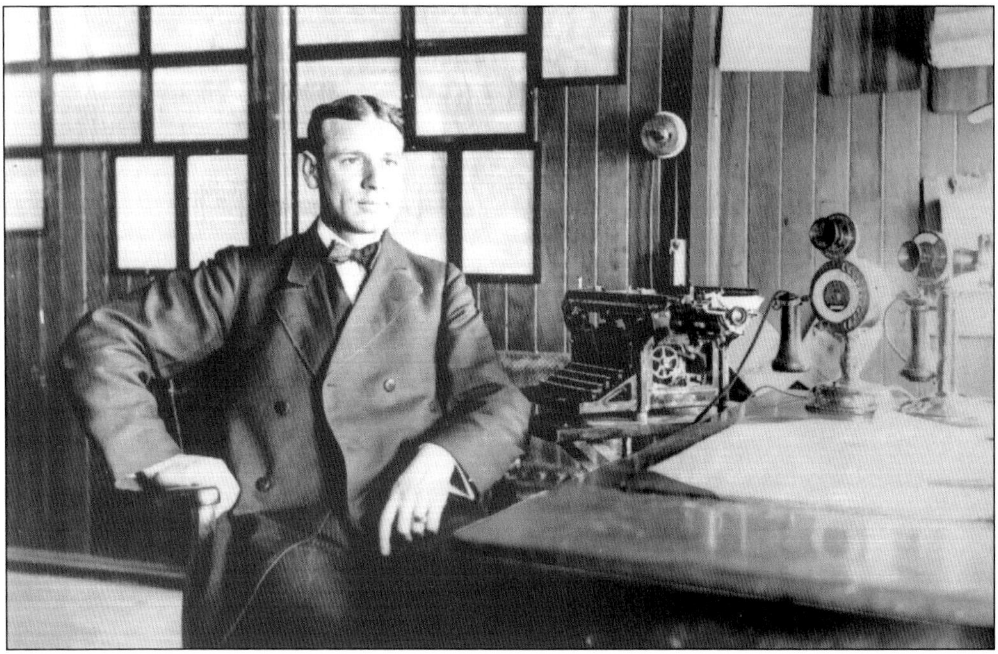

Nattily attired PRL&P dispatcher Joseph F. Roach, seen here at his desk in 1909, had at his disposal the latest technology. In addition to the typewriter and bulletin board, he had telephones from the Home Telephone and Pacific Telephone Companies. Two phones were necessary because there were two competing systems at the time. Roach also worked as a motorman, then an inspector and, by 1920, was interurban division assistant superintendent.

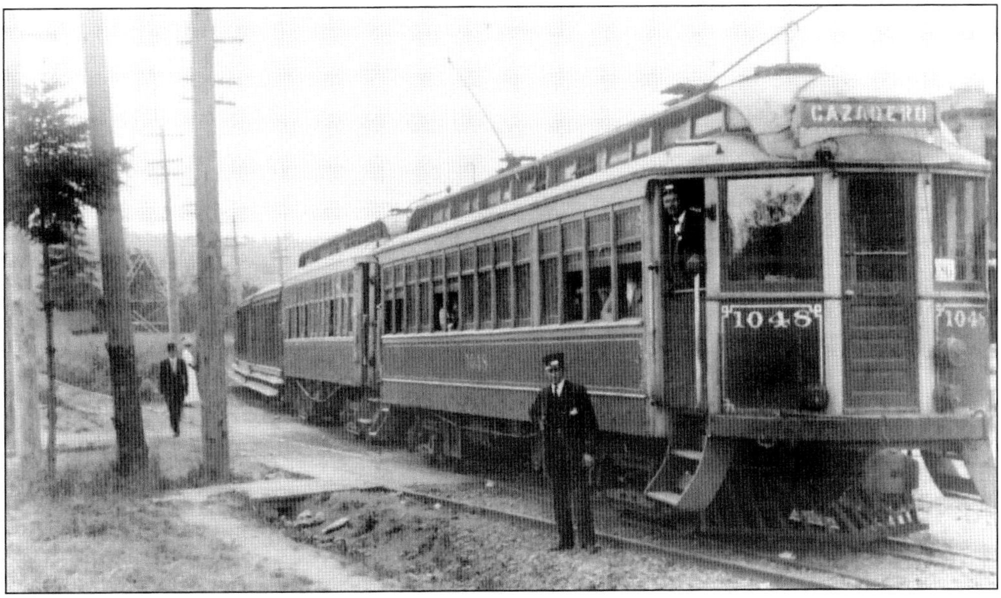

The conductor looks impatient as Cazadero-bound train No. 86 waits on the mainline across from the Sellwood Club House. No. 1048, and one of the 1060s, are pulling a string of open trailers. During a 1908 remodeling from a mail and express car to a standard passenger car, No. 1048 lost its original 1893 Holman five-windowed ends.

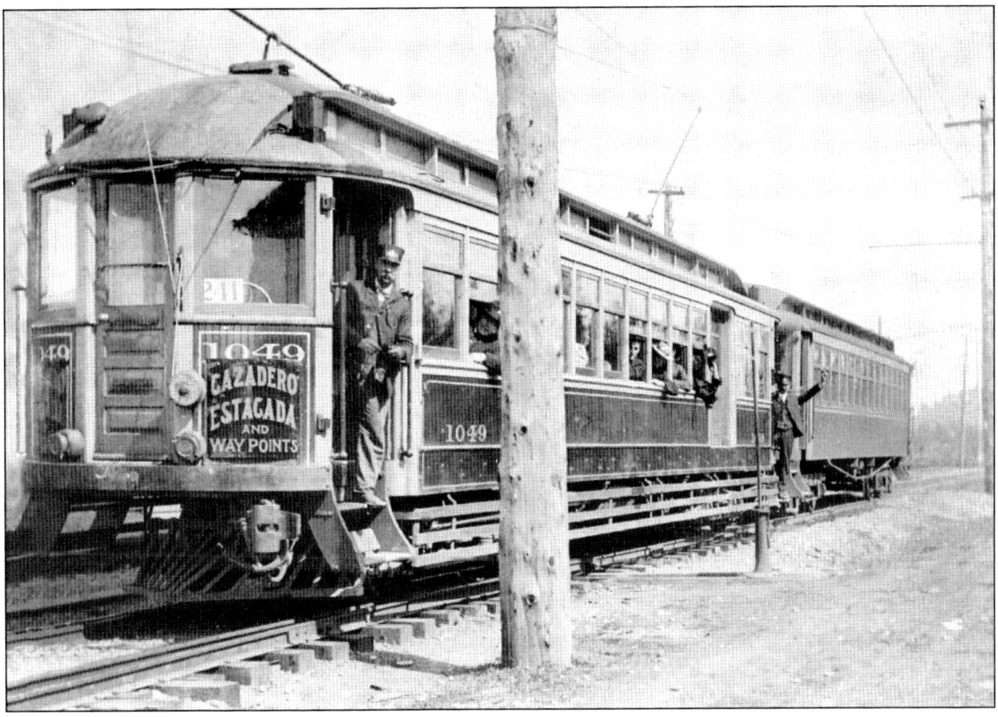

The crew and passengers of Estacada Line No. 1049 are waving and tipping their hats to motorman Albert A. Reck at Lents Junction in 1911. The large stenciled metal destination signs have not yet been installed on the front and side of the roof. (Photograph Albert A. Reck; courtesy Mark Moore.)

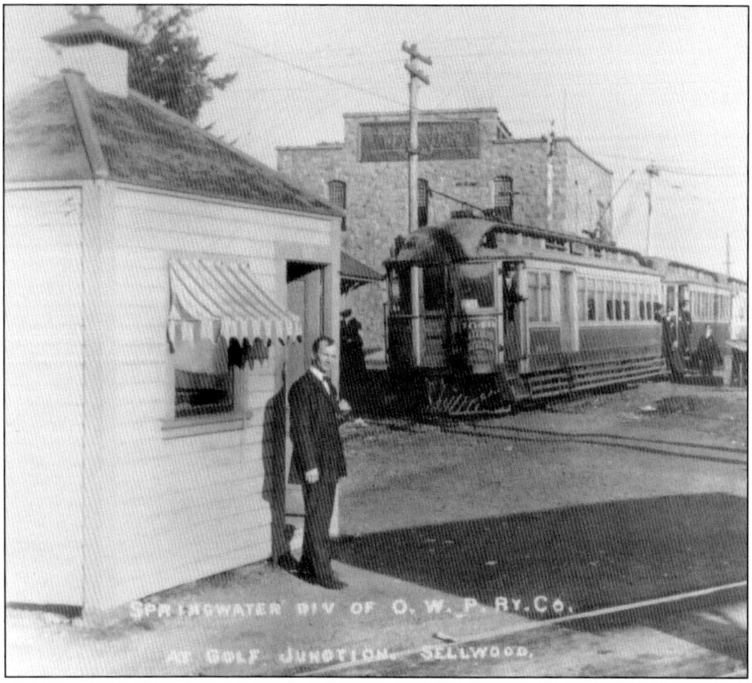

The agent squints into the sun as inbound Estacada train No. 251 arrives at Southeast Thirteenth and Ochoco Streets on an afternoon in 1908. A corner of Golf Links Station and the OWP substation can be seen behind car No. 1049. Around 1910, the station was moved closer to the Oregon City Line (seen at lower right) and renamed Golf Junction. (Courtesy Norm Gholston.)

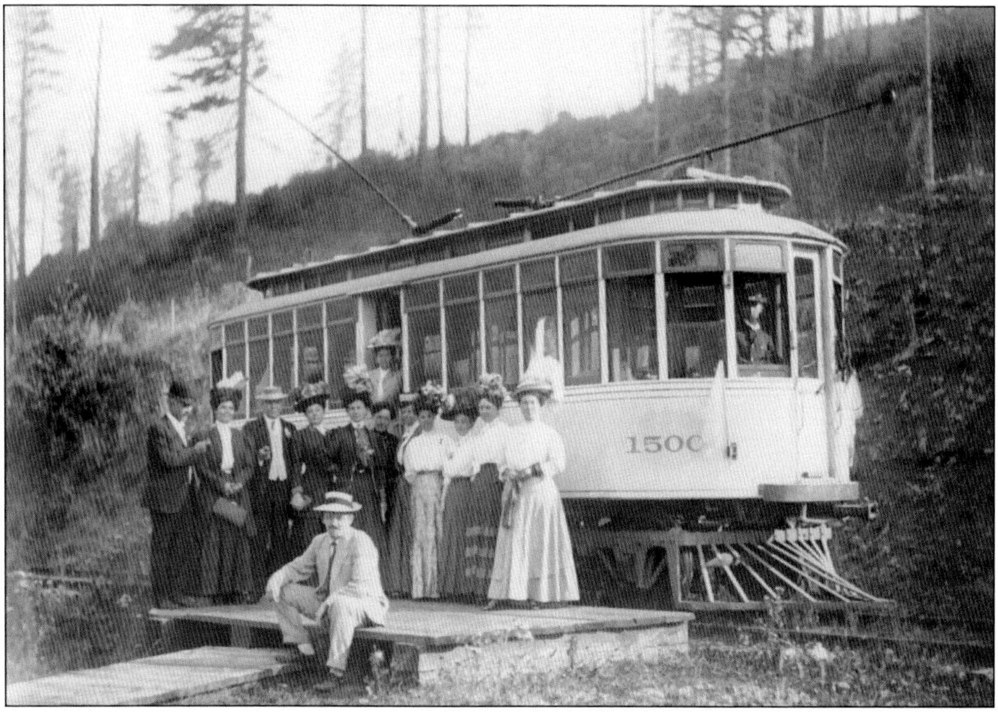

Like steam railroads, interurban railways had "parlor" cars for use by company officials and for charters. PRL&P's first parlor car, No. 1500, had a long and varied history, starting (unsuccessfully) as a Portland & Vancouver Railway gas electric motor in 1892, then becoming, in succession: a parlor car in 1903, a funeral car in 1909, a mail car in 1914, and a stub line shuttle in 1917. It is seen here with a Cazadero excursion party.

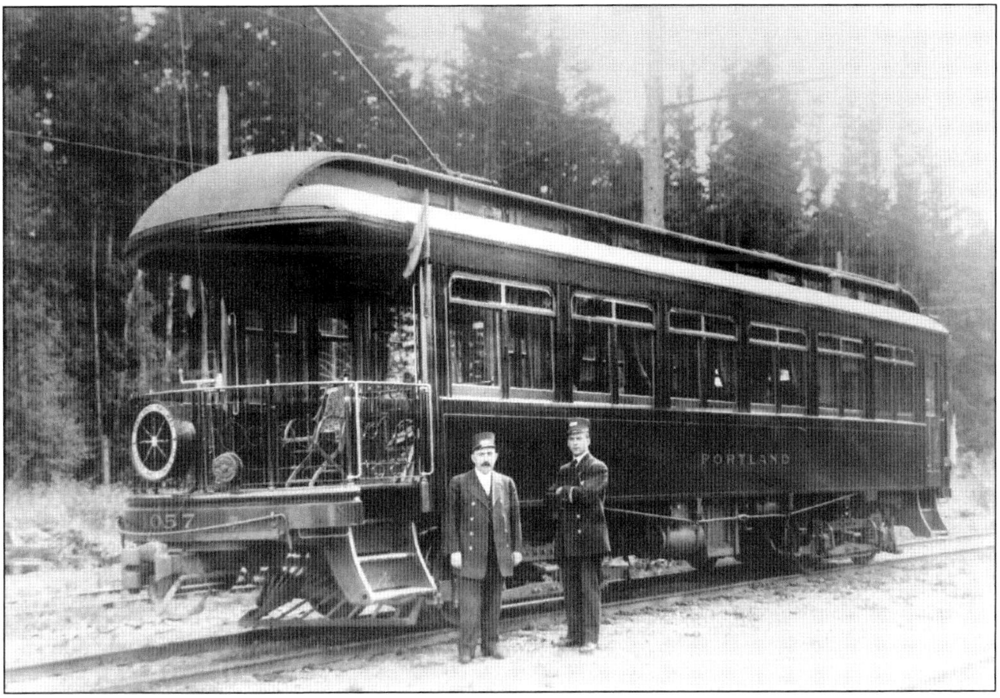

The Niles Car and Manufacturing Company built interurbans No. 57 and No. 58 for OWP in 1903. In 1909, car No. 1057, renumbered by PRL&P, was rebuilt as the parlor car *Portland*. When not being used by company executives, it was available for charter. The *Portland* is seen here at Linnemann Junction in 1912 with conductor Leon M. Fernandez (left) and motorman Albert A. Reck. Note the illuminated corporate "drumhead" and the folding chair on the observation platform.

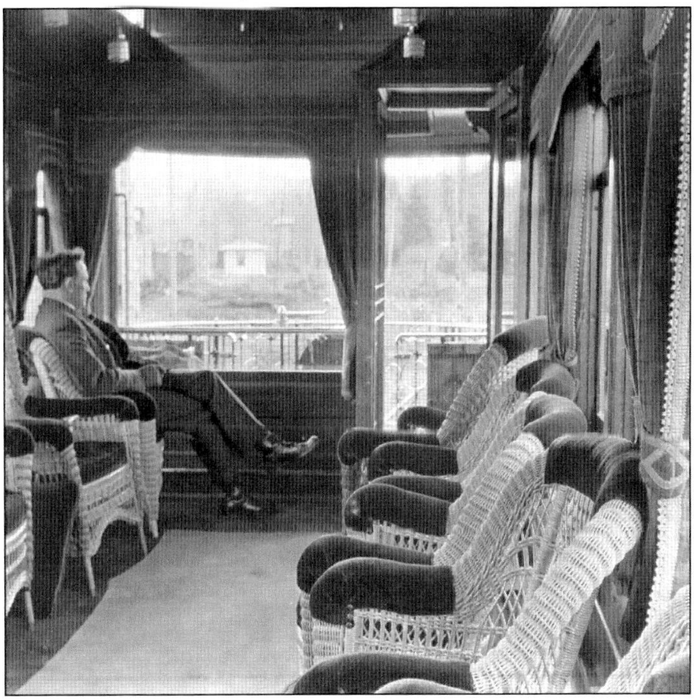

Charles Blaugus peers out of the rear window of the parlor car *Portland* at River Mill Station on the Cazadero Line in a photograph snapped by motorman Albert A. Reck. His plush surroundings include heavy velvet curtains, upholstered wicker armchairs, art glass ceiling lamps, and carpeting. (Photograph Albert A. Reck; courtesy Mark Moore.)

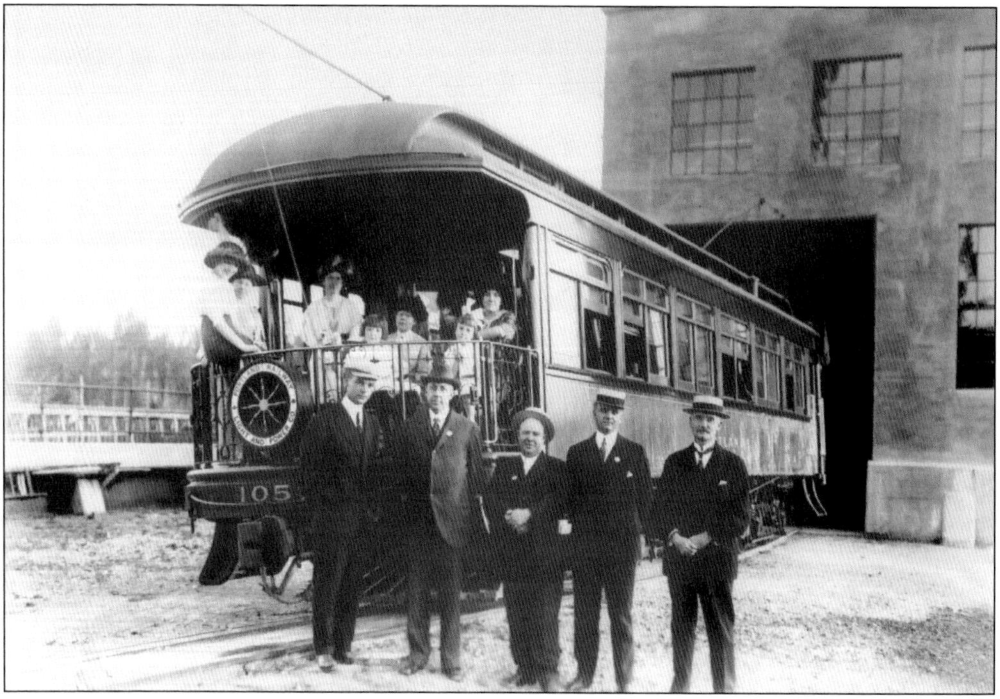

Serious-looking VIPs from the Chicago & Northwestern Railway pose with PRL&P OWP division traffic manager Fred D. Hunt (center) during a tour stop at the River Mill powerhouse in August 1913. At least the wives and children looking on from the observation platform of the parlor car *Portland* appear to be enjoying themselves.

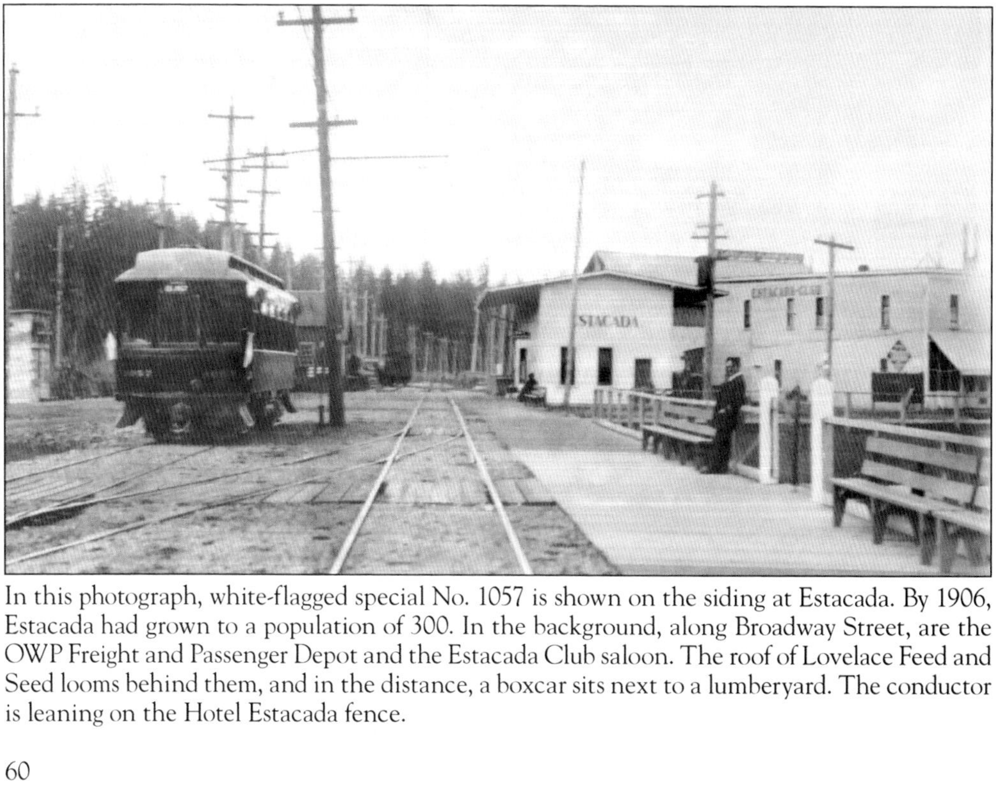

In this photograph, white-flagged special No. 1057 is shown on the siding at Estacada. By 1906, Estacada had grown to a population of 300. In the background, along Broadway Street, are the OWP Freight and Passenger Depot and the Estacada Club saloon. The roof of Lovelace Feed and Seed looms behind them, and in the distance, a boxcar sits next to a lumberyard. The conductor is leaning on the Hotel Estacada fence.

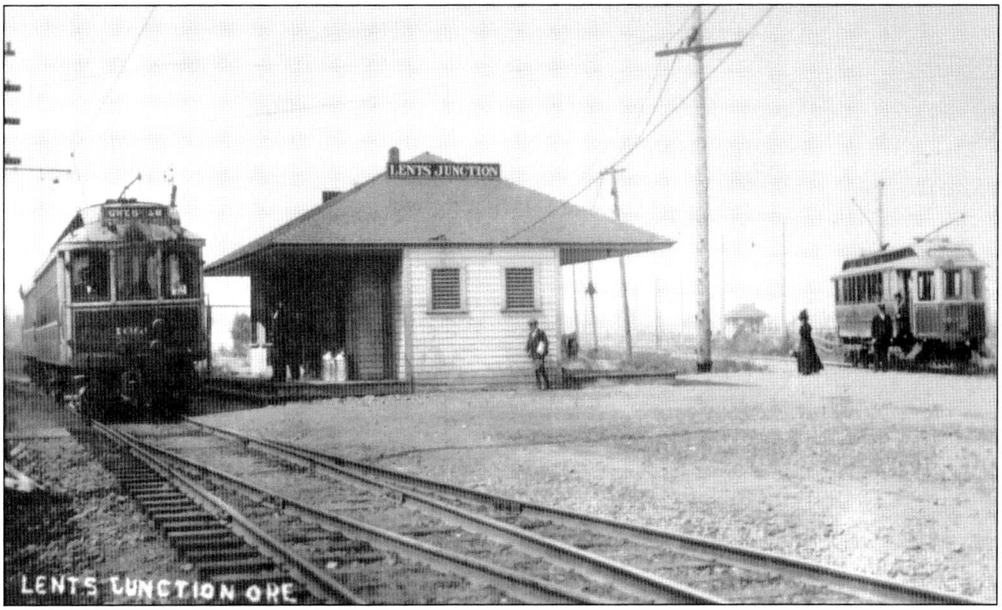

In this c. 1919 photograph, a boy in short pants and a woman hurry between Mount Scott Line No. 1037 and Gresham local train No. 72 at Lents Junction. Interesting details in this scene include milk cans on the station platform and two kinds of block signals: a birdhouse-like semaphore above No. 1060, and a disk-type indicator on the other track. These cars are East Side Railway veterans from the early 1890s.

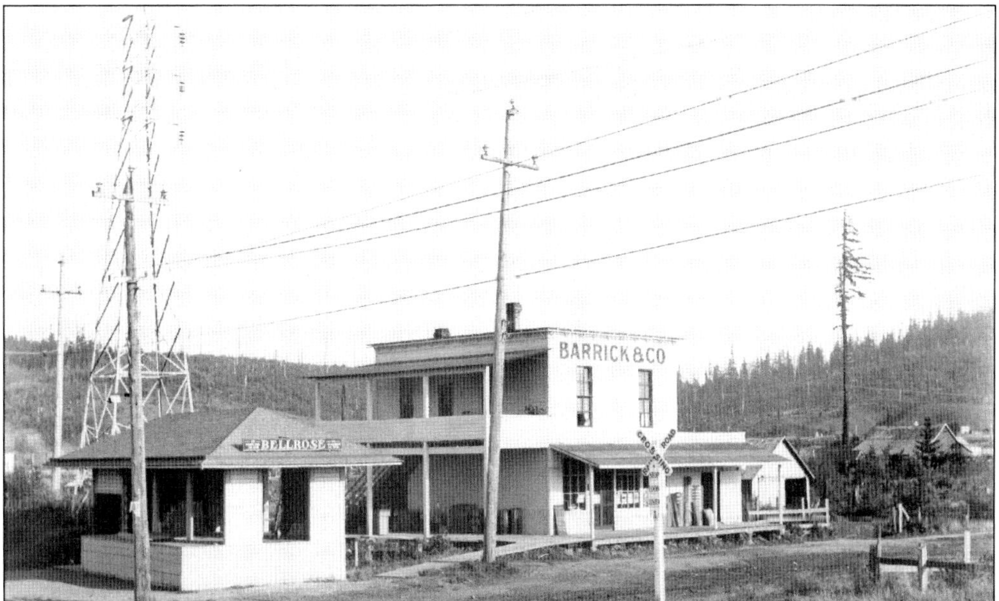

This photograph of Bellrose Station is from the early days, when the Barrick & Company Store was located nearby. In 1949, this station, on what is now Southeast 136th, north of Foster Road, would become the final eastern terminus for the Springwater Division. Since Bellrose was located 12 miles from downtown Portland, this made the last two interurban routes nearly equal in length (the Oregon City Line was 14 miles long).

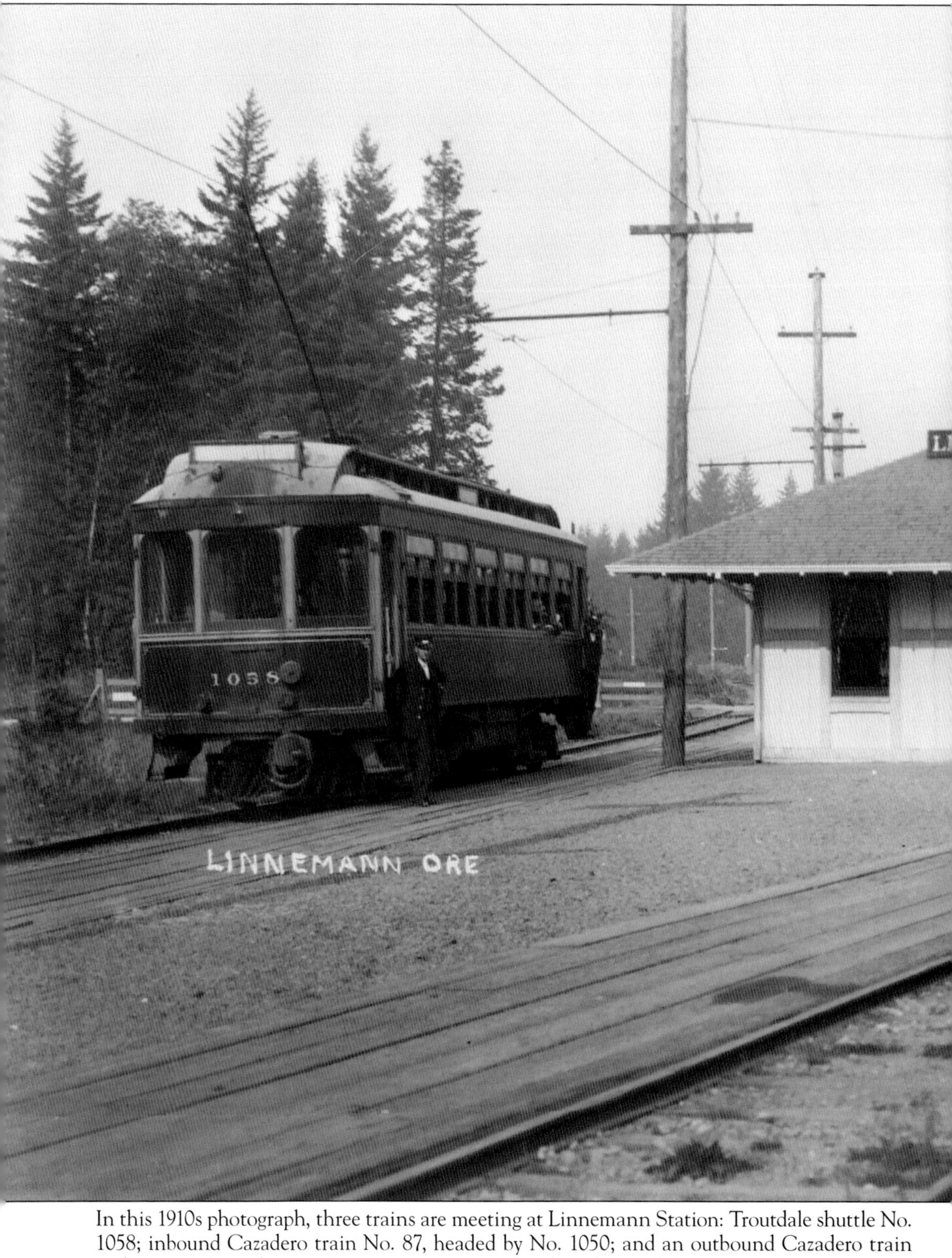

In this 1910s photograph, three trains are meeting at Linnemann Station: Troutdale shuttle No. 1058; inbound Cazadero train No. 87, headed by No. 1050; and an outbound Cazadero train with No. 1067 on the rear. Passengers are waiting to board one of the two-car Cazadero trains.

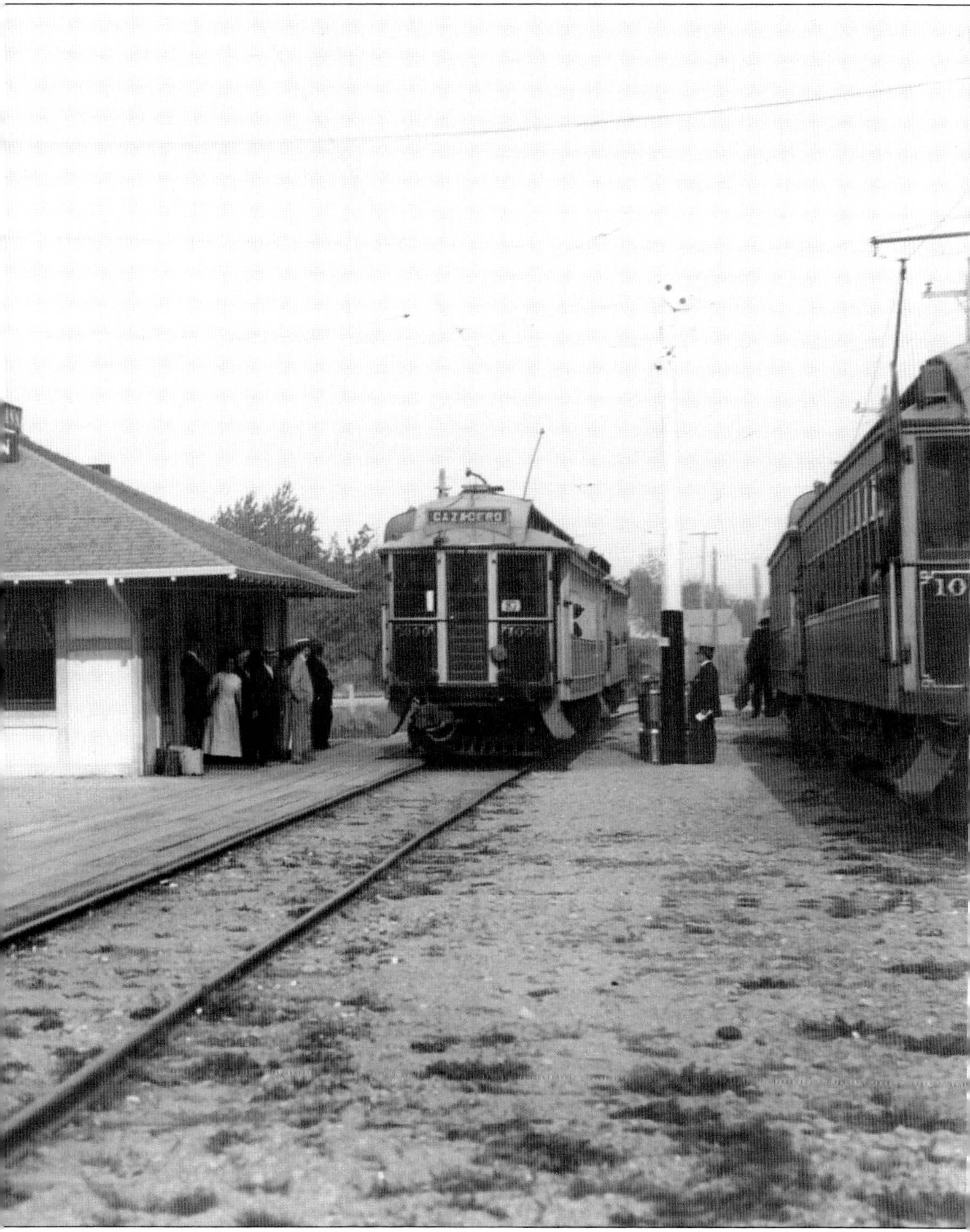

Linnemann station was located west of Gresham at Linnemann Junction, the point where the Troutdale branch met the mainline to Estacada and Cazadero.

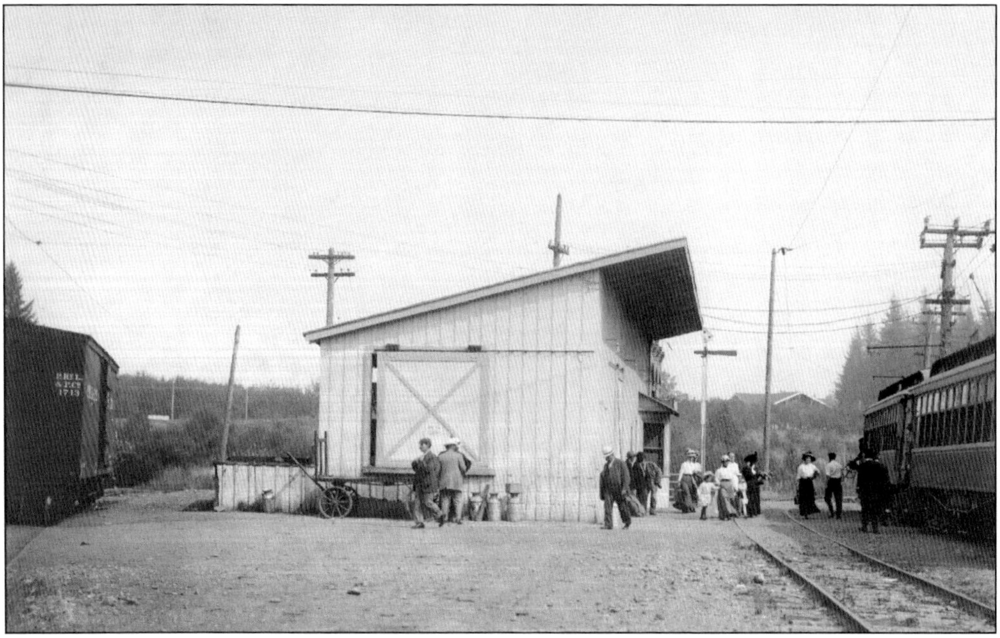

In this photograph, the motorman is climbing down from the rear car with his stool, while two conductors assist passengers boarding No. 1060 and its mate at Gresham's Springwater Division Station. Service to this, the largest town on the line, began in 1903. Milk cans, a baggage wagon, and a boxcar can be seen next to the station, and on the far side, the brick substation is just visible. (Courtesy Norm Gholston.)

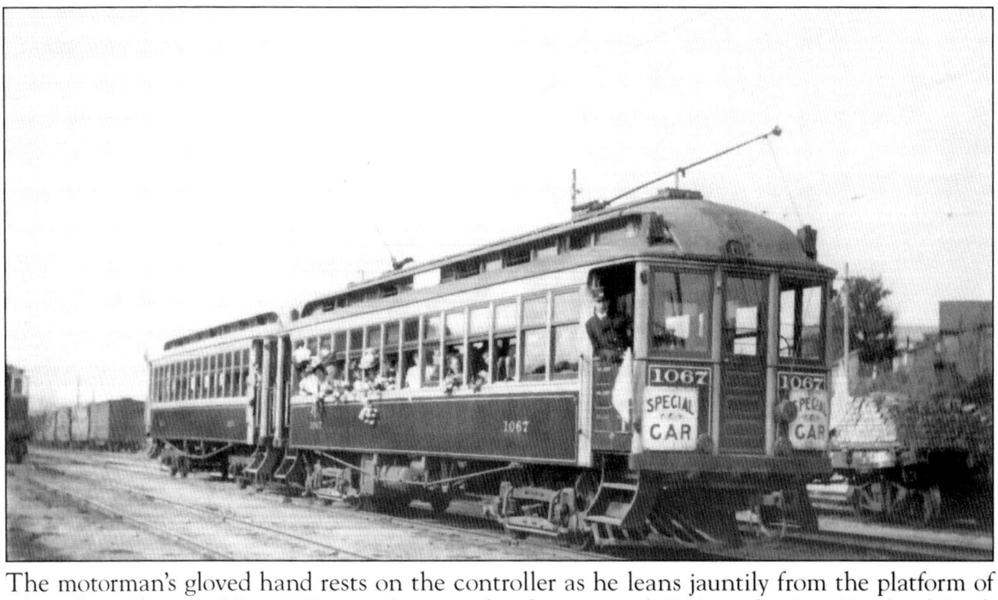

The motorman's gloved hand rests on the controller as he leans jauntily from the platform of white-flagged motor No. 1067 in a photograph taken around 1910 in the East Portland Yard. Special motor 1067, and matching trailer No. 1122, are outbound with a party of women. Large bouquets and fancy hats are on display as the eager excursionists claim their seats.

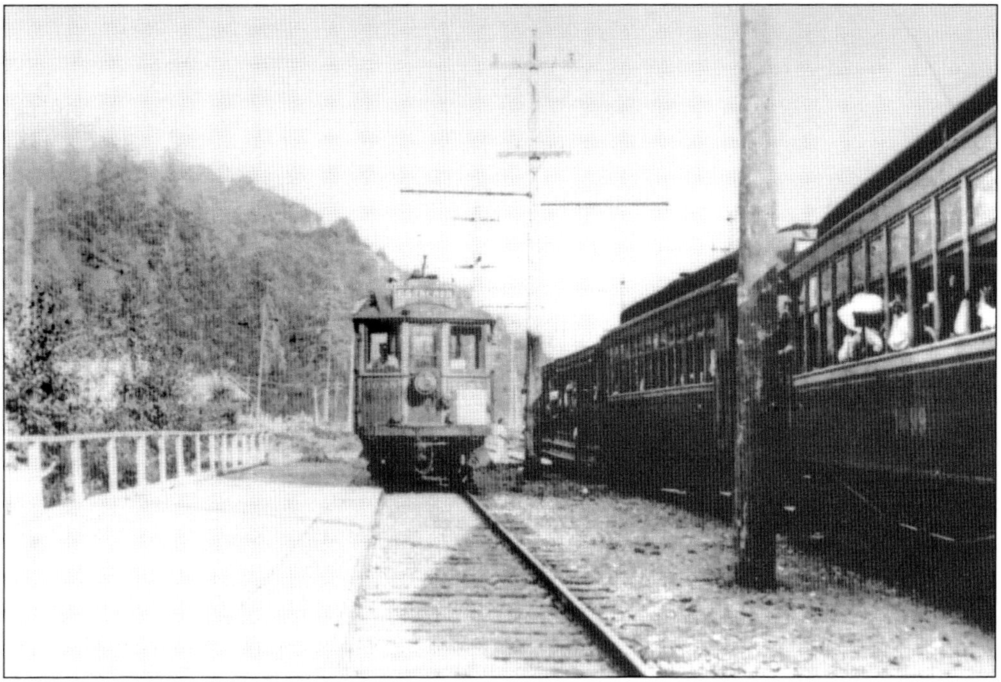

As the evening shadows grow, the headlight has been hung on No. 1098. The Estacada local is getting ready to depart the terminus in front of the Hotel Estacada, while a picnic special, led by sister interurban No. 1099, waits "in the hole," ready to take the mainline after the other train leaves.

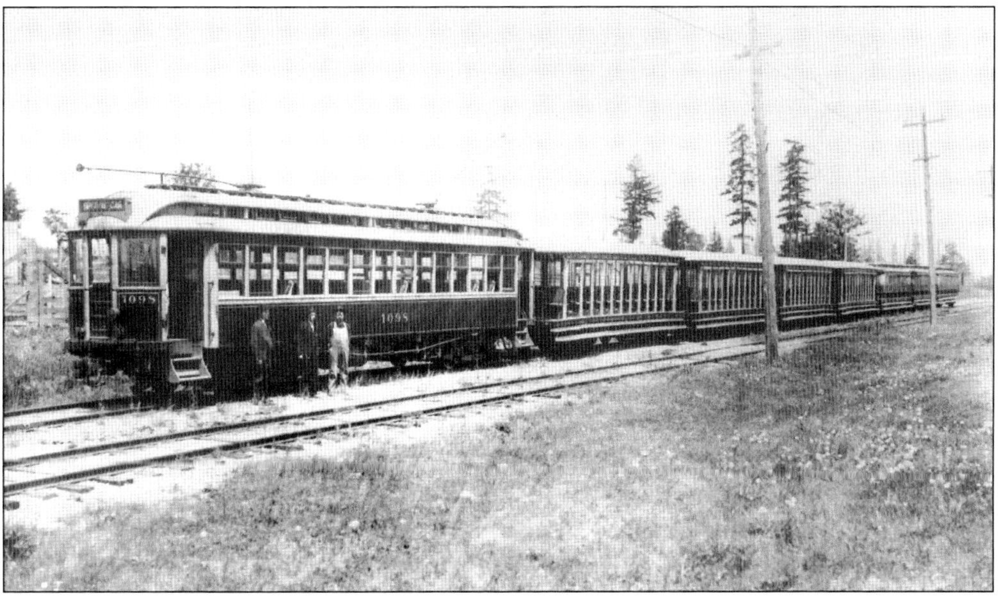

Pictured from left to right in this 1912 photograph are shop foreman John C. Wilkinson, conductor Harry Simmons, and shop man Albert Hildebrand. They have assembled an excursion train with seven open trailers, which was no challenge for No. 1098, since it weighed 61,600 pounds and was equipped with four motors. After retirement, this car served as a store on Southeast Foster Road until 1956. (Photograph Albert A. Reck.)

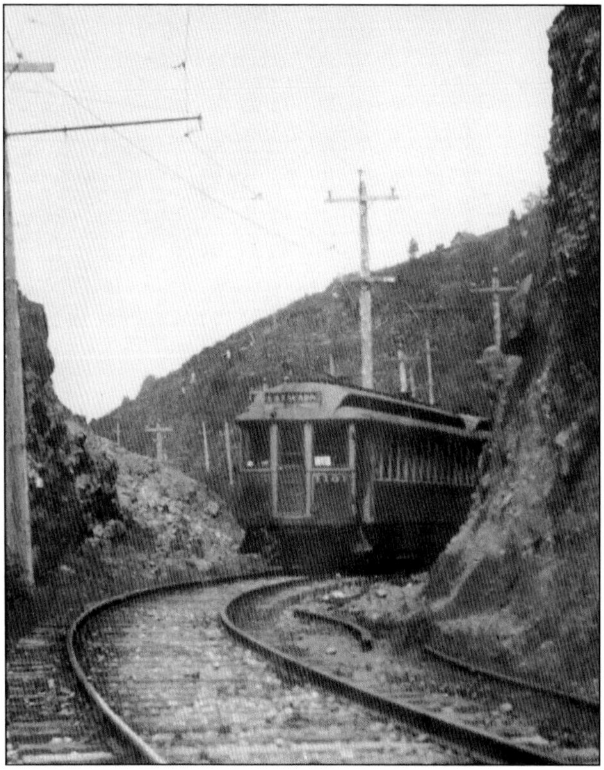

Cars No. 1101 and No. 1102, heading northbound as train No. 9, round a corner on the Estacada Line on a morning in 1915. Car No. 1101 holds the distinction of having been the last wooden interurban car in service, when it was used for a fan trip to Boring on June 21, 1953.

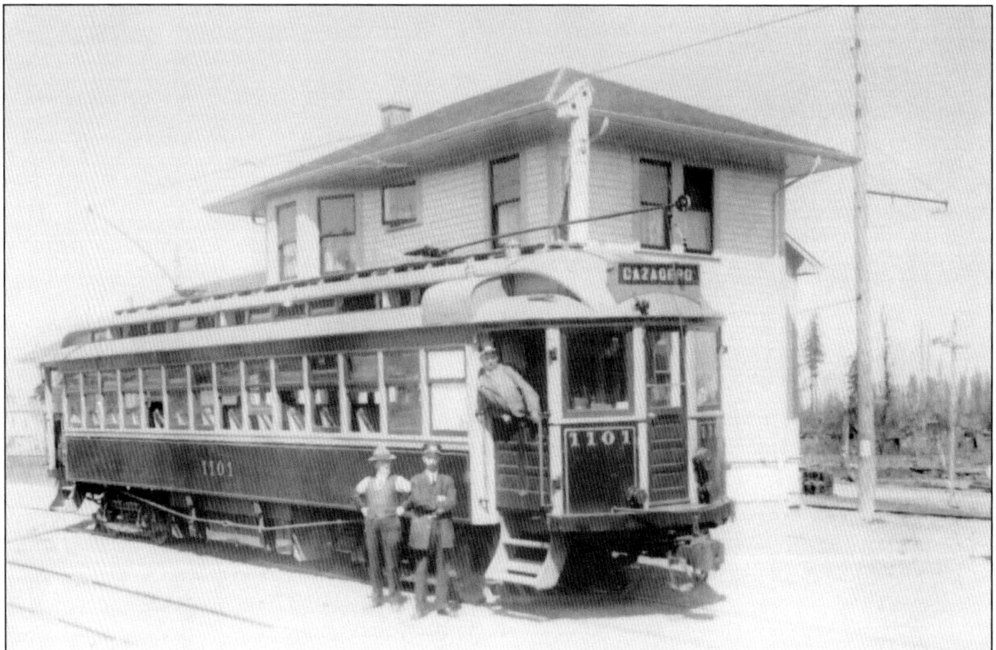

Shown here at Boring Station are, from left to right, an unidentified station agent, conductor Leonard T. Compton, and motorman Charles Lewis. No one seems to be aboard Cazadero-bound No. 1101. Note the birdhouse-like signal mechanism atop the pole behind the car.

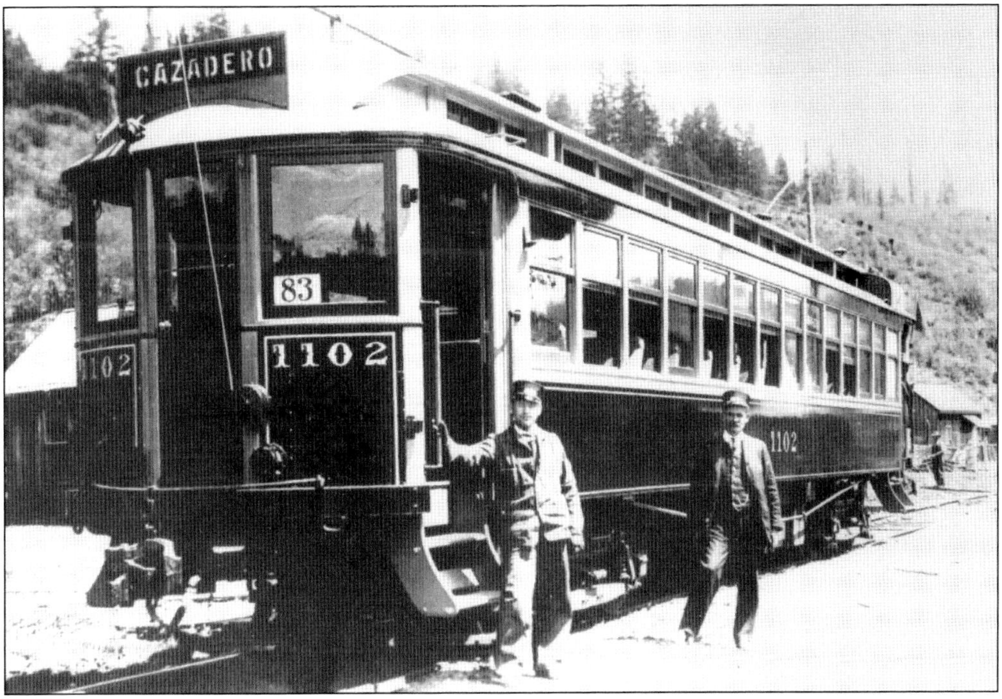

Train No. 83 was usually a Mount Hood Division local from Troutdale to Montavilla or Linnemann Junction to Troutdale, so it is interesting to notice that No. 1102 is displaying that number as it gets ready to leave Cazadero on the Springwater Division. Car 1102, the last of 10 interurbans built by PRL&P in 1912, looks new in this photograph above.

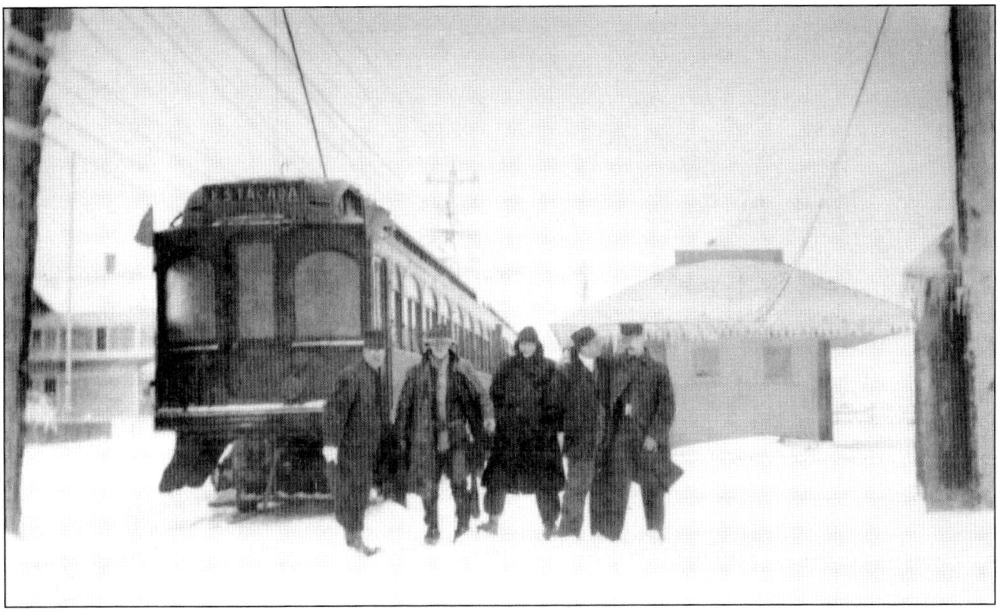

No. 1124 was built in 1911 by G.C. Kuhlman of Cleveland for the Mount Hood Railway & Power Company. Like its sisters, it was a trailer until electrification by PRL&P in 1914. This Jack Frost scene finds the beautiful Mount Hood Division interurban and its stalwart crew at Lents Junction on the Estacada Line, probably providing emergency service during the great snow of 1916.

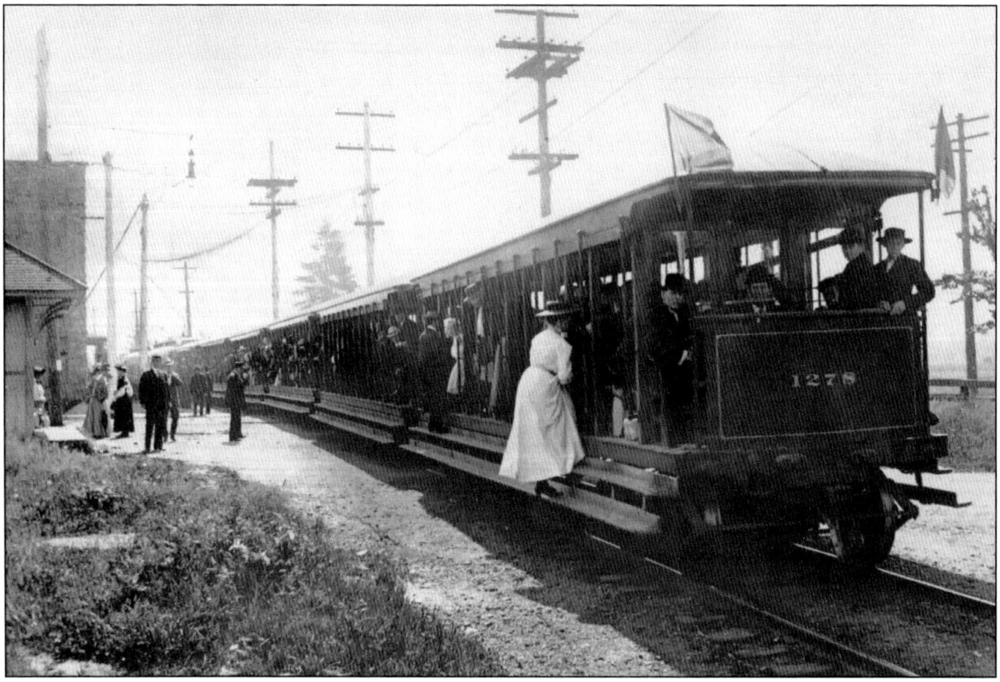

Flags snap in the breeze as the last passengers board No. 1278 on the rear of an Estacada excursion train at Golf Junction on a bright Sunday morning around 1908. During the hobble skirt craze of the first decade of the 1900s, female passengers found the dual running boards on these OWP open cars difficult to negotiate. Golf Links Station and the OWP substation are in the background.

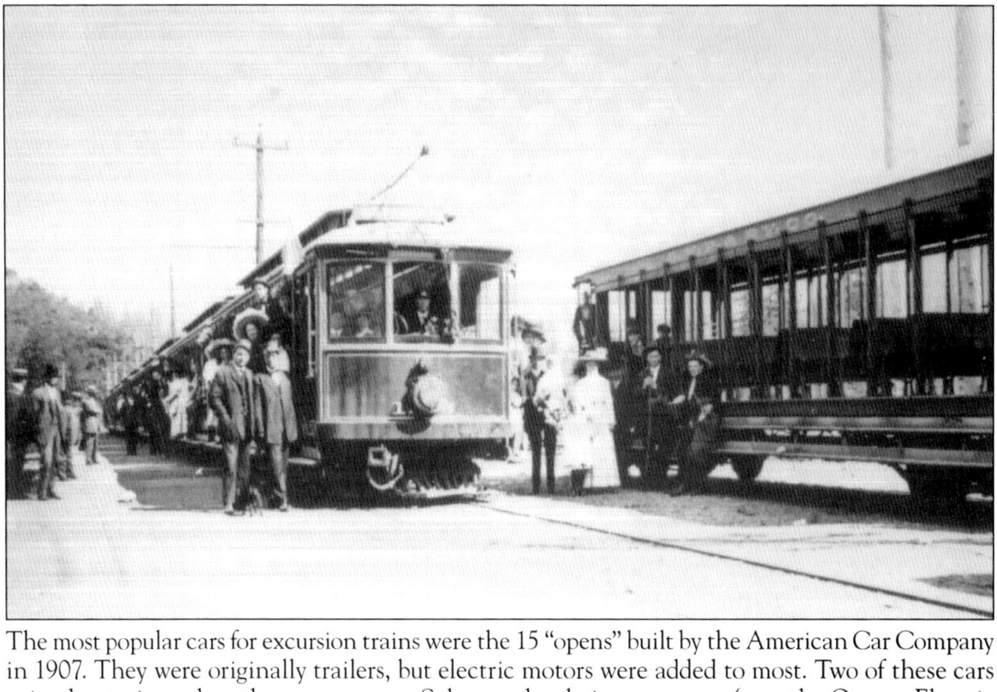

The most popular cars for excursion trains were the 15 "opens" built by the American Car Company in 1907. They were originally trailers, but electric motors were added to most. Two of these cars gained notoriety when they were sent to Salem under their own power (over the Oregon Electric Railway) for use at the state fair. No. 1308 is seen here in Estacada next to a 1200 series trailer.

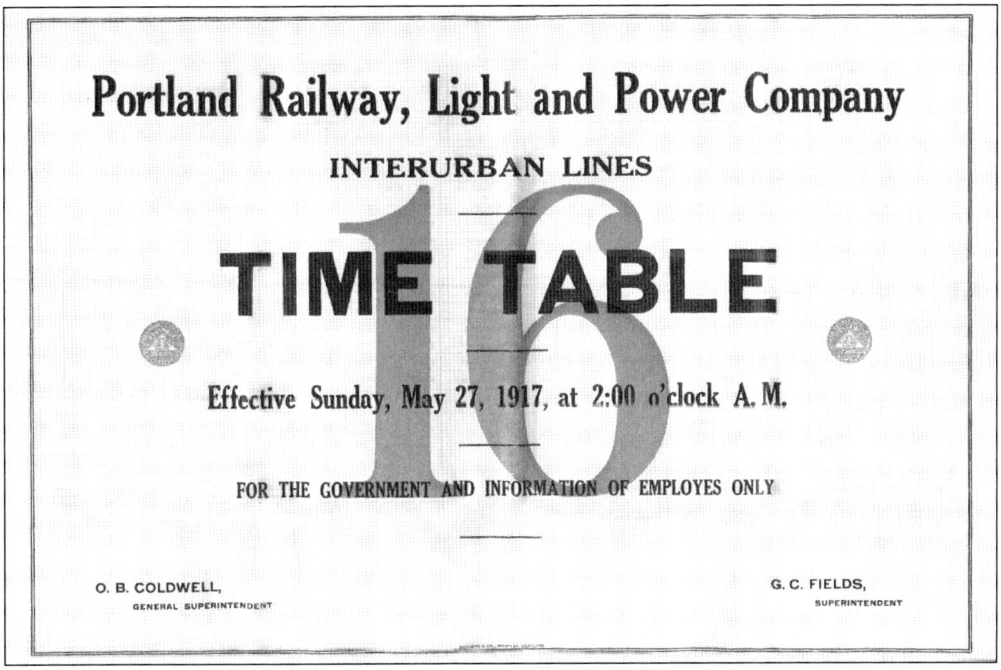

Portland Railway, Light and Power Company

INTERURBAN LINES

16

TIME TABLE

Effective Sunday, May 27, 1917, at 2:00 o'clock A. M.

FOR THE GOVERNMENT AND INFORMATION OF EMPLOYES ONLY

O. B. COLDWELL,
GENERAL SUPERINTENDENT

G. C. FIELDS,
SUPERINTENDENT

The pages of this 1917 interurban timetable show 53 passenger trains departing Portland daily: 36 were bound for Oregon City, 5 for Cazadero, 8 for Gresham, and 4 for Bull Run. "Trippers" to stations part of the way along the line went to Milwaukie, Bellrose, and Stanley. There were also nine trains from Montavilla to Troutdale and six from Linnemann Junction to Bull Run. Trains left Southwest First Avenue and Alder Street from 4:30 a.m. until midnight.

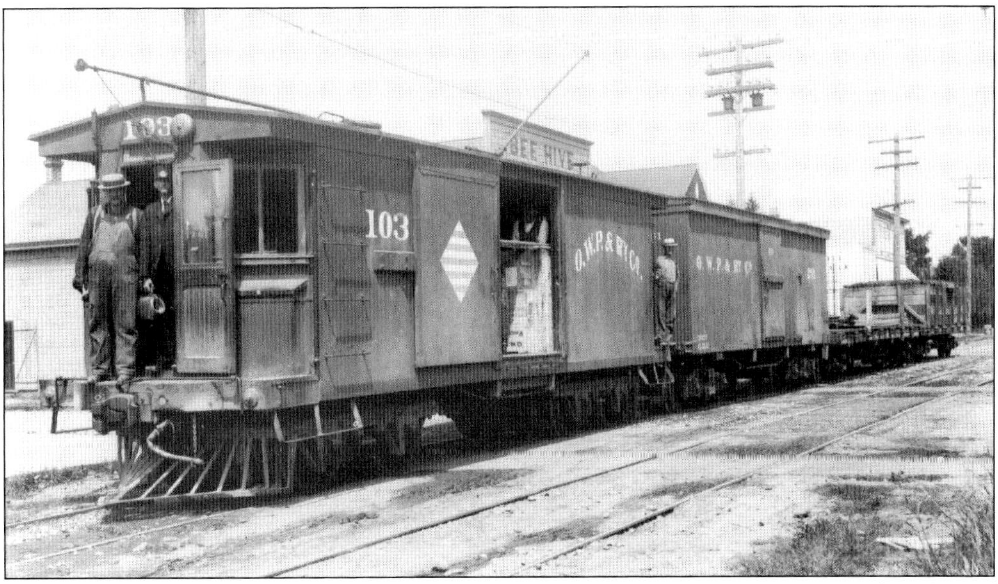

When OWP took over in 1902, new freight motors were created by adding four-motored trucks and motormen's cabs to boxcars. These box motors were configured as mail and express cars partly in order to avoid an Oregon City ordinance banning the operation of regular freight trains on city streets. (In 1907, No. 103 was rebuilt again, this time as caboose No. 1452; see the photograph on page 52). (Courtesy Mark Moore.)

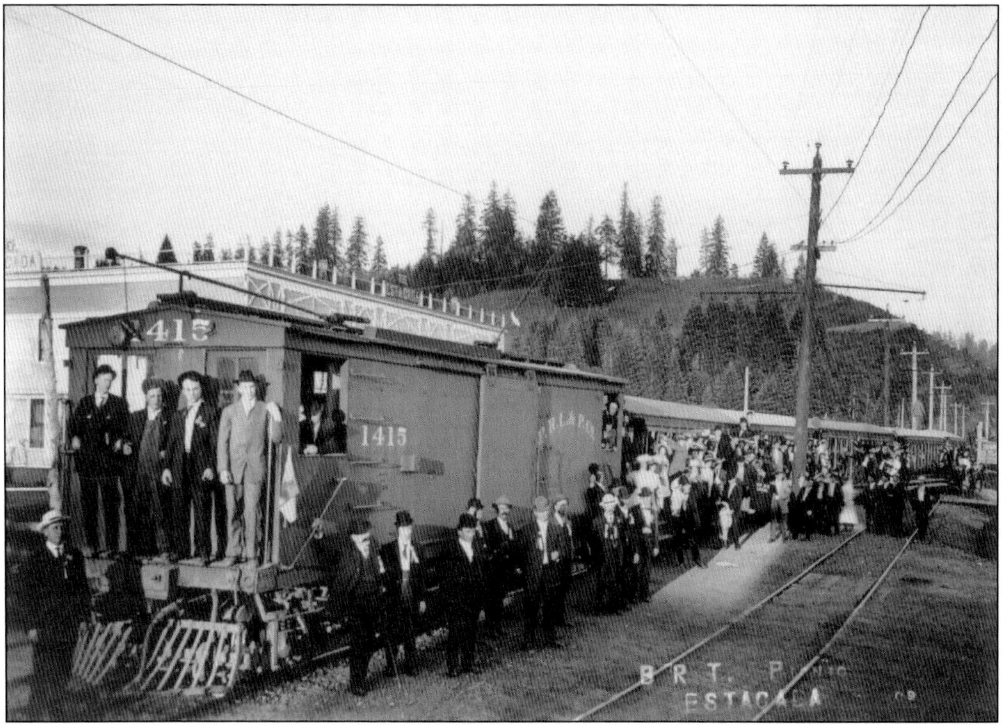

Freight motors were often assigned to pull excursion trains. Box motor No. 1415 is seen here with a long train in front of the Hotel Estacada. The occasion was the Brotherhood of Railway Trainmen's 1909 picnic. This 1904 vintage former OWP electric locomotive survived for many years after retirement as an oil storage house. (Courtesy Mark Moore.)

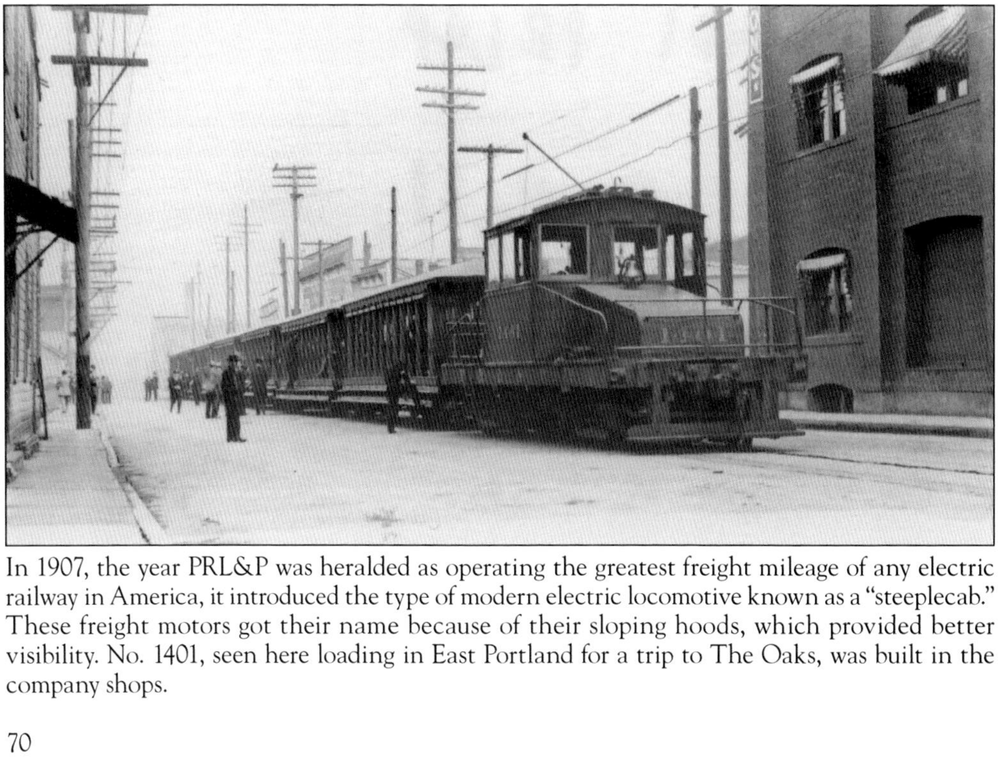

In 1907, the year PRL&P was heralded as operating the greatest freight mileage of any electric railway in America, it introduced the type of modern electric locomotive known as a "steeplecab." These freight motors got their name because of their sloping hoods, which provided better visibility. No. 1401, seen here loading in East Portland for a trip to The Oaks, was built in the company shops.

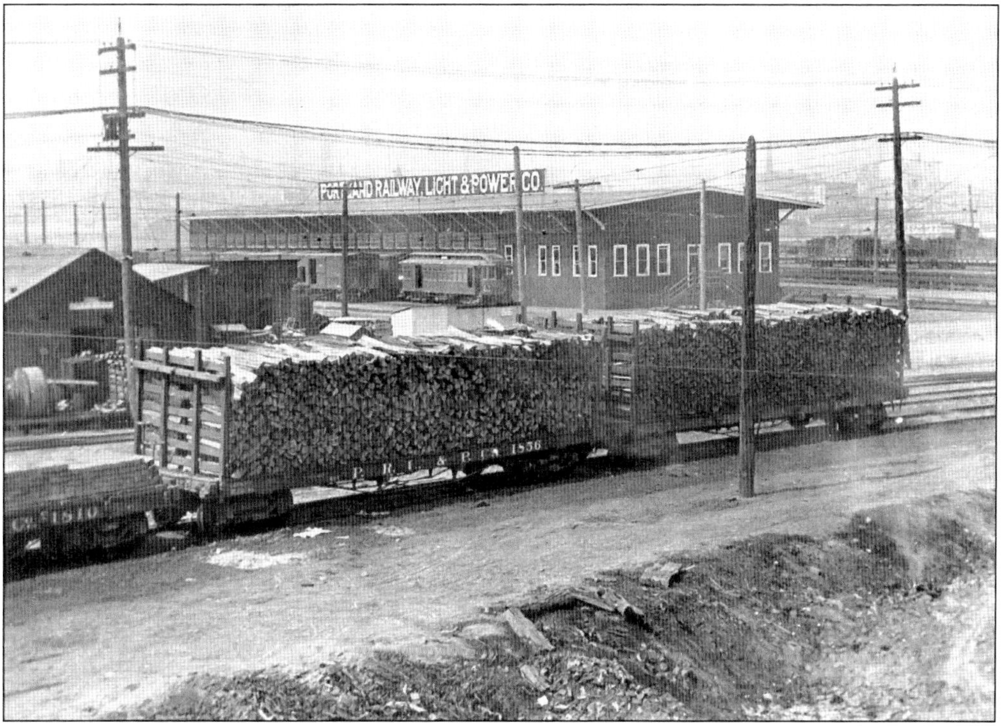

Although passenger traffic was the primary source of revenue, freight hauling soon grew in importance for Portland's interurbans. One of the things that distinguished the East Side Railway from other early electric railroads was that it carried freight. A mail and express combine is seen here around 1908 next to the Eastside Freight Depot built by OWP near Southeast Hawthorne Boulevard and Water Street. (Photograph Albert A. Reck; courtesy Mark Moore.)

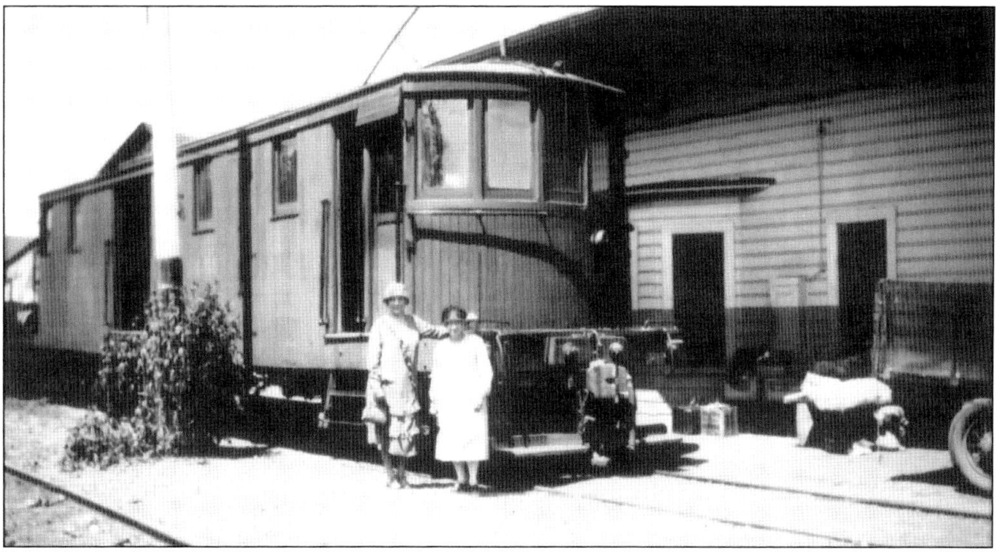

Less than glamorous motive power was still in use when these ladies posed with box motor No. 1461 at Estacada about 1922. It was built as a mail and express car by PRL&P in 1910. The daily mail train arrived at Cazadero at 4:30 p.m. After retirement in 1941, No. 1461 became a storeroom for old records at the Center Street Shops. It was burned in 1948, records and all.

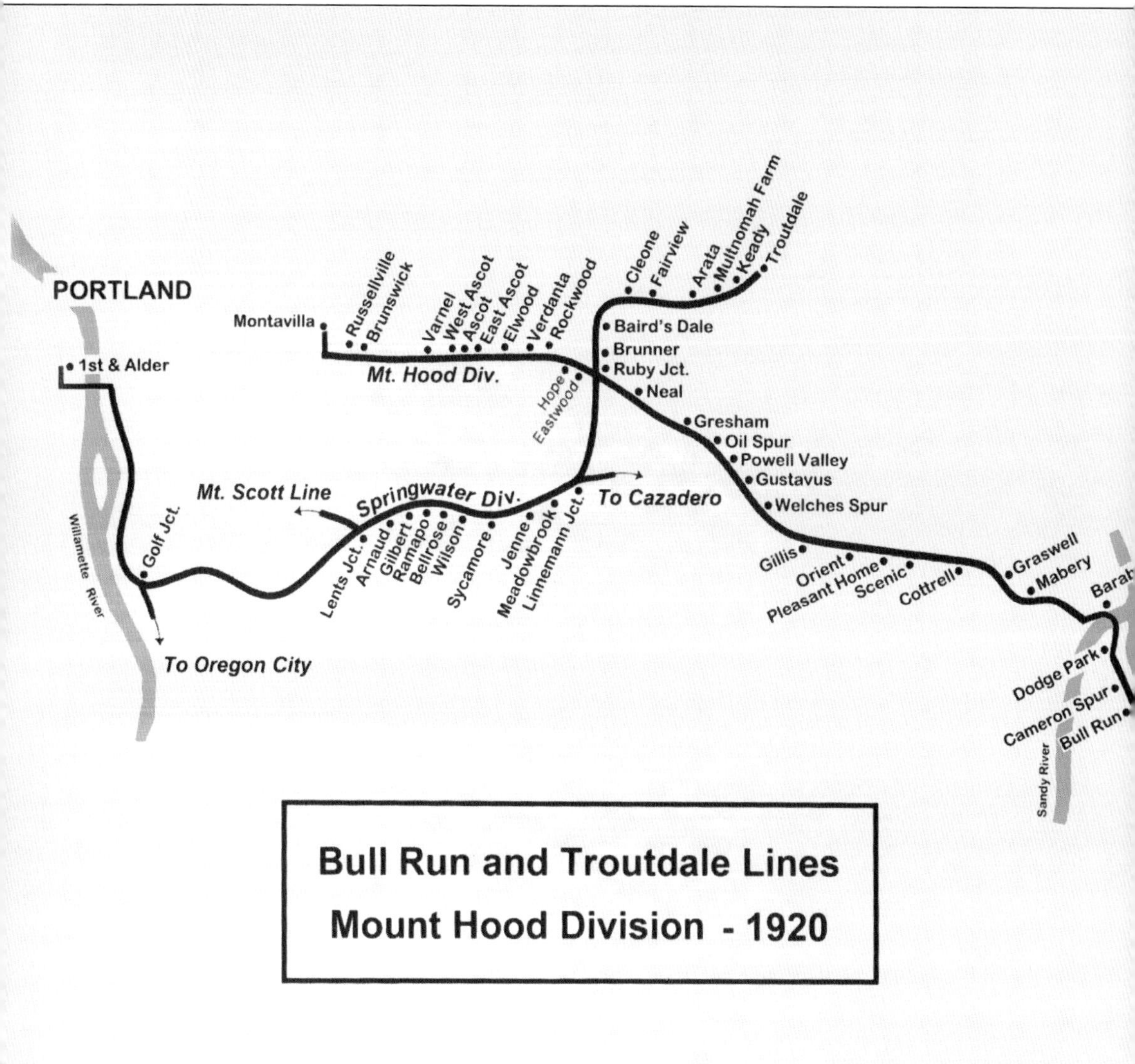

This map shows stations on the PRL&P Mount Hood Division lines to Bull Run and Troutdale at their peak in 1920. The Troutdale Line was begun by OWP in 1905 and completed by PRL&P in 1907. The line to Bull Run was built by the Mount Hood Railway & Power Company in 1911, and electrified by PRL&P in 1913. At the time of this map, four daily Bull Run trains ran from downtown Portland on the Springwater Division, crossing over to Mount Hood Division tracks at Linnemann Junction, and then turning east toward Bull Run at Ruby Junction. There were also eight Gresham locals. Nine trains ran from Montavilla to Troutdale, while six operated from Linnemann Junction to Troutdale. Cuts in Mount Hood Division service began with the Troutdale Line closure in 1927. (Courtesy Tom Hatch.)

Four

Branching Out

THE BULL RUN AND TROUTDALE LINES

The East Side Railway aspired to build an electric railway from Portland to Mount Hood and beyond. The enterprise that finally got the job done, however, was the Mount Hood Railway & Power Company, which incorporated on October 29, 1906. Construction got under way in 1907 and was finished in 1911.

The Mount Hood line was isolated at first, running from a connection with the Union Pacific Railroad on Northeast Eighty-second Street, six miles from Portland's city center. Crossing the Sandy River at Dodge Park, the 20 miles of track terminated at the powerhouse near Bull Run Dam.

Service to Bull Run began in 1911, with steam locomotives pulling cars designed for electric operation. Electrification of the line started after the Portland Railway, Light & Power Company (PRL&P) bought the Mount Hood Railway & Power Company on April 4, 1912. It was completed on March 1, 1913. Motors were added to the former Mount Hood Railway interurbans in 1914.

In 1905, the Oregon Water Power Company had started construction on a six-and-a-half-mile branch to Troutdale as part of a proposed ferry connection across the Columbia River to Washington. The crossing never developed, but the Troutdale Line was completed in 1907 by PRL&P.

PRL&P used the western end of the newly acquired Mount Hood Railway for its Troutdale trains, which connected with city streetcars at a depot on Northeast Ninetieth Avenue and Irving Street in Montavilla. Passengers for Bull Run transferred at Ruby Junction. Bull Run cars first used Linnemann Junction as a starting point. After electrification, the western terminus became Southwest First Avenue and Alder Street in Portland. There were 20 stations between Montavilla and Troutdale and 18 between Ruby Junction and Bull Run.

The building of roads, and slow population growth, doomed the Mount Hood Division interurbans after less than 20 years. Troutdale passenger service ended on June 15, 1927. Passenger trains to Bull Run ceased on December 26, 1930, although from 1944 until 1949, rerouted Gresham trains used a portion of the old right-of-way to reach the Mount Hood Depot.

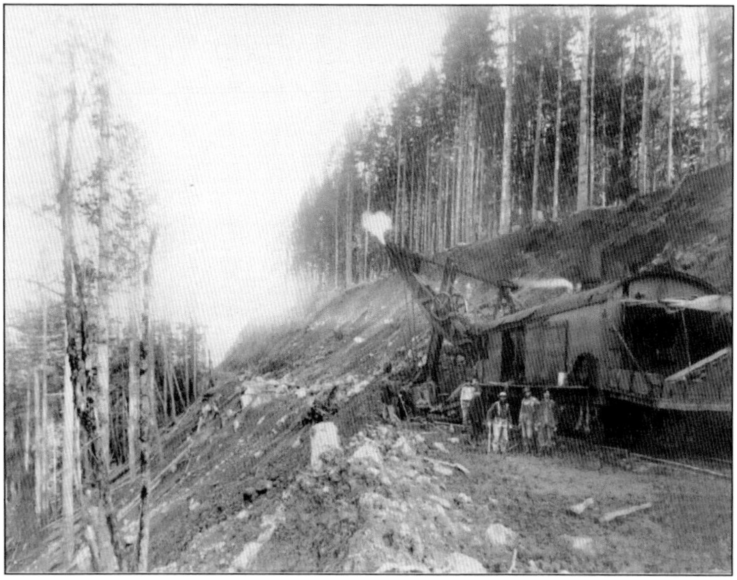

Building the Mount Hood Railway was a long and convoluted affair. Construction began in 1907, not long after the company was incorporated; however, the 20-mile route from Montavilla Station in Northeast Portland to the powerhouse at Bull Run was not completed until 1911. Here, a railroad steam shovel is working on a cut on June 19, 1911.

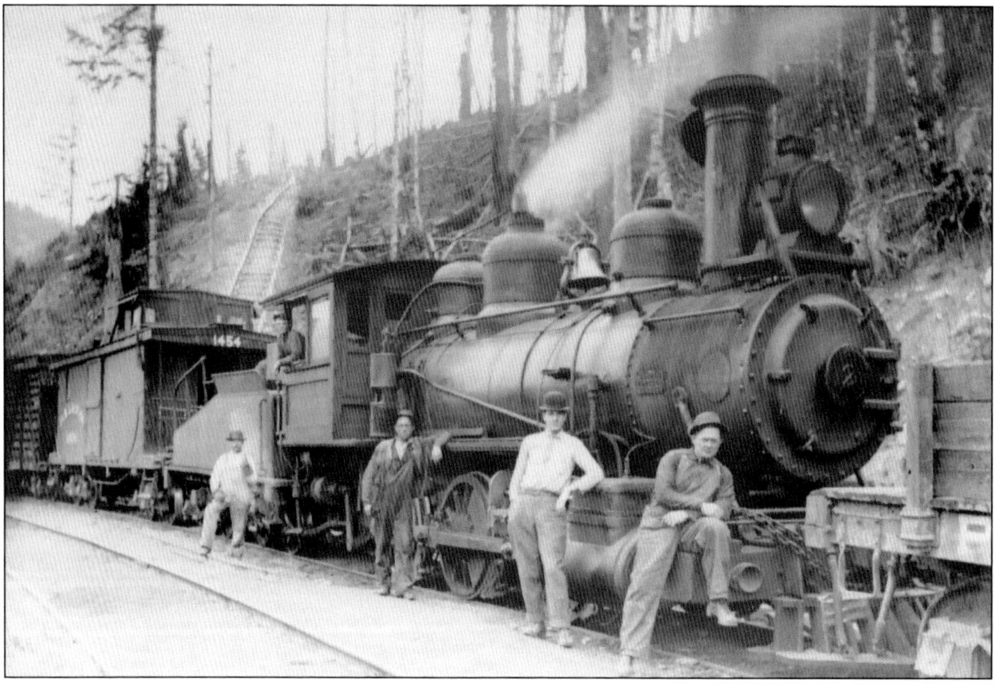

PRLP, desiring its power generation and distribution network, bought the Mount Hood Railway Company on April 4, 1912. When preliminary freight and passenger service began, railroad steam engines were used. In this photograph, locomotive No. 2 and caboose No. 1454 are shown at Bull Run in 1912. Both were inherited from the OWP, which built the caboose from a boxcar in 1903. Note the steep logging incline track in the background.

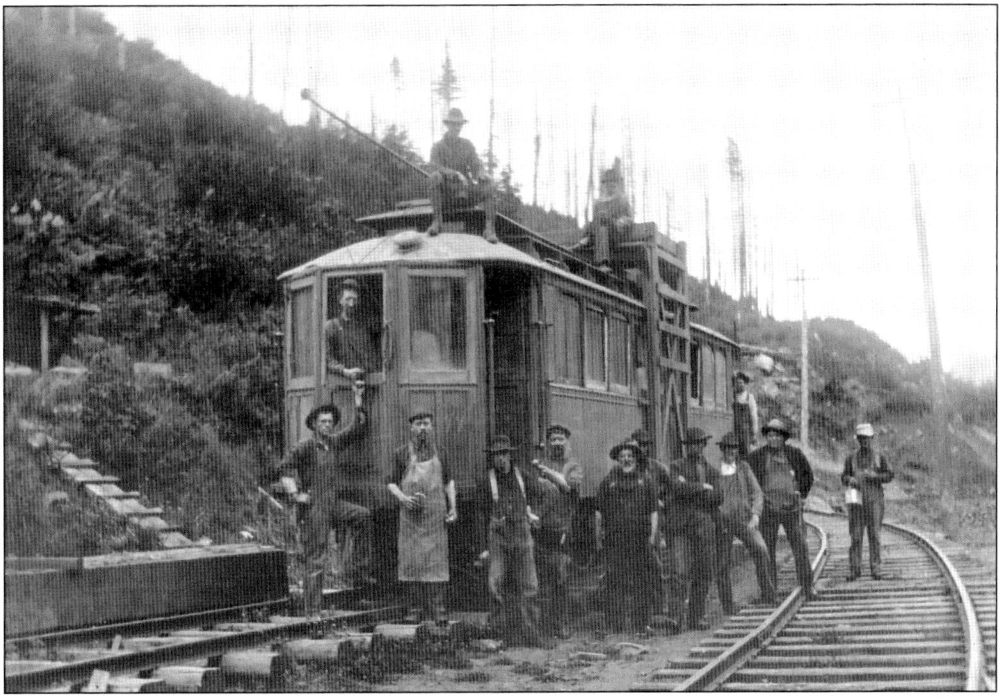

Former OWP No. 44 was converted to a tower car (for overhead line work) in 1910 and used during construction of the Bull Run Line. One of the oldest interurban cars in America, No. 44 is thought to have begun life as the East Side Railway's *Helen*. That 1890 Vulcan Manufacturing interurban made the first trip to Oregon City in 1893. (Courtesy Mark Moore.)

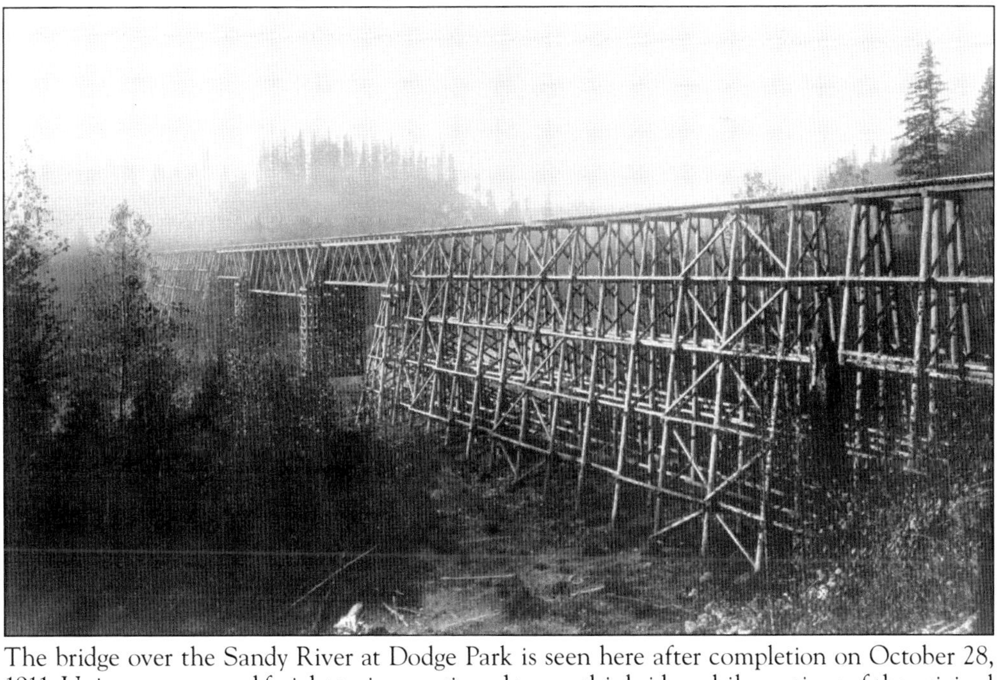

The bridge over the Sandy River at Dodge Park is seen here after completion on October 28, 1911. Unique unmanned freight trains continued to use this bridge while portions of the original wooden structure were being replaced by a steel bridge in the 1920s (see page 85).

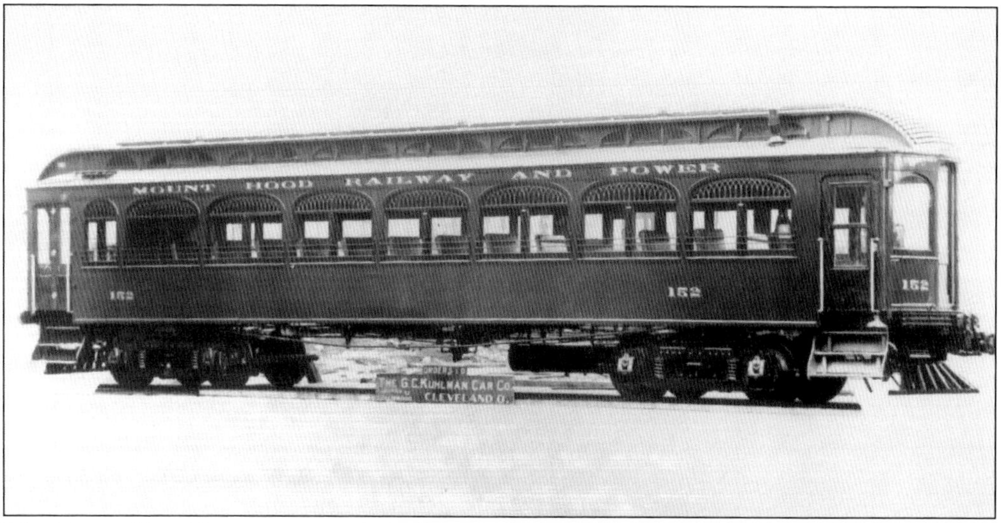

The Mount Hood Division sported the finest rolling stock seen on any interurban in the state, including the long-distance electric railways to Eugene and Corvallis, as can be seen in this 1912 builder's photograph of No. 152. The beautiful coaches and express motors from Kuhlman, as well as the elegant Niles cars used on the Troutdale Branch, represented the peak of the car builder's art. (Courtesy Mark Moore.)

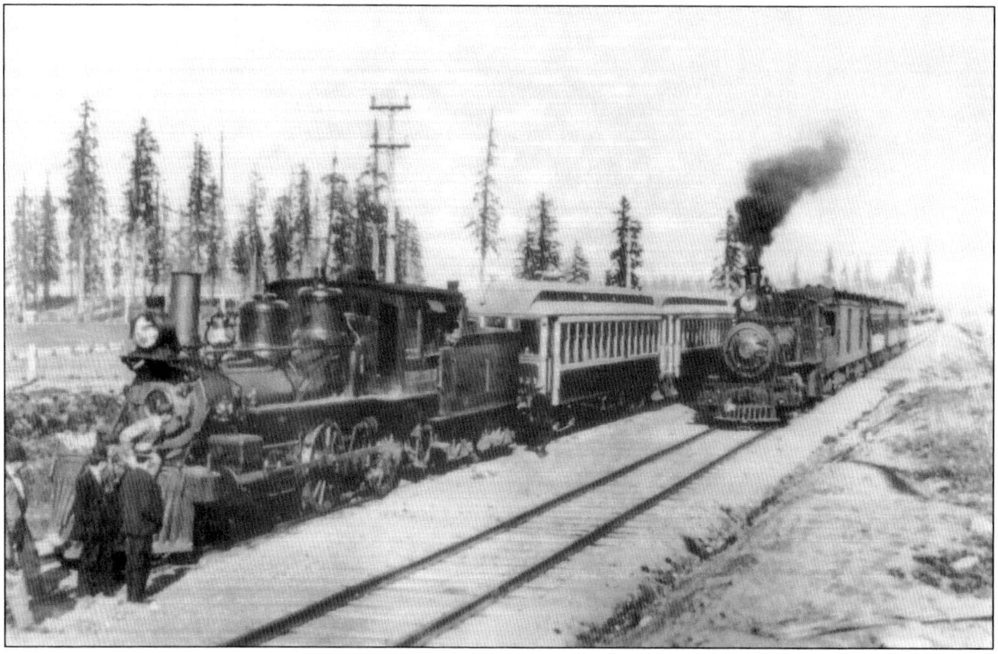

A group of businessmen are watching in front of locomotive No. 1 while sister No. 2 speeds past with a Bull Run Line train. The photograph was taken in 1912, before electrification. The moving train includes a baggage and express car and three passenger trailers, all originally Mount Hood Railway rolling stock. The train waiting "in the hole" consists of three PRL&P trailers headed by No. 1121.

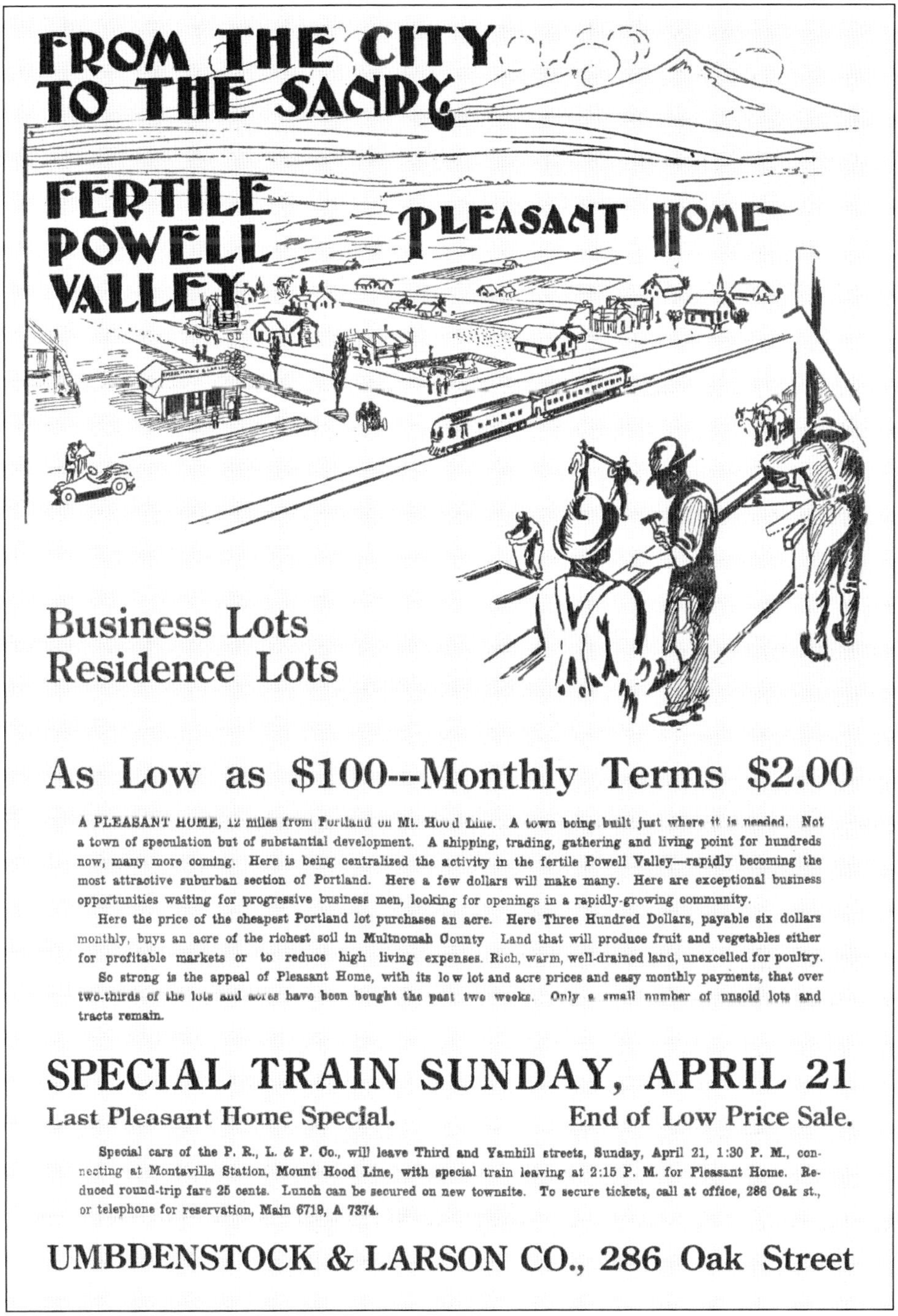

This real estate promotion for business and residential lots in the new community of Pleasant Home on the Bull Run Line depicts a two-car "Special Train" running "From the City to the Sandy." The train is headed by what looks like a McKeen gasoline motor car, although none of those were ever used on this line. The artist might have meant to depict an electric interurban train, since the Mount Hood Railway was electrified several months after this advertisement appeared in the April 19, 1912, *Oregonian*.

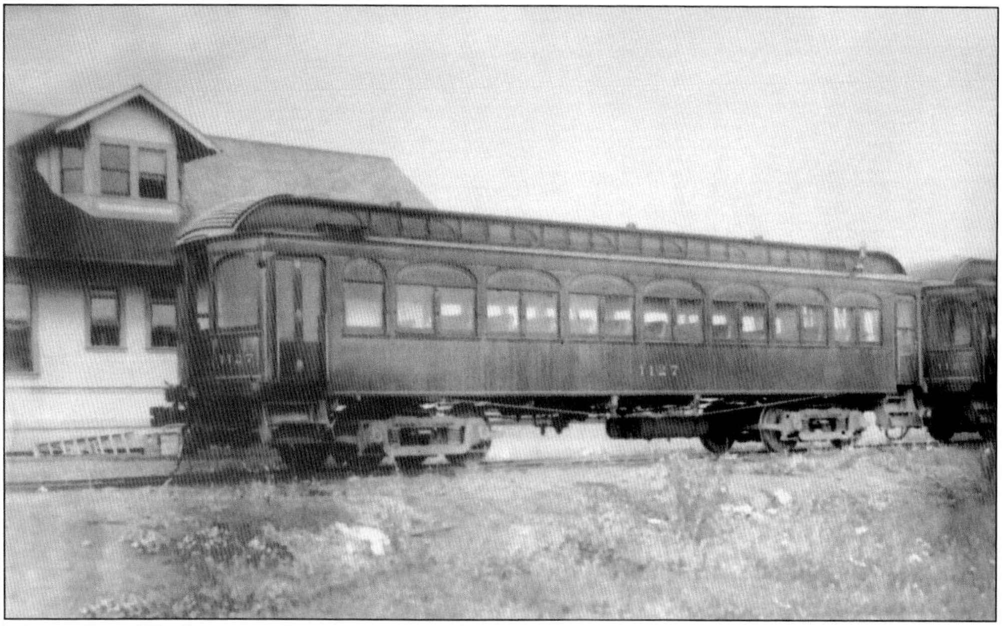

Mount Hood Railway coaches No. 1127 and No. 1125 have been renumbered by PRLP, but not yet motorized, in this 1912 snapshot taken by motorman Fred Blaisdell at Gresham Station. Four nonpowered smoking section cars like this were ordered from the G.C. Kuhlman Car Company. They sported interiors of African mahogany with leather seats, bronze hardware, oil lamps, hot water heaters, and toilets. (Photograph Fred L. Blaisdell.)

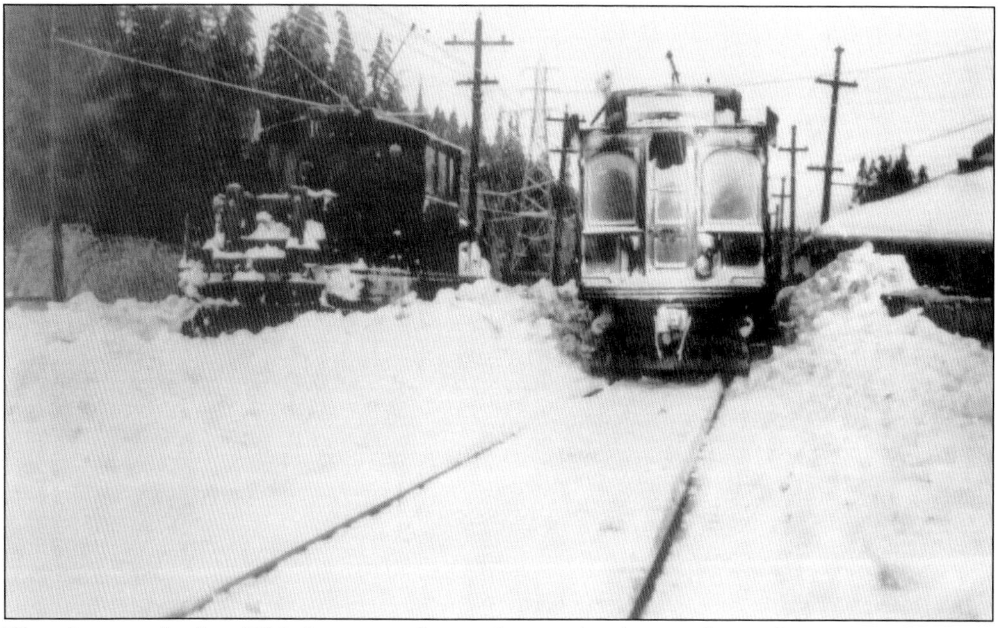

This photograph of an 1124 class interurban and a steeplecab was taken at Linnemann Junction during the big snow of 1916 (see similar picture at Lents Junction on page 67). Until 1913, Linnemann Junction had been the western terminus of the Bull Run Line. Afterward, trains originated in downtown Portland, ran east along Springwater Division tracks, and then switched to the Mount Hood Division at Linnemann Junction.

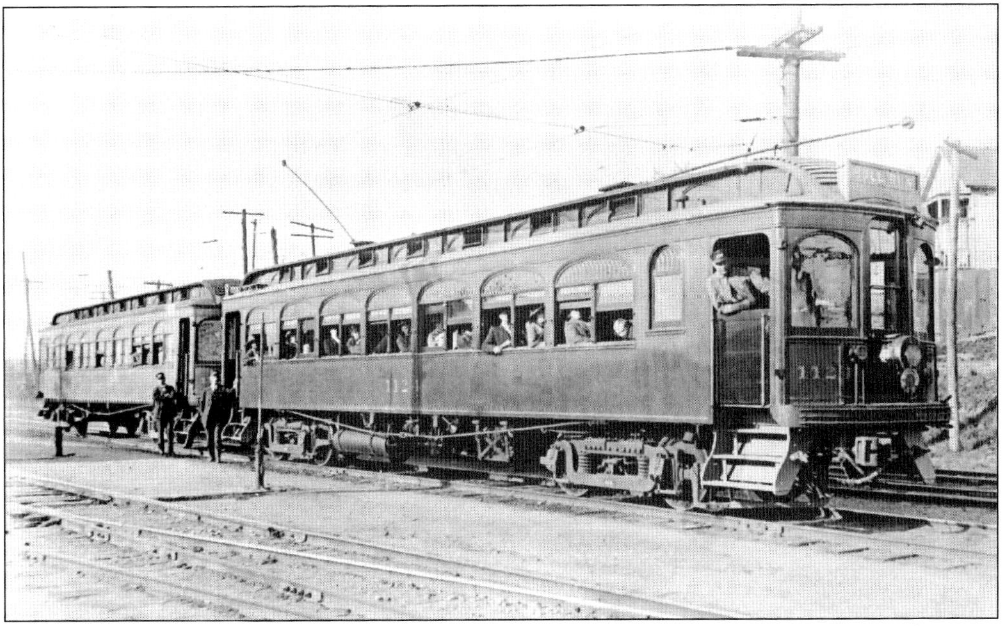

One of the former Mount Hood Railway passenger cars has not yet received motors, in this 1914 photograph of No. 1124, and a sister, outbound at Southeast Eleventh Avenue in Sellwood. The crewmen on this Bull Run train included motorman James A. Van Ham and conductor Harry S. Trick (the other conductor is not identified). The photograph was taken by another crewman, Fred Blaisdell. (Photograph Fred L. Blaisdell.)

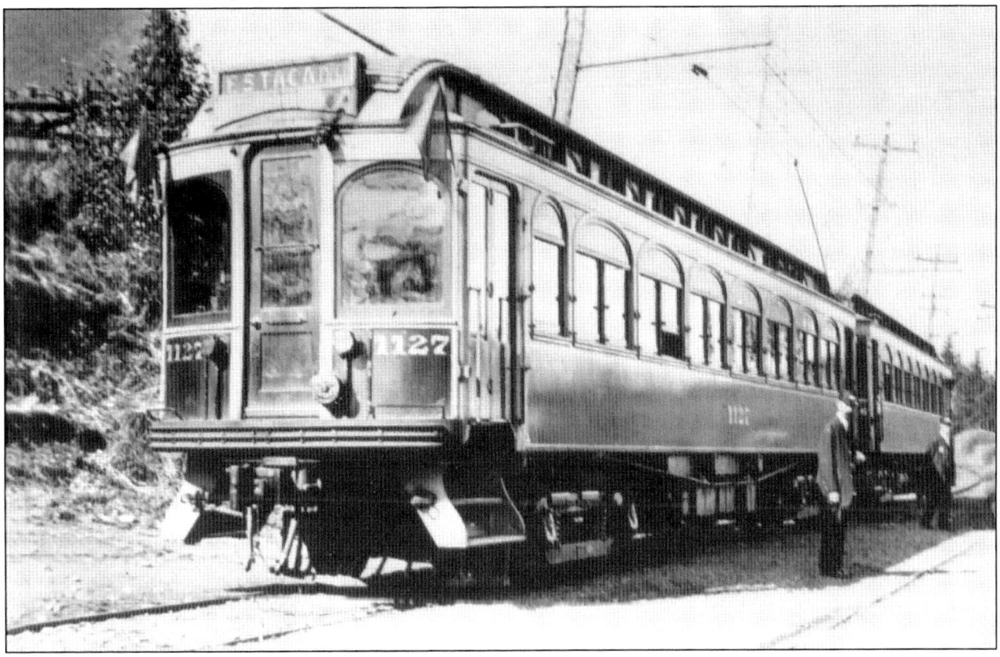

At times, the elegant Mount Hood Railway interurbans saw service on the Springwater Division. In this undated photograph, cars No. 1126 and No. 1127 are working as an Estacada Line excursion train. The end came for excursion traffic during the 1920s. No. 1126 was retired in 1933, and No. 1127 followed in 1936.

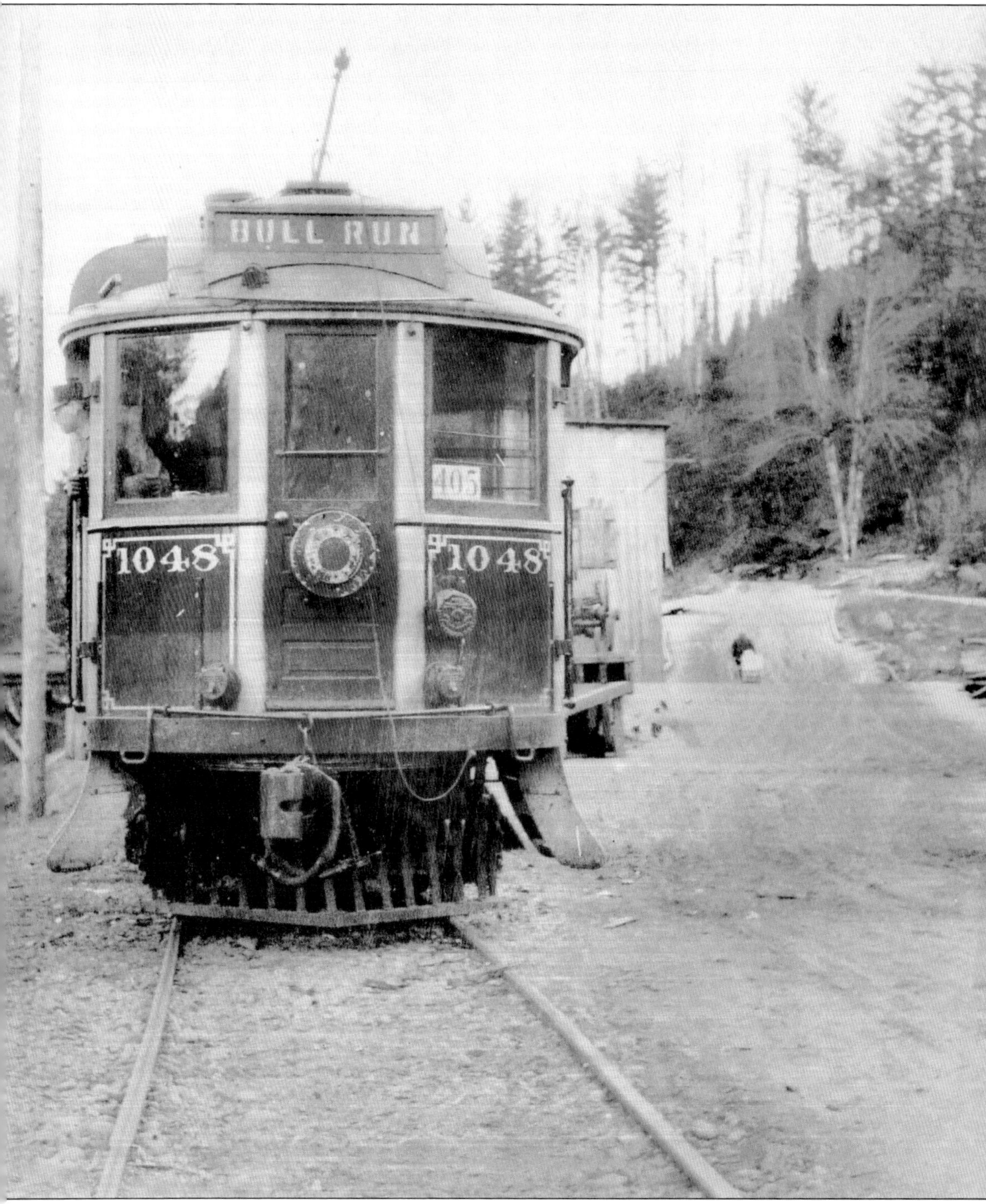

After 1912, PRL&P rolling stock like No. 1048 augmented the original Mount Hood Railway fleet. In this undated postcard, motorman Lee Fagg leans from the vestibule as he prepares to depart the Bull Run Line terminus. The large arc headlight has been hung on the front of the train in preparation for its 4:35 p.m. arrival in downtown Portland. Note the wagon on the freight dock in the background. (Courtesy Mark Moore.)

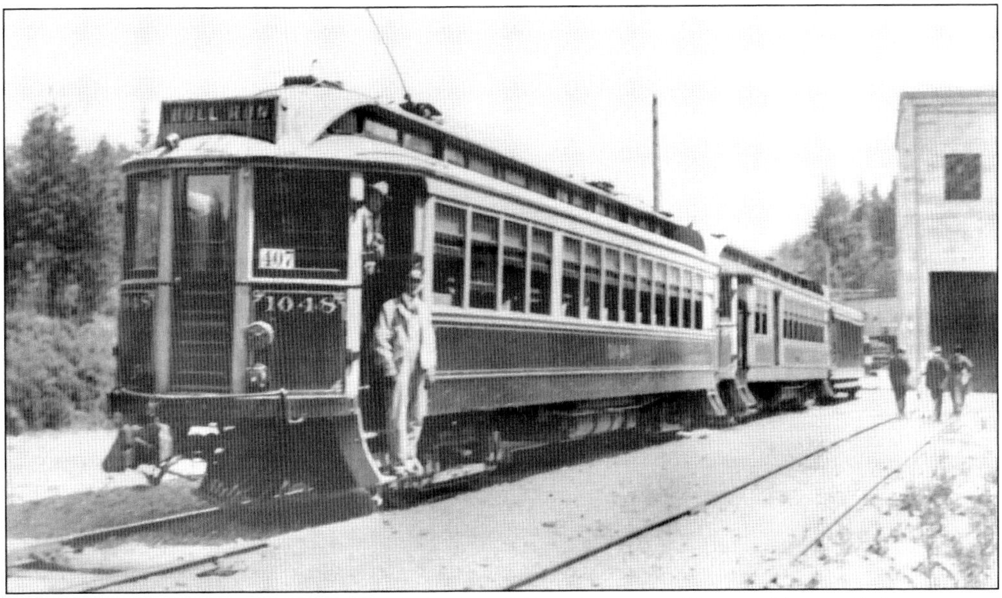

Train No. 407, consisting of cars No. 1048, No. 1050, and an open "breezer," has pulled up next to the powerhouse at the end of the Bull Run Line. It will be the last train of the day when it departs at 6:00 p.m. No. 1048 and No. 1050 were combines when received from the W.L. Holman Company in 1893, but were remodeled as regular passenger coaches with smoking sections in 1908.

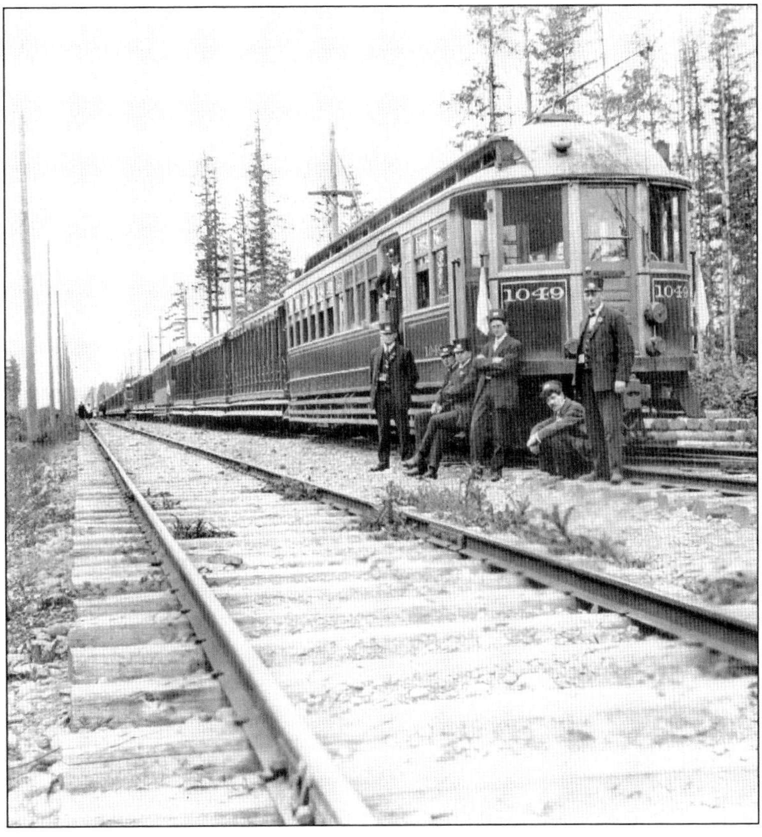

The reason for the excursion, captured here at Ruby Junction by motorman Albert A. Reck, is unknown, but it was a big occasion. Cars stretch as far as the eye can see, and seven carmen are taking a break next to No. 1049. Several trains are behind them, with at least 18 open cars, as well as a steeplecab and another motor. (Photograph Albert A. Reck; courtesy Mark Moore.)

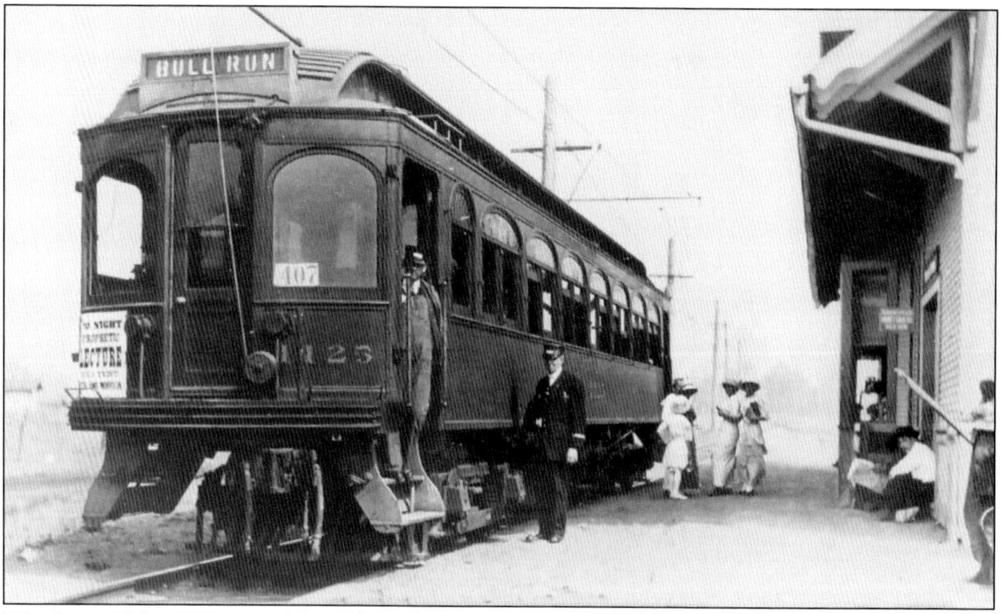

Westbound No. 1125, train No. 407, makes a stop at Gresham's Mount Hood Station during the 1910s. The advertising sign on the dash reads "To Night Prophetic Lecture Big Tent 10th and Morrison." (Courtesy Mark Moore.)

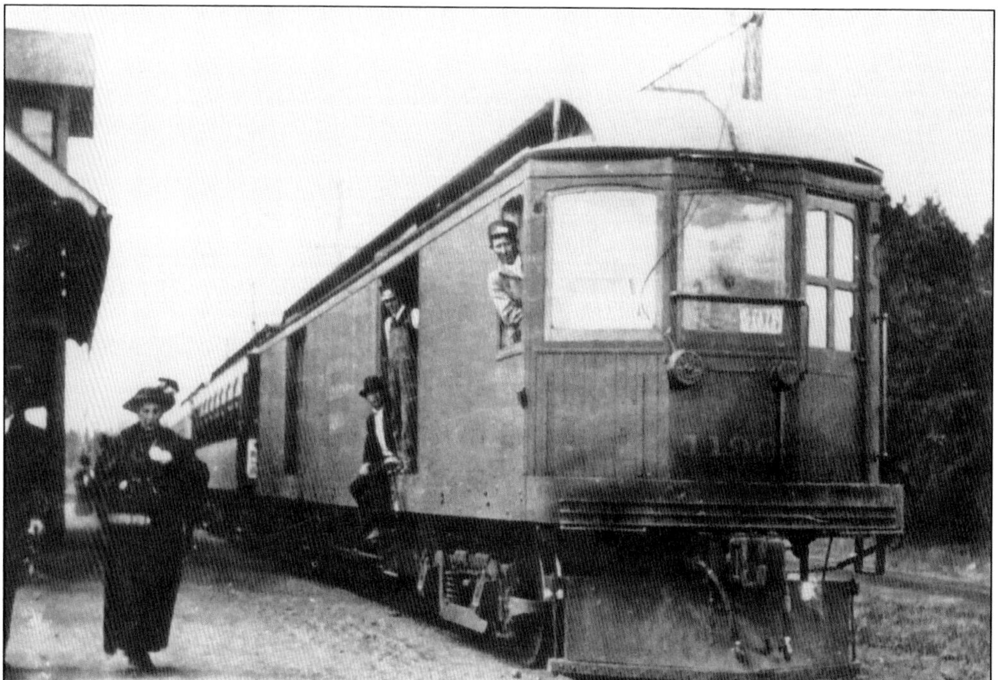

A woman carrying a parcel hurries past newly motorized express car No. 1190 at Gresham in 1914. The car, originally No. 101, was one of two express freight motors purchased in 1912 by the Mount Hood Railway. They were often at the head of long Bull Run passenger trains, as seen here. Upon retirement in 1936, the No. 1190 became a fire car, a kind of fire engine on rails.

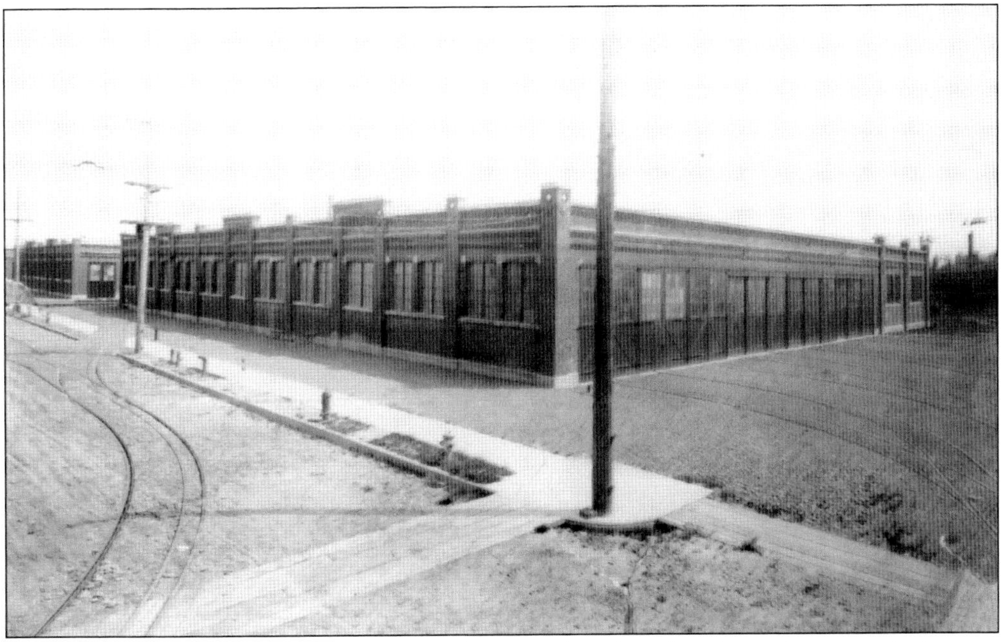

In October 1912, PRL&P completed a new shop complex along Southeast Seventeenth Avenue, between Southeast Rhone and Southeast Mall Streets. The Center Street Shops were designed to serve the entire railway system, both standard-gauge and narrow-gauge, eliminating other shop facilities inherited when PRL&P merged all Portland streetcar and interurban companies. This photograph was taken during construction.

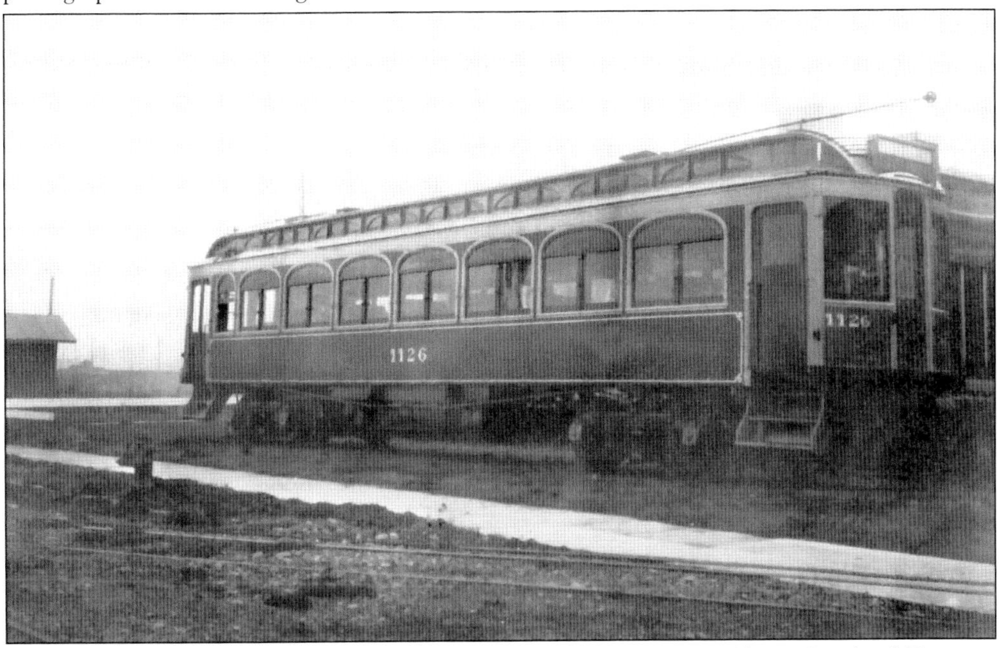

On the back of this 1920s photograph, taken at the Center Street Shops, Portland Traction Company superintendent of equipment Earl B. Richardson labeled car No. 1126 a "Fancy Dan." He was referring to the arched art glass windows on this series of four Mount Hood Railway interurbans, which may have required a bit of work to keep clean.

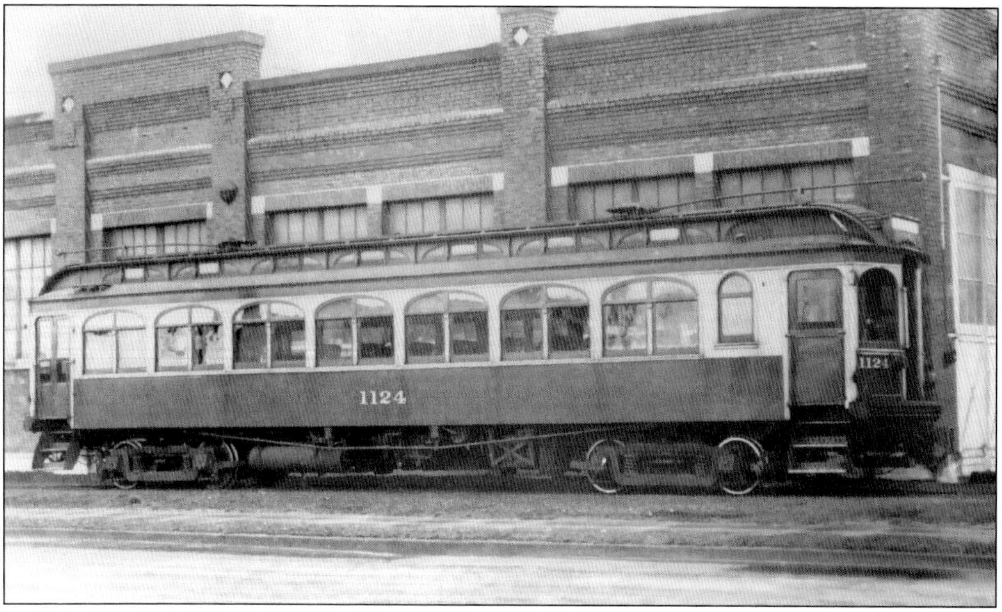

This photograph of Portland Electric Power Company (PEPCO) No. 1124 was taken at the Center Street Shops after the abandonment of passenger service on the Mount Hood Division in 1930. The side view highlights the car's elegant, curved design as well as its underbody equipment and Master Car Builder (MCB) high-speed trucks.

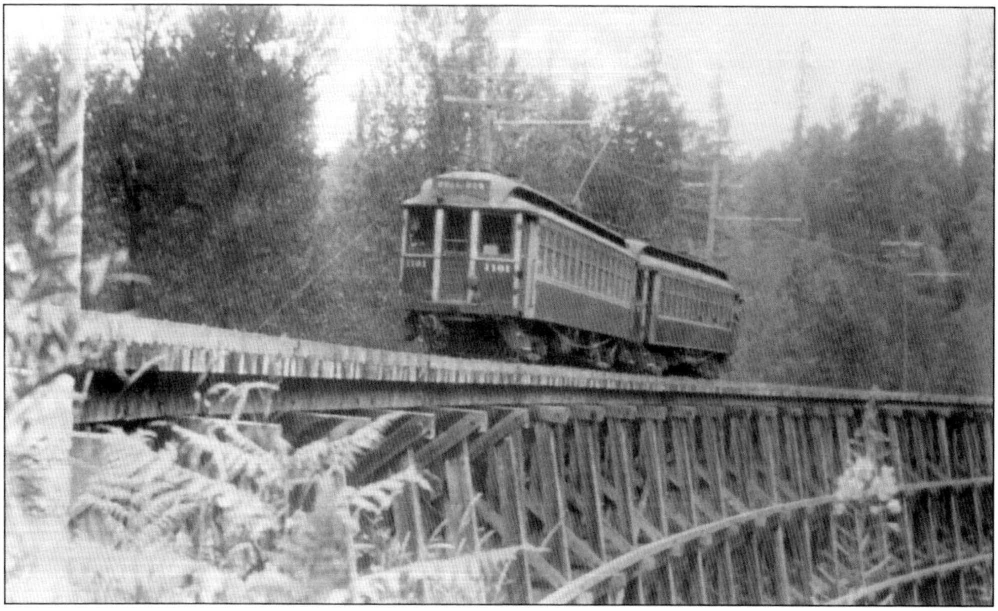

A two-car train led by No. 1101 is seen crossing the original wooden bridge over the Sandy River at Dodge Park in 1928. The bridge, completed by the Mount Hood Railway & Power Company on October 28, 1911, was replaced by a steel bridge in the 1920s. The second bridge was removed in 1932 after the Bull Run Line was abandoned.

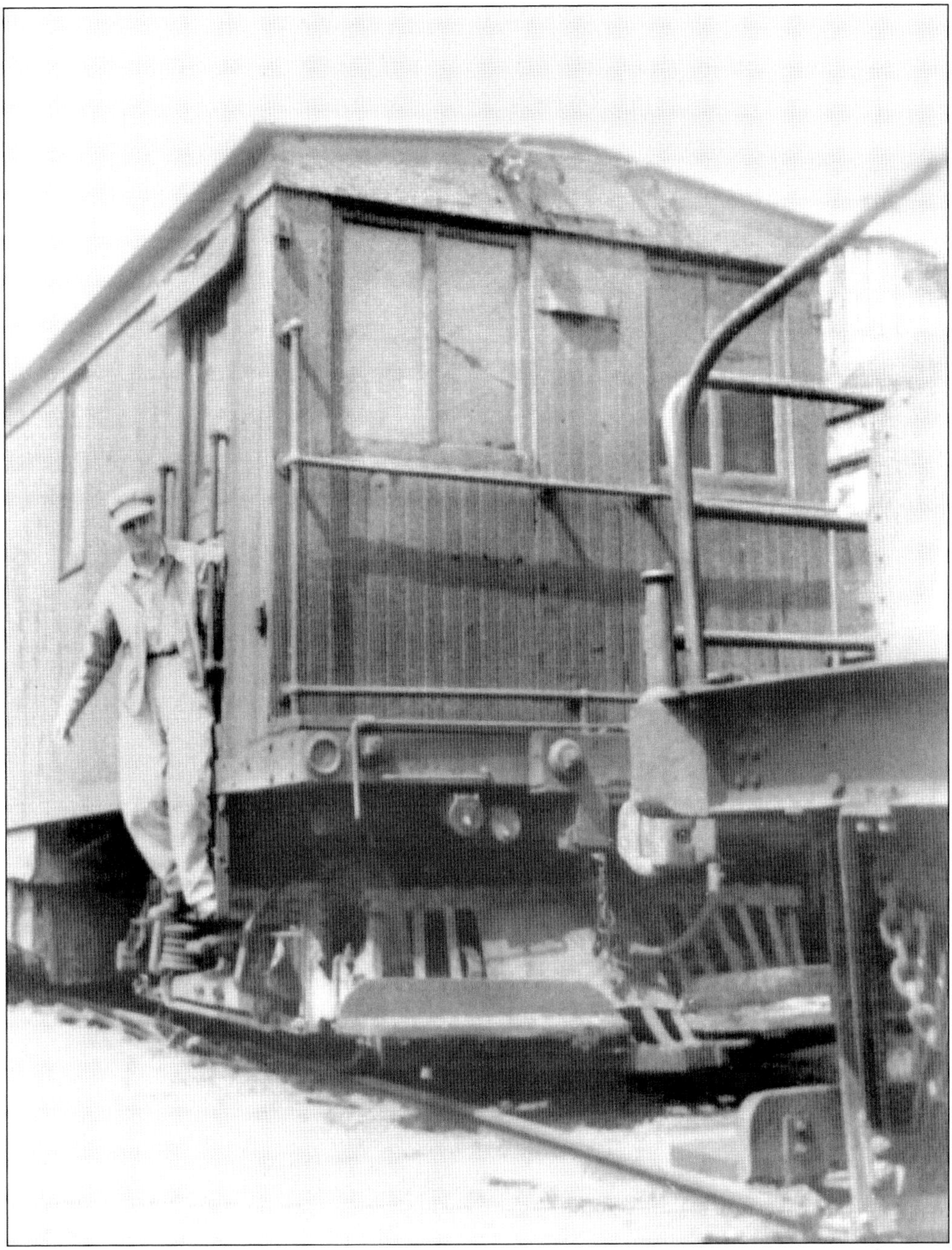

This photograph of a trainman climbing down from box motor No. 1415 brings to mind a 1939 *Railroad Magazine* article describing the crewless operation of freight trains across the Sandy River Bridge during its 1920s reconstruction. PEPCO did not want to cancel freight trains while the bridge was closed. So, a supposedly safe scheme was worked out whereby trains would be sent across in unmanned four-car segments. A brakeman, or "trolley pup," first walked across the bridge and signaled the go-ahead using a bridge telephone. Crews would start a train rolling, then hop off the "juice hog" (motor). As the train reached the other side, the brakeman would jump aboard and stop the train!

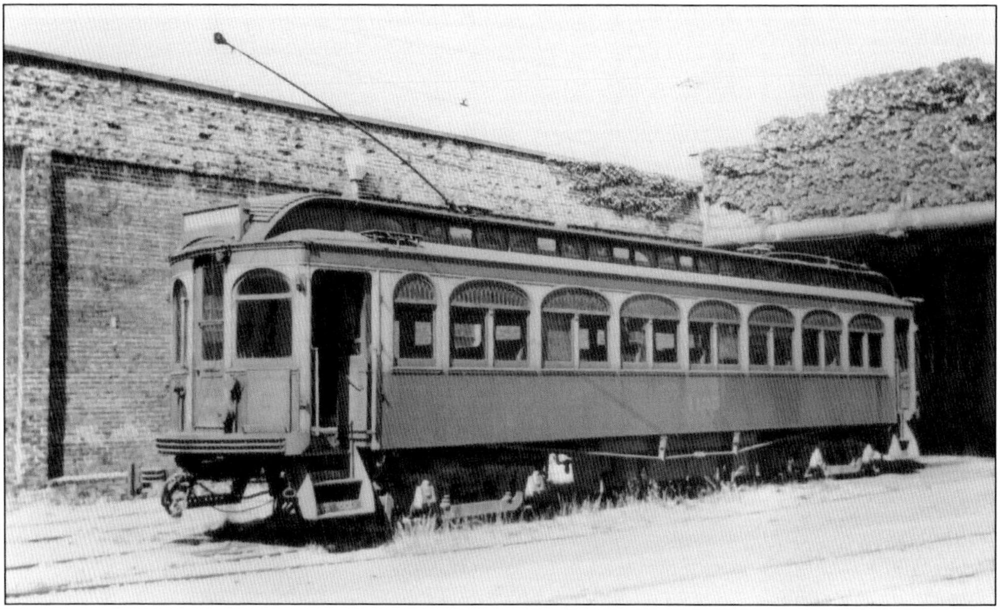

It is May 23, 1935. With the line to Bull Run gone and the Springwater Division cut back to Gresham, the end is rapidly approaching for the old Mount Hood Railway cars. PEPCO No. 1125 is seen here at the Sellwood carbarn a few months before retirement. It would be converted into a wrecker. (Photograph by Charles Savage.)

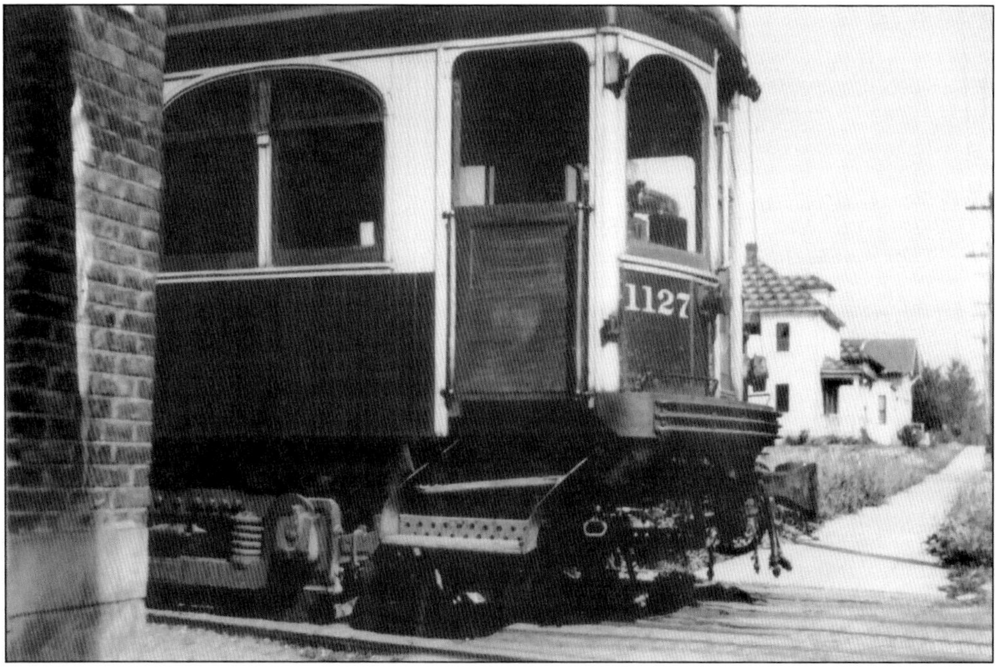

Superintendent Charles Snook took this photograph of No. 1127 at the Sellwood barn, showing the damage it received after having been struck by an automobile near Sellwood Gardens (one-half mile east of Golf Junction) on September 6, 1933. Most of the damage seems to have been to the steps. Within three years, all four former Mount Hood Railway cars had been retired. (Photograph Charles C. Snook.)

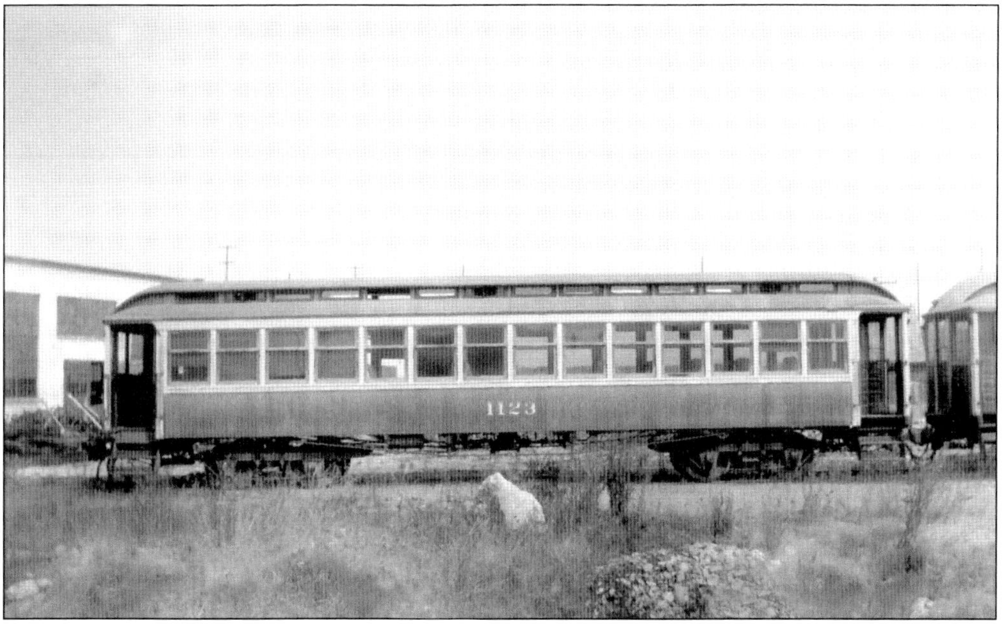

PTC No. 1123, seen here in the East Side Yards on August 26, 1934, was one of a pair of interurban trailers (the other was No. 1121) built by PRL&P in 1907. They were likely rebuilt OWP open trailers. In 1911, these cars inaugurated steam train passenger service on the Bull Run Line. Later, they were standard equipment on both Bull Run and Estacada excursion trains. (Photograph by Edward Maas.)

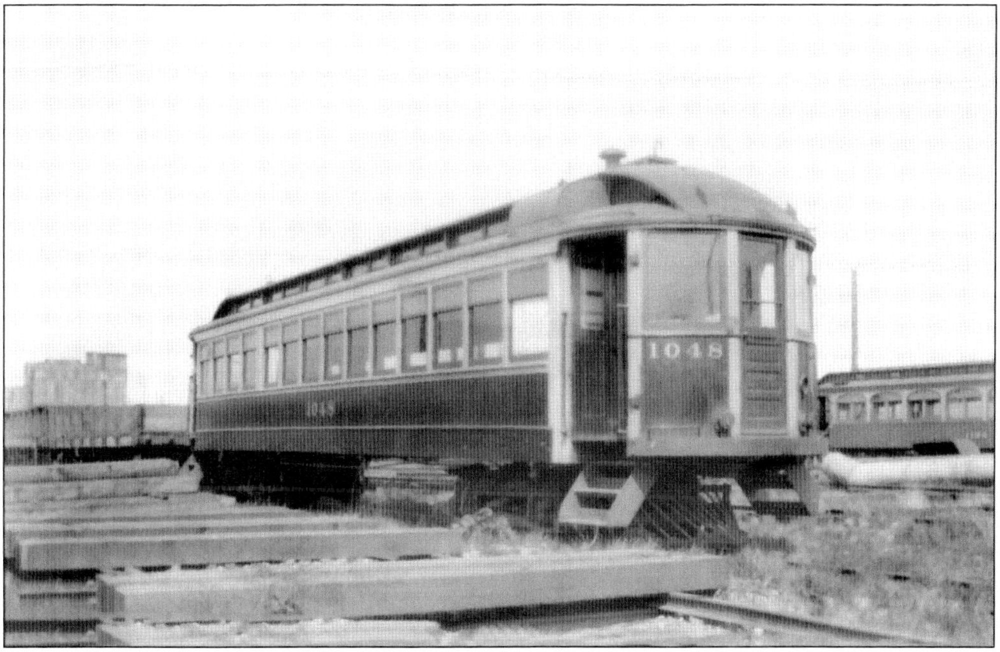

The clock is ticking for interurbans No. 1048 and No. 1124, seen here on the "rip tracks" at the Center Street Shops in 1936. Trolley poles and other equipment have already been removed from these cars as they await the scrapper's torch. The Mount Hood Division had been abandoned by this time, and the Springwater Division cut back to Boring. (Photograph Robert Kurkinen.)

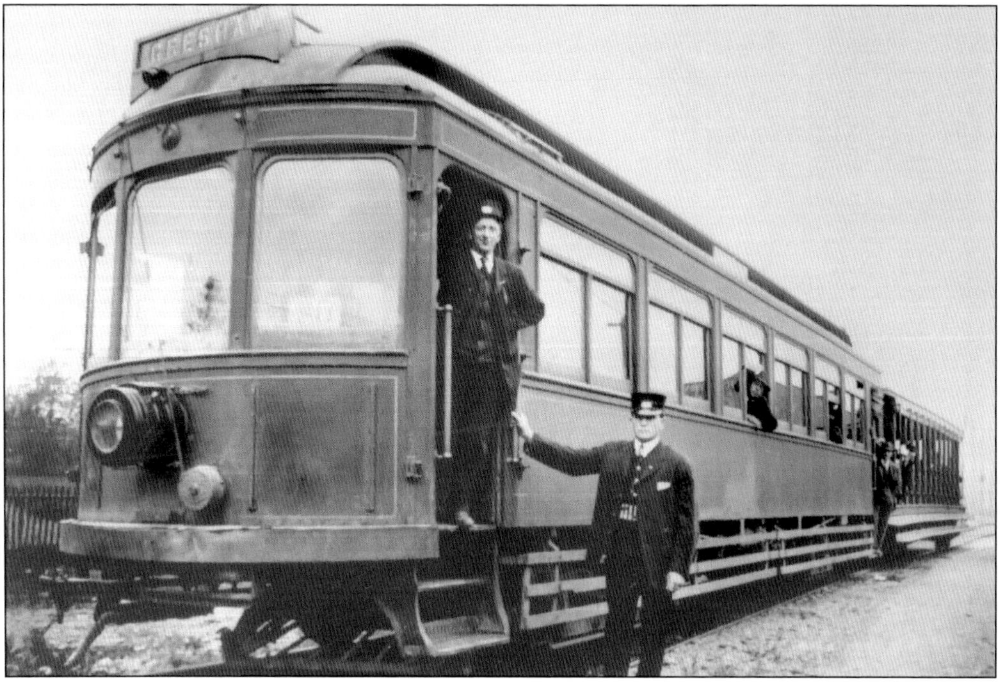

In 1903, OWP ordered beautiful interurban cars No. 57 and No. 58 from the Niles Car and Manufacturing Company. Instead of classic arched windows, they featured two-pane sightseeing windows with colored glass upper sash. No. 57 is seen here at Linnemann Junction several years before its transformation into the parlor car *Portland*. Although signed as a Gresham local, the Niles cars worked mainly on the Troutdale Line.

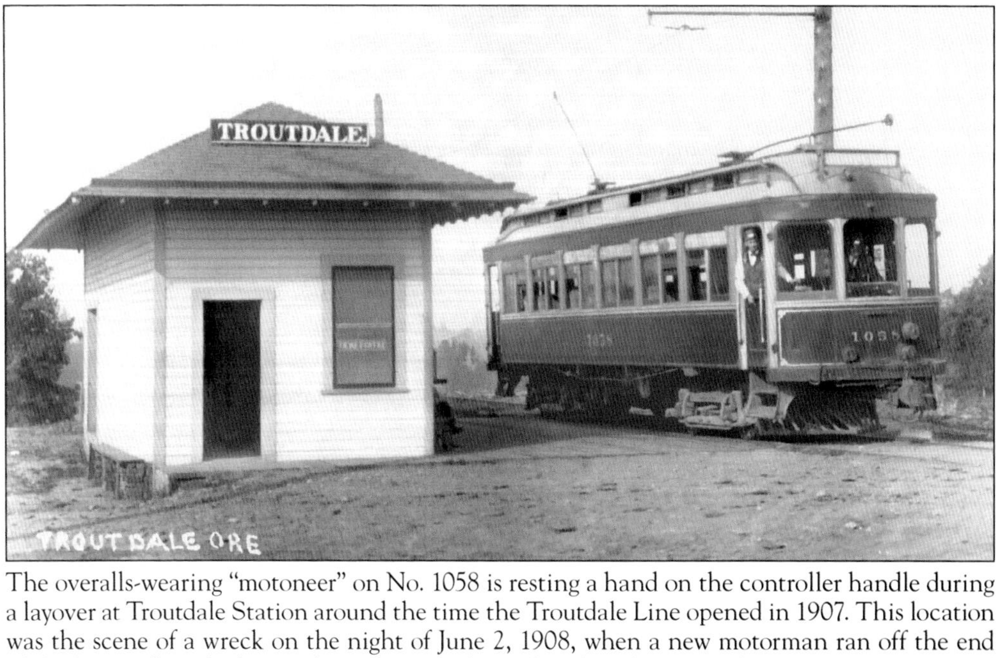

The overalls-wearing "motoneer" on No. 1058 is resting a hand on the controller handle during a layover at Troutdale Station around the time the Troutdale Line opened in 1907. This location was the scene of a wreck on the night of June 2, 1908, when a new motorman ran off the end of the line and crashed onto the Union Pacific Railroad tracks. Several passengers were injured and the car destroyed.

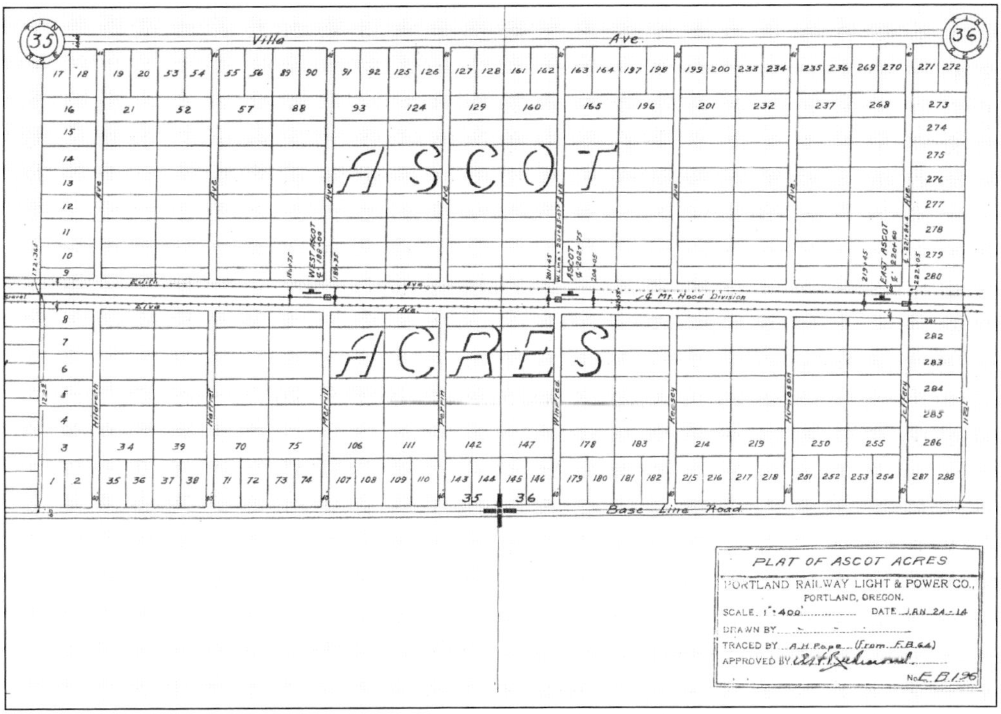

This 1914 PRL&P plat for Ascot Acres illustrates the close ties between real estate development and railway building. The stations of East Ascot, Ascot, and West Ascot are just two to three blocks apart (unusually close for an interurban) along the Mount Hood Division right-of-way (now East Burnside Street). The neighborhood straddled the line between present-day Northeast and Southeast Portland between Glisan and Stark Streets.

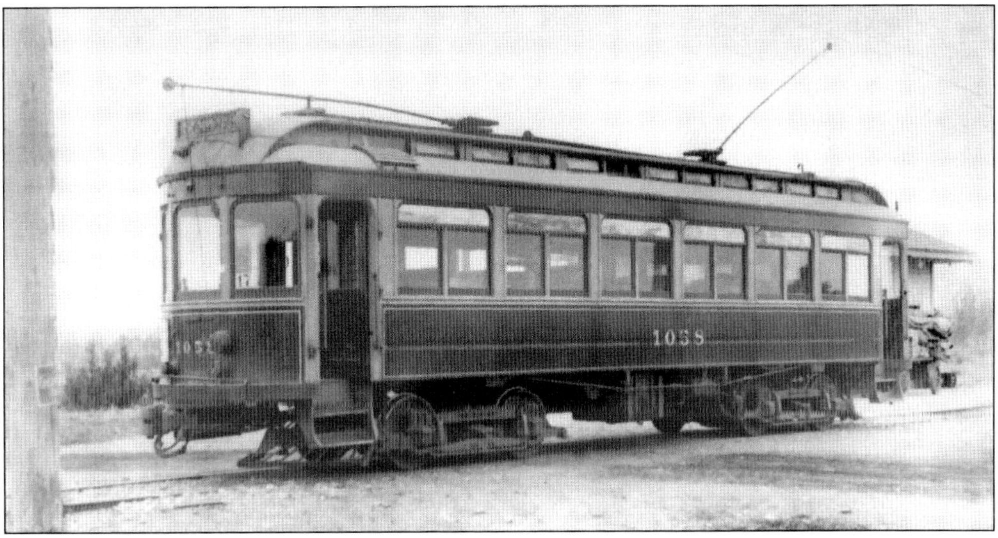

Car No. 58, now renumbered No. 1058, is seen at the Troutdale terminus in 1912. Before electrification had been completed on the neighboring line to Bull Run, eight daily trains were already running to Troutdale from Montavilla. Another four shuttled between Troutdale and Linnemann Junction, linking the Mount Hood and Springwater Divisions. Note the loaded baggage cart on the Troutdale Station platform to the right.

CALIFORNIA PLATING WORKS Gold, Silver, Brass and Nickel Plating. Metal Coloring a Specialty. 248 Second Street, Portland, Main 7218 9

– R. L. & P. CO.
– st and Alder Streets

CAZADERO (Estacada, Gresham) to PORTLAND

*Daily except Sunday. ‡Sunday only. A. M. in light face. P. M. in black face.

	*3 AM	9 AM	11 AM	15 AM	17 PM	19 PM	21 PM	25 PM	27 PM	*31 PM	33 PM	35 PM	37 PM	39 PM	*1 AM	†301 AM
Lv. CAZADERO	....	6.40	8.45	....	....	12.45	....	....	4.45	....	....	....	8.50	....	....	1.20
Estacada	....	6.48	8.52	....	....	12.52	....	....	4.52	....	6.30	....	9.00	....	....	1.31
Currensville	....	6.56	8.57	....	....	12.57	....	....	4.57	....	6.36	....	9.08	....	....	1.36
Eagle Creek	....	7.02	9.04	....	....	1.04	....	....	5.04	....	6.41	....	9.14	....	....	1.40
Barton	....	7.09	9.10	....	....	1.10	....	....	5.10	....	6.47	....	9.21	....	....	1.45
Seifer	....	7.14	9.15	....	....	1.15	....	....	5.15	....	6.51	....	9.27	....	....	1.49
Boring	....	7.18	9.19	....	....	1.19	....	....	5.19	....	6.53	....	9.30	....	....	1.52
Haley	....	7.20	9.22	....	....	1.22	....	....	5.22	....	6.55	....	9.32	....	....	1.55
Anderson	....	7.23	9.25	....	....	1.25	....	....	5.25	....	6.58	....	9.35	....	....	1.57
Hogan	A. M.	7.28	9.29	A. M.	P. M.	1.29	P. M.	P. M.	5.29	P. M.	7.02	P. M.	9.40	P.M.	A. M.	2.00
Gresham	5.40	7.33	9.34	10.40	12.40	1.34	2.40	4.40	5.34	6.40	7.06	9.15	9.45	11.15	12.30	2.04
Linnemann Jct.	5.45	7.40	9.40	10.44	12.44	1.40	2.44	4.44	5.40	6.45	7.10	9.20	9.50	11.20	12.34	2.08
Sycamore	5.50	7.45	9.45	10.48	12.48	1.45	2.48	4.48	5.45	6.50	7.13	9.25	9.55	11.25	12.40	2.12
Bellrose	5.54	7.48	9.48	10.52	12.52	1.48	2.52	4.52	5.48	6.53	7.17	9.28	9.58	11.28	12.42	2.14
Lents Jct.	5.59	7.53	9.53	10.57	12.57	1.53	2.57	4.57	5.53	6.58	7.22	9.32	10.03	11.33	12.45	2.16
Kendall	6.03	7.57	9.57	11.00	1.00	1.57	3.00	5.00	5.57	7.01	7.25	9.35	10.08	11.38	12.48	2.19
Stanley	6.07	8.03	10.03	11.05	1.05	2.03	3.05	5.05	6.03	7.05	7.29	9.39	10.13	11.43	12.52	2.23
Ardenwald	6.11	8.08	10.08	11.10	1.10	2.08	3.10	5.10	6.08	7.10	7.33	9.43	10.17	11.47	12.57	2.26
Golf Jct.	6.16	8.12	10.12	11.14	1.14	2.12	3.14	5.14	6.12	7.15	7.36	9.46	10.20	11.50	1.00	2.30
Ar. PORTLAND	6.45	8.35	10.35	11.35	1.35	2.35	3.35	5.35	6.35	P. M.	7.55	10.05	10.4J	P.M.	A. M.	A. M.

No. 7—Bellrose Local (Daily except Sun.) Lv. Bellrose 7.00 A. M. Ar. Portland 7.45 A. M.
No. 23—Stanley Local (Daily except Sun.) Lv. Stanley 4.45 P. M. Ar. Portland 5.10 P. M.
No. 29—Daily except Sun. Lv. Lents Jct. 6.54 P. M., Ar. Golf. Jct. 7.10 P. M.

MONTAVILLA (Mt. Hood Depot) TROUTDALE and WAY POINTS

Take Montavilla car at Third and Yamhill, marked Mt. Hood on dash sign.

From Montavilla--Read Down — **To Montavilla--Read Up**

90	88	86	84	82	80	78	76	74	72	70	68	66	64	NUMBERS	*63	65	67	L69	71	L73	75	L77	79	L81	83	85	87	L89	P91
PM	PM	PM	PM	PM	PM	PM	PM	AM	AM	AM	AM	AM	AM	STATIONS	AM	AM	AM	AM	AM	AM	PM	PM	PM	PM	PM	PM	PM	PM	PM
....	6.55	5.50	4.30	....	2.35	....	12.35	....	10.35	....	8.45	7.15	6.15	lv.Montavilla ar	6.15	7.10	8.35	....	10.35	....	12.35	....	2.35	....	4.30	5.40	6.45	....	....
....	6.57	5.52	4.32	....	2.37	....	12.37	....	10.37	....	8.47	7.17	6.17	..Russellville..	6.10	7.05	8.32	....	10.30	....	12.30	....	2.30	....	4.25	5.35	6.42	....	....
....	6.58	5.53	4.33	....	2.38	....	12.38	....	10.38	....	8.48	7.18	6.18	..Brunswick..	6.09	7.04	8.31	....	10.29	....	12.29	....	2.29	....	4.24	5.34	6.41	....	....
....	7.00	5.55	4.35	....	2.40	....	12.40	....	10.40	....	8.50	7.20	6.20	.Ventura Park	6.07	7.02	8.29	....	10.27	....	12.27	....	2.27	....	4.22	5.32	6.39	....	....
....	7.01	5.56	4.36	....	2.41	....	12.41	....	10.41	....	8.51	7.21	6.21	...Varnell...	6.06	7.01	8.28	....	10.26	....	12.26	....	2.26	....	4.21	5.31	6.38	....	....
....	7.02	5.57	4.37	....	2.42	....	12.42	....	10.42	....	8.52	7.22	6.22	..West Ascot..	6.05	7.00	8.27	....	10.25	....	12.25	....	2.25	....	4.20	5.30	6.37	....	....
....	7.03	5.58	4.38	....	2.43	....	12.43	....	10.43	....	8.53	7.23	6.23	....Ascot....	6.04	6.59	8.26	....	10.24	....	12.24	....	2.24	....	4.19	5.29	6.36	....	....
....	7.04	5.59	4.39	....	2.44	....	12.44	....	10.44	....	8.54	7.24	6.24	..East Ascot..	6.03	6.58	8.25	....	10.23	....	12.23	....	2.23	....	4.18	5.28	6.35	....	....
....	7.05	6.00	4.40	....	2.45	....	12.45	....	10.45	....	8.55	7.25	6.25	....Elwood....	6.02	6.57	8.24	....	10.22	....	12.22	....	2.22	....	4.17	5.27	6.34	....	....
....	7.06	6.01	4.41	....	2.46	....	12.46	....	10.46	....	8.56	7.26	6.26	....Verdante..	6.01	6.56	8.23	....	10.21	....	12.21	....	2.21	....	4.16	5.26	6.33	....	....
....	7.07	6.02	4.42	....	2.47	....	12.47	....	10.47	....	8.57	7.27	6.27	...Rockwood..	6.00	6.55	8.22	....	10.20	....	12.20	....	2.20	....	4.15	5.25	6.32	....	....
PM	7.08	6.03	4.43	PM	2.48	PM	12.48	AM	10.48	AM	8.58	7.28	6.28	...Edgewood...	5.59	6.54	8.21	AM	10.19	AM	12.19	PM	2.19	PM	4.14	5.24	6.31	PM	PM
7.45	7.10	6.05	4.45	3.46	2.50	1.46	12.50	11.46	10.50	9.46	9.00	7.41	6.30	...Ruby Jct...	5.58	6.53	8.20	9.28	10.18	11.28	12.18	1.28	2.18	3.28	4.13	5.23	6.30	7.31	8.11
7.47	7.11	6.06	4.46	3.47	2.51	1.47	12.51	11.47	10.51	9.47	9.01	7.42	6.31	...Base Line...	5.55	6.50	8.11	9.25	10.15	11.25	12.15	1.25	2.15	3.25	4.10	5.20	6.25	7.30	8.10
7.51	7.16	6.11	4.51	3.51	2.56	1.51	12.56	11.51	10.56	9.51	9.06	7.47	6.36	...Fairview...	5.50	6.45	8.06	9.20	10.10	11.20	12.10	1.20	2.10	3.20	4.05	5.15	6.20	7.25	8.05
7.53	7.17	6.12	4.53	3.53	2.57	1.53	12.57	11.53	10.57	9.53	9.07	7.48	6.37	....Arata....	5.48	6.43	8.04	9.18	10.08	11.18	12.06	1.18	2.08	3.18	4.03	5.13	6.18	7.23	8.03
8.00	7.20	6.15	4.55	4.00	3.05	2.00	1.05	12.00	11.05	10.00	9.10	7.52	6.40	ar.Troutdale.lv.	5.45	6.40	8.00	9.15	10.05	11.15	12.05	1.15	2.05	3.15	4.00	5.10	6.15	7.20	8.00

Trains marked "L" run to Linnemann; "P" to Portland.
Trains 63 and 64 Daily except Sunday. Trains 70, 74, 78, 82 and 90 start from Linnemann.

This 1915 official timetable lists 14 daily Troutdale Line trains in each direction; five from Ruby Junction, and nine from Montavilla. The trains served 17 stations. Passengers were advised to catch the Montavilla streetcar at Southwest Third Avenue and Yamhill Street, which would carry dash signs marked "Mount Hood." The advertisement for a fishing outfit was aimed at recreational riders on PRL&P's "Trout Route."

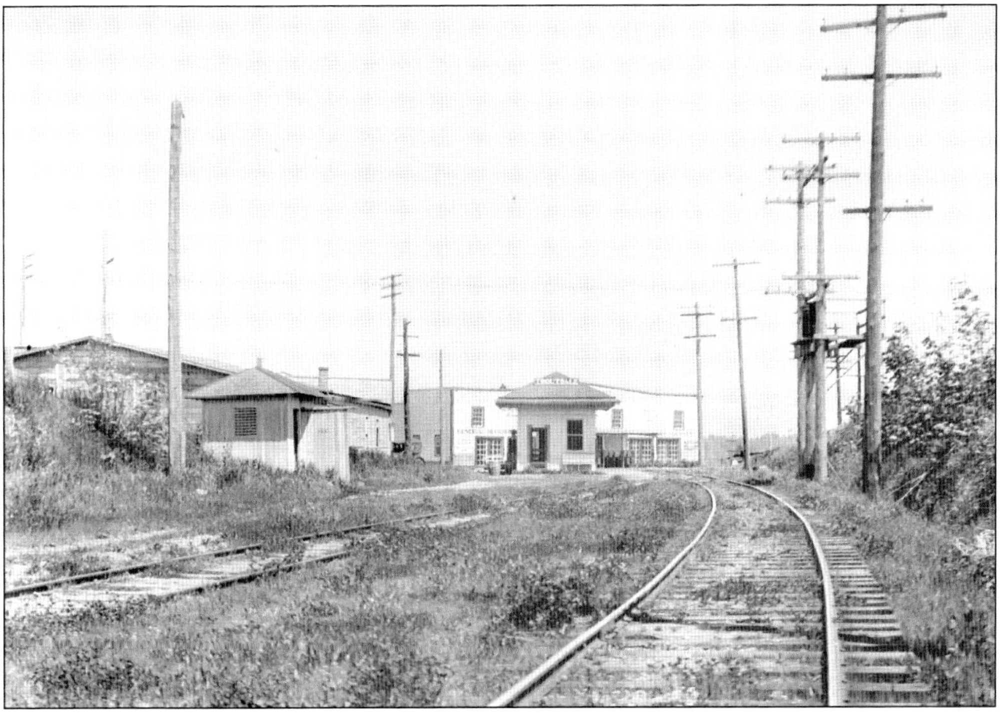

Two years remained for the Troutdale Line when this 1925 photograph of Troutdale Station was taken. Signs on the adjacent automobile garage read, "LADIES REST ROOM" and "Wait for Cars HERE." The men's restroom was less conveniently located in the out building to the left. The little station itself originally housed a ticket office and baggage area.

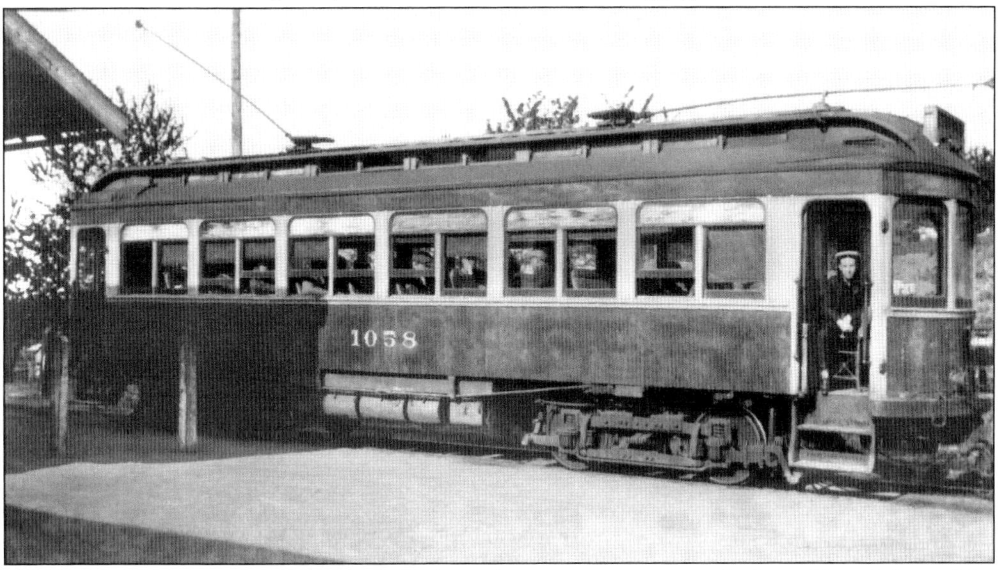

The colored glass windows gleam in the late afternoon sun as worn-looking Troutdale car No. 1058 waits at the depot on Northeast Ninetieth Avenue in Montavilla in the 1920s. In 1929, bins were placed inside No. 1058, a large side door installed, and a tower built on the roof, converting this formerly elegant interurban into an overhead line repair car (compare with the photograph on page 123).

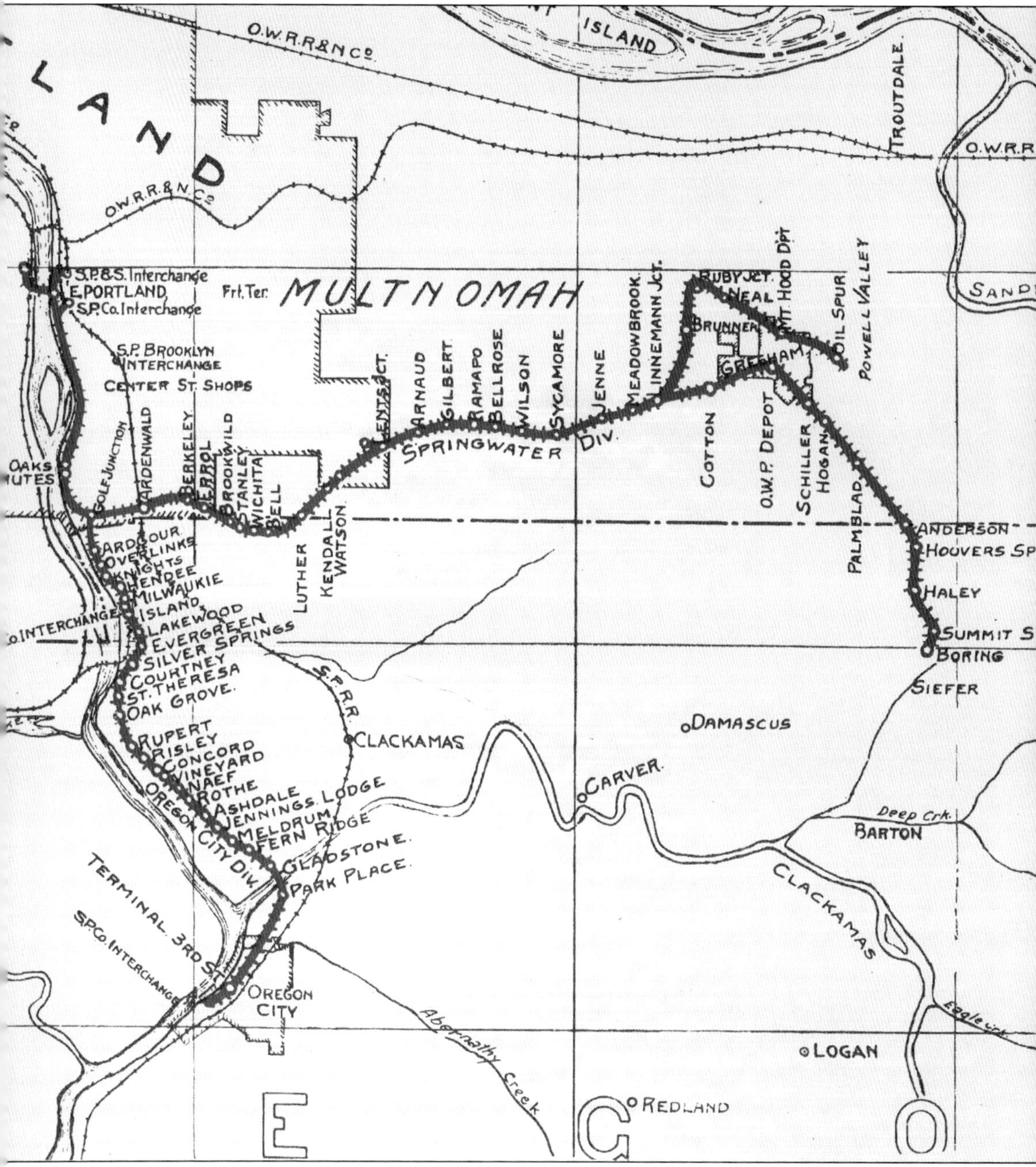

This Portland Traction Company map shows the nation's oldest interurban railway in its final form, in 1950. The original 14.6-mile Oregon City Line was still in use, however passenger service had been discontinued beyond Bellrose, 12 miles from Portland, on the Springwater Division. Only freight trains still made the trip to Boring and Gresham.

Five

Save Our Streetcars

THE LAST LINES

The nation's first interurban, the East Side Railway, failed for the same reasons that later ones did: unrealistic expectations and low return on investment. But, when the Portland Railway, Light & Power Company (PRL&P) finished consolidating all Portland street and interurban railways in 1908, the nationwide boom in interurban railway construction was still under way, and PRL&P was building more lines and adding streetcars. Freight traffic, as well as passenger traffic, remained strong for several years after mileage and new car orders peaked in 1912.

The first major interurban abandonments came after the Portland Electric Power Company (PEPCO) took over in 1924. The Mount Hood Division, which had not made a profit from the start, saw the first cuts. The Montavilla-Troutdale route was discontinued on June 15, 1927. Passenger trains over the Bull Run Line ceased operating on December 28, 1930. Springwater Division reductions were next. Passenger trains to Estacada ceased in 1932, and the terminus was cut back to Boring. On May 1, 1934, it was further cut to the Springwater depot in Gresham. A 1944 rerouting via Ruby Junction changed the Gresham terminus to the more centrally located Mount Hood depot.

Following a service reduction on January 31, 1949, Bellrose (sometimes spelled Bell Rose) and Oregon City became the last two interurban lines. During the 1940s, PEPCO began supplementing Portland's aging wooden interurbans with secondhand streetcars for use on these remaining lines. By the time eight Pacific Electric "Hollywood" cars arrived in 1953, the Railway and Terminal Division of Portland Traction Company (PTC) was at the helm.

In 1952, believing a freight-only railroad would attract buyers, PTC requested permission to abandon passenger service. Four years later, they allowed Multnomah County to cut interurban access to downtown via the Hawthorne Bridge. However, when a citizen's group called Transit Savers stepped up their "Save Our Streetcars" (SOS) campaign, the Public Utilities Commission declared passenger service essential and continued to deny abandonment. The debate stopped when PTC abruptly ceased passenger service on January 25, 1958, in defiance of PUC orders. The longest-lasting interurban was gone.

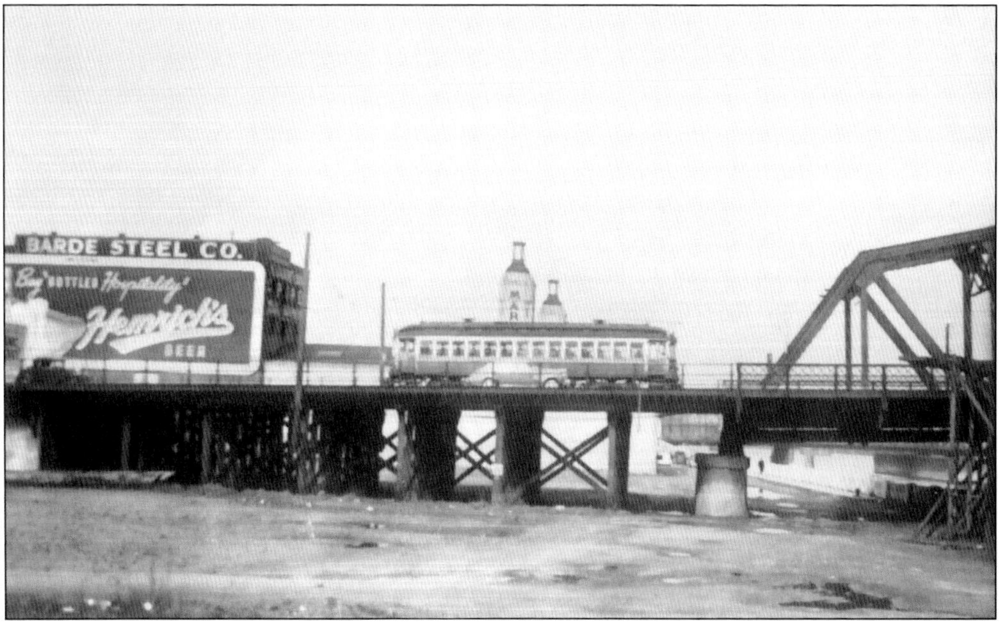

One of the locally built wooden interurbans is outbound across the Hawthorne Bridge in the years prior to 1956, when the Portland Traction Company allowed Multnomah County to remodel the bridge ramps without reinstalling tracks. During their last two years, the Oregon City and Bellrose Lines had no direct access downtown. The old Farmers Market towers can be seen in the background. (Photograph Alfred L. Haij.)

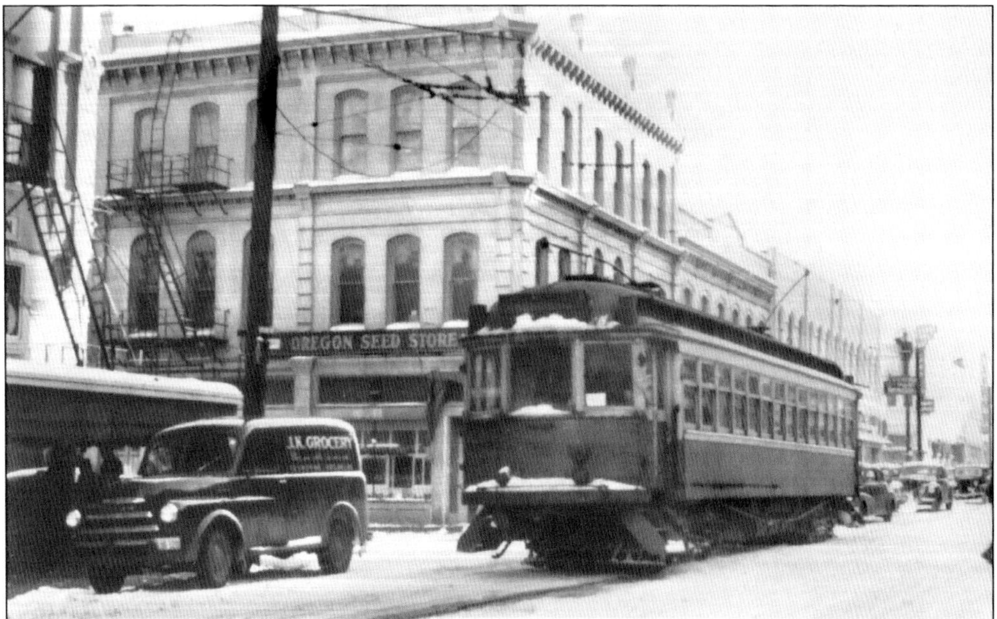

The No. 1093 is outbound through the winter slush on Southwest First Avenue and Yamhill Street in Portland during the early 1950s. The days are numbered for both the interurban car and the tracks through downtown. Some of the buildings in the background would survive to become part of a new farmers market called Yamhill Marketplace.

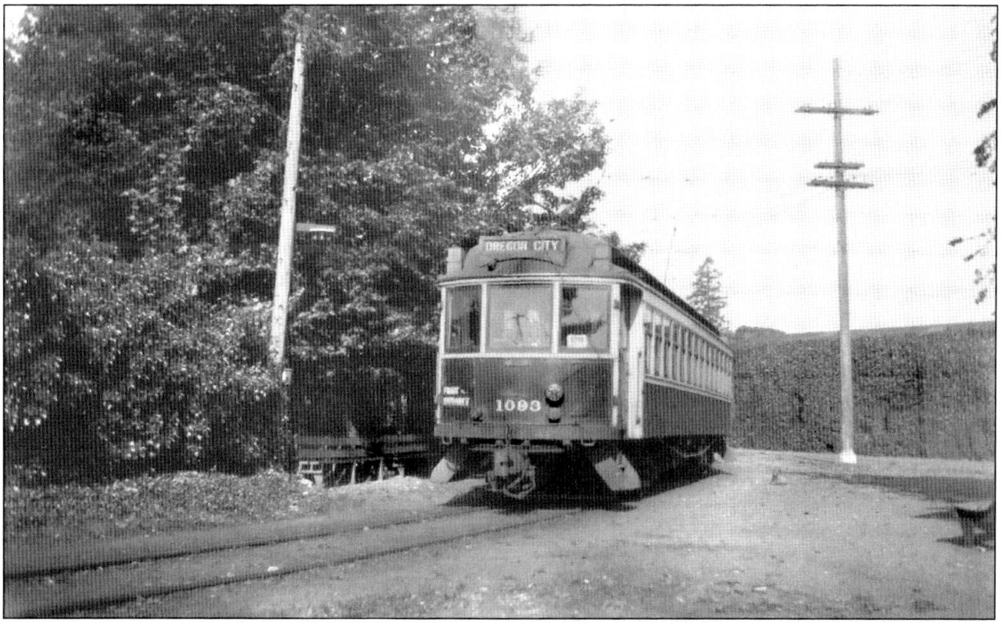

In this photograph, No. 1093 is headed south at Golf Junction. The ivy-covered building in the background is the former Sellwood carbarn, which had been sold to private enterprise before World War II. When the 11 cars in this class were converted to one-man operation in the 1930s, their train doors were removed and controls moved to the center of the platform. They were no longer operated with multiple unit (MU) control.

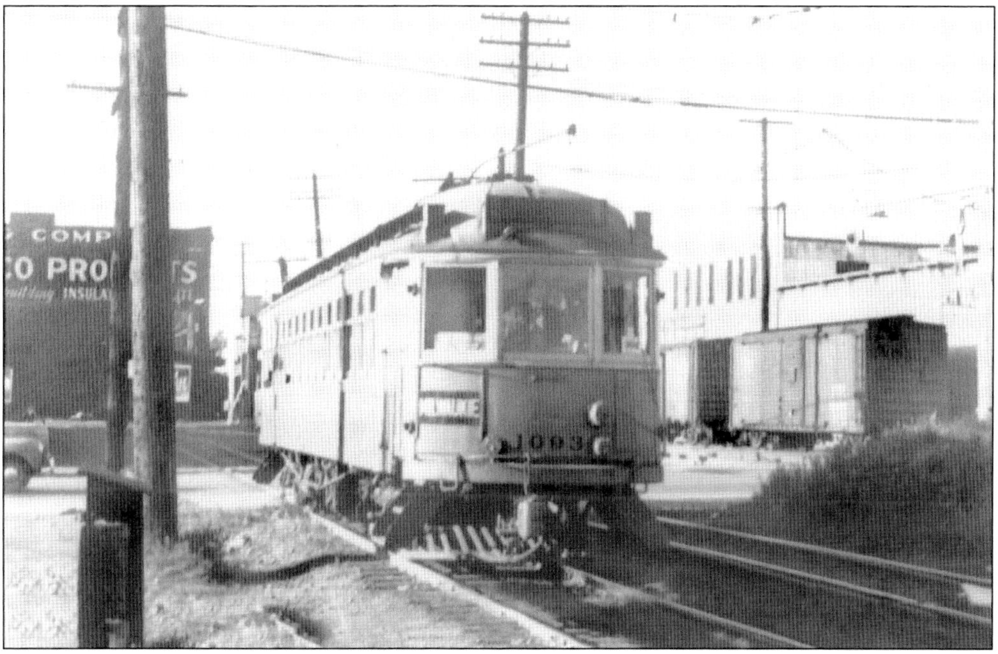

Milwaukie Local No. 1093 is wearing an experimental orange-and-cream color scheme as it crosses Southeast Clay Street in East Portland in the early 1950s. The area in the background became the final northern terminus for the Oregon City Line after the Hawthorne Bridge tracks were cut in 1956. (Photograph Alfred L. Haij.)

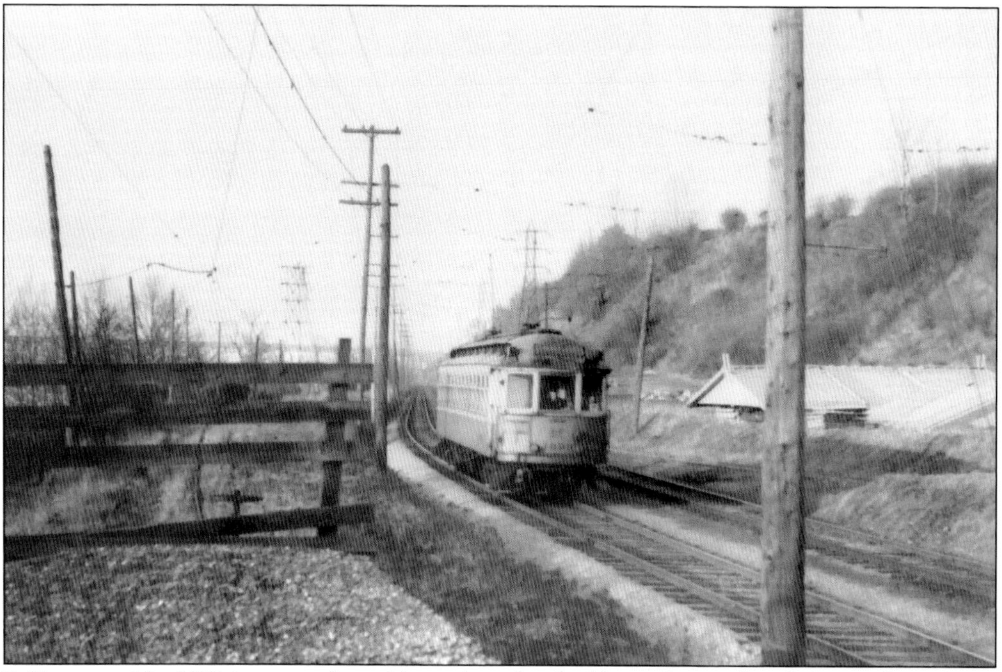

Bellrose car No. 1093 is at speed southbound on the double track mainline below Sellwood in a photograph taken after Bellrose became the terminus of the former line to Estacada in 1949. The right-of-way seen here, which closely followed the Willamette River, opened in August 1904.

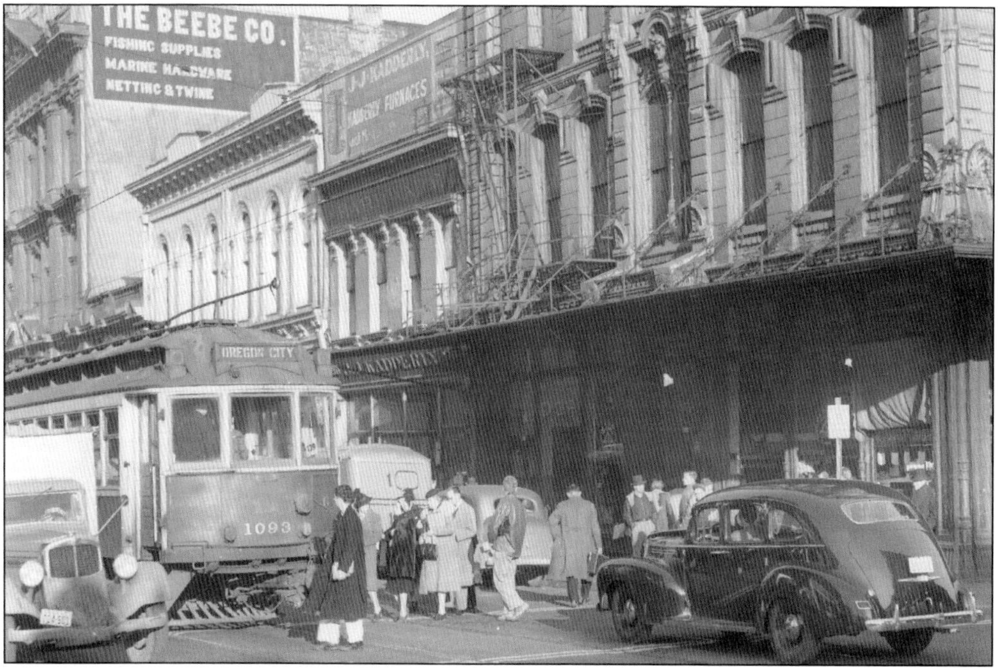

This bustling rush hour scene shows Oregon City No. 1093 loading passengers at the interurban station at Southwest First Avenue and Alder Streets about 1939. The Mount Hood Division was already gone and cuts had begun on the Springwater Division, but World War II would briefly boost ridership to Gresham and Oregon City.

Streetcars were an important means of student transportation. This interurban school ticket was issued in the 1930s, during the Portland Electric Power Company years. The top half includes 22 Oregon City Line stations, while the bottom half has 18 stops on the Gresham Line. Portland's streetcar companies had provided discounted student tickets since the turn of the 20th century. (Courtesy Mark Moore.)

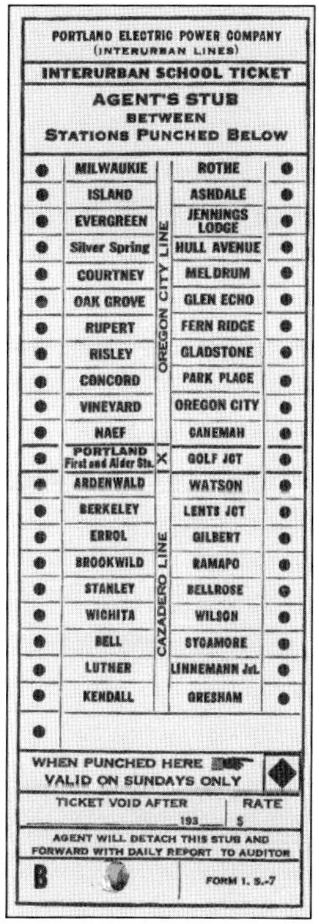

PORTLAND ELECTRIC POWER COMPANY
(INTERURBAN LINES)

INTERURBAN SCHOOL TICKET

AGENT'S STUB
BETWEEN
STATIONS PUNCHED BELOW

		OREGON CITY LINE	
MILWAUKIE		ROTHE	
ISLAND		ASHDALE	
EVERGREEN		JENNINGS LODGE	
Silver Spring		HULL AVENUE	
COURTNEY		MELDRUM	
OAK GROVE		GLEN ECHO	
RUPERT		FERN RIDGE	
RISLEY		GLADSTONE	
CONCORD		PARK PLACE	
VINEYARD		OREGON CITY	
NAEF		CANEMAH	
PORTLAND First and Alder Sts.	X	GOLF JCT	
		CAZADERO LINE	
ARDENWALD		WATSON	
BERKELEY		LENTS JCT	
ERROL		GILBERT	
BROOKWILD		RAMAPO	
STANLEY		BELLROSE	
WICHITA		WILSON	
BELL		SYCAMORE	
LUTHER		LINNEMANN Jct.	
KENDALL		GRESHAM	

WHEN PUNCHED HERE VALID ON SUNDAYS ONLY

TICKET VOID AFTER ______ 193__ | RATE $

AGENT WILL DETACH THIS STUB AND FORWARD WITH DAILY REPORT TO AUDITOR

B FORM I. S.-7

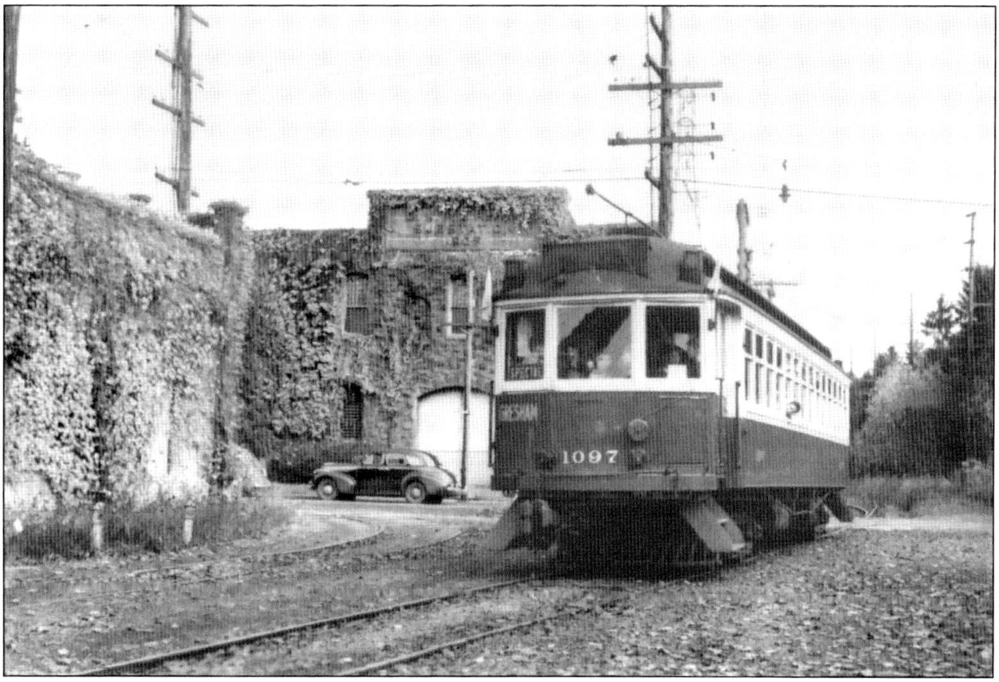

The old substation and carbarn at Southeast Thirteenth Avenue and Ochoco Street provide an Ivy League–like background for a Portland Traction Company school special. No. 1097 is seen inbound from Gresham at Golf Junction with a load of kids during an autumn in the 1940s.

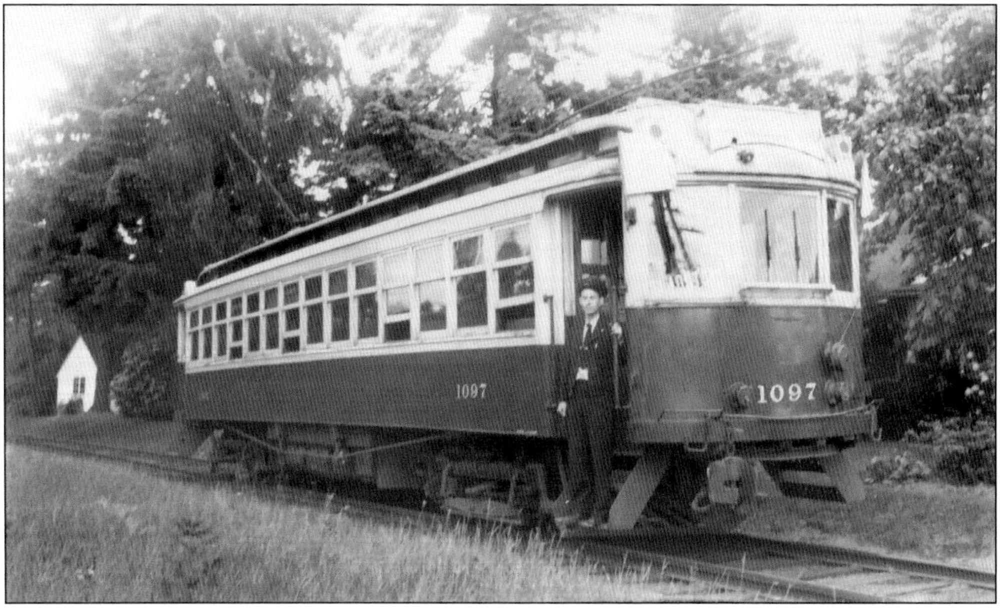

New operator Charles Hayden poses with Oregon City car No. 1097 at Fern Ridge Station in 1953. He is wearing the bus driver–style uniform phased in during the 1940s. No. 1097 was one of the last six wooden cars remaining in service. All cars in this series, built by PRL&P in 1910 and 1912, were scrapped a few months after this photograph was taken. The new "Hollywood" cars replaced them.

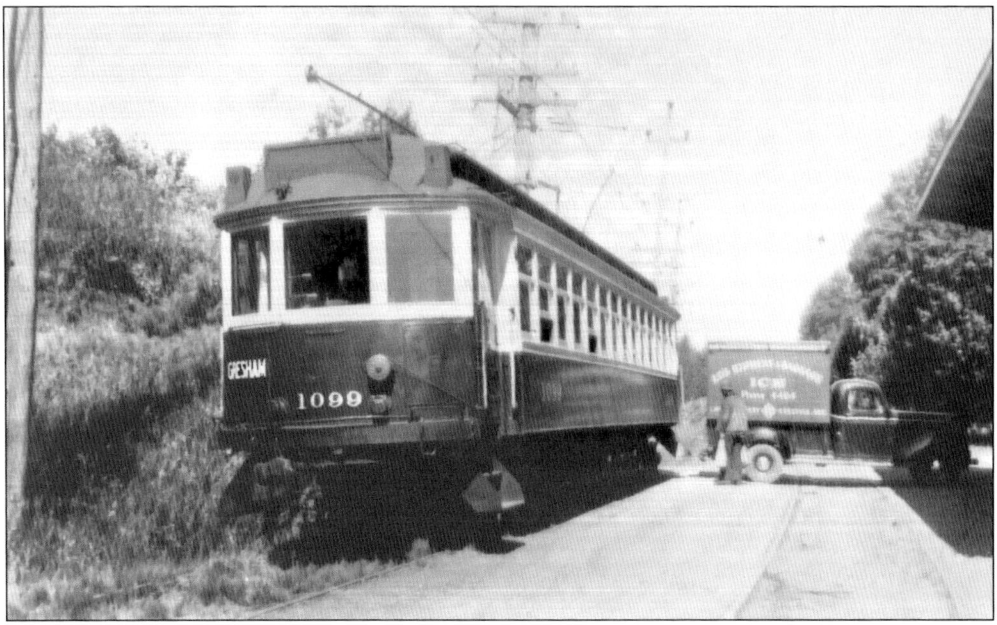

An employee is transferring packages from an Ed's Express, Baggage and Ice delivery truck to the rear platform of No. 1099 at the Springwater Division Gresham Station. This is either a nonpassenger trip, or the photograph was taken before trains were rerouted to use the former Mount Hood Division Gresham Station in 1944. (Photograph Alfred L. Haij.)

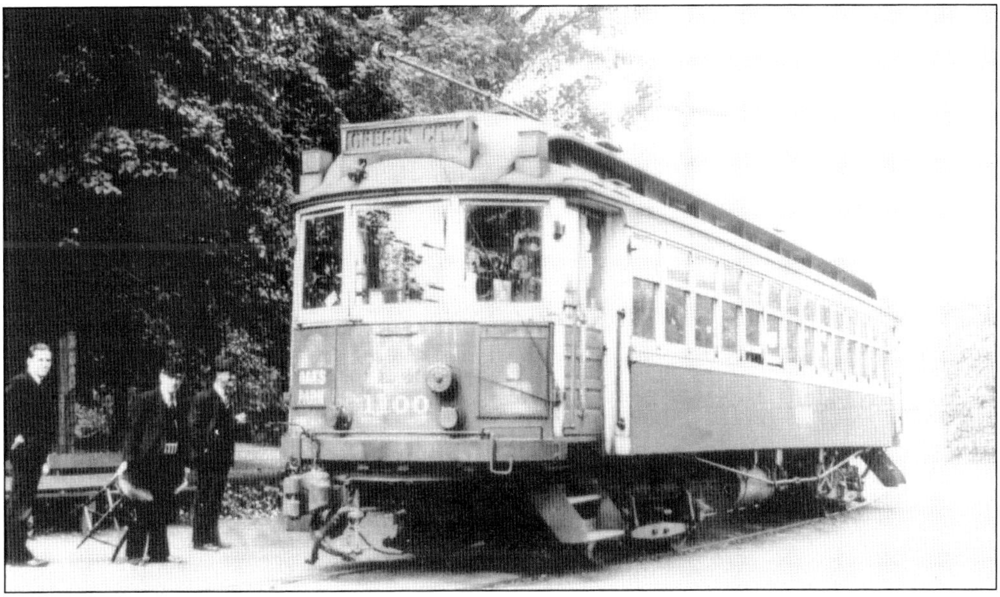

This bench at the start of the tracks to Oregon City at Golf Junction was a waiting place for car men about to make a crew change. The motorman (or operator, as they were called after streetcars were converted to one-man operation in the 1930s) about to climb aboard the No. 1100 is following the long-held practice of bringing a stool so that he would not have to stand while operating. (Photograph Alfred L. Haij.)

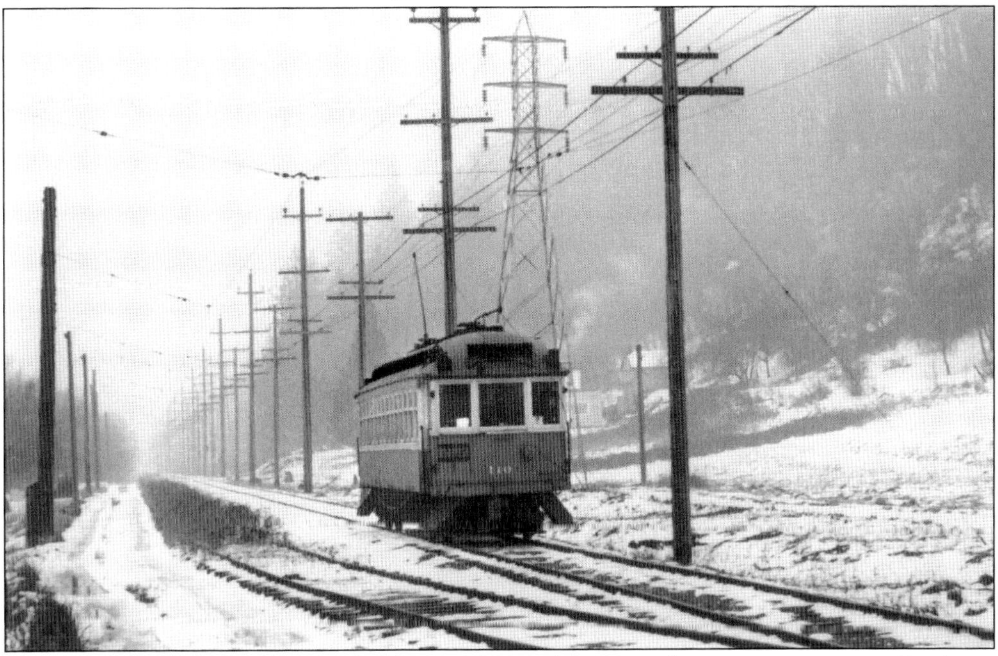

Motorman Delos H. Pond piloted old No. 1101 on the next-to-last passenger trip to Gresham, on January 31, 1949. This photograph shows the car inbound at Jenne Station, east of Bellrose. Railfans aboard for the snowy ride included George Chope and James West. There were three daily trains to Gresham at this time, but PTC claimed that only about 20 passengers rode all the way there each month.

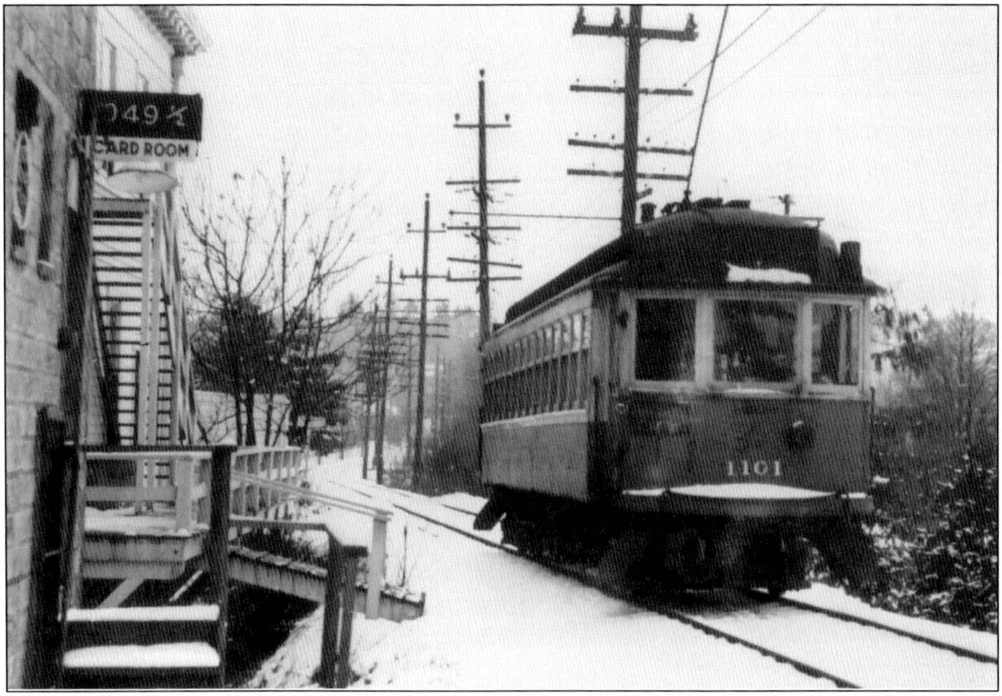

No. 1101 leaves Milwaukie Station on a frosty January 16, 1950. The interurban tracks seen here had long since been relocated from Milwaukie's Main Street to "back door" right-of-way behind the shops on McLoughlin Boulevard. The next stop would be Island Station, where the author saw his first streetcar.

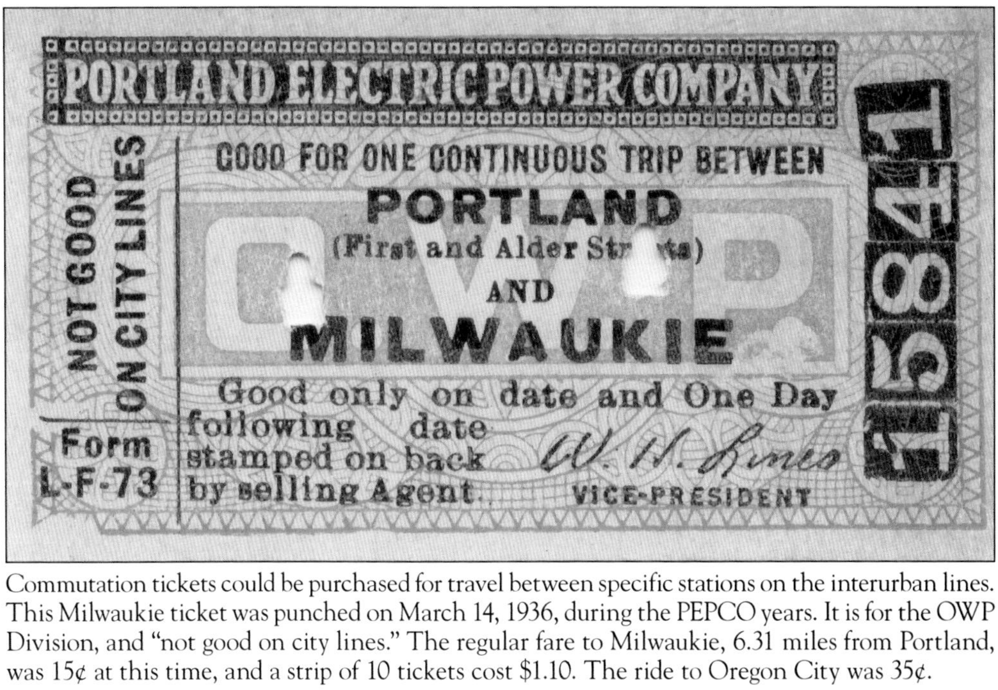

Commutation tickets could be purchased for travel between specific stations on the interurban lines. This Milwaukie ticket was punched on March 14, 1936, during the PEPCO years. It is for the OWP Division, and "not good on city lines." The regular fare to Milwaukie, 6.31 miles from Portland, was 15¢ at this time, and a strip of 10 tickets cost $1.10. The ride to Oregon City was 35¢.

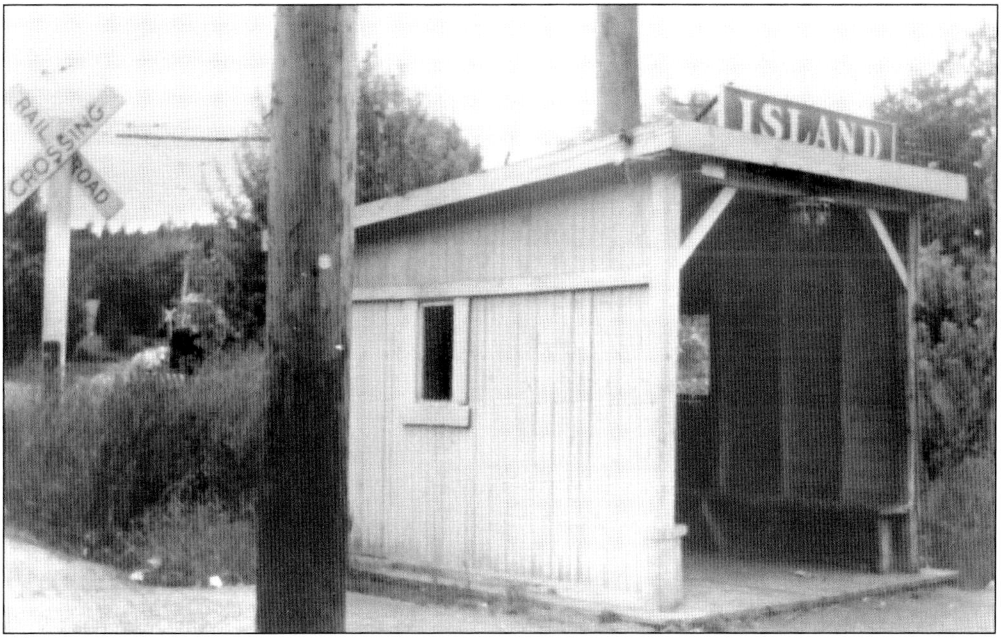

The author's lifelong passion for trolleys got its start here at Island Station as he waited "to catch a car" on the Oregon City Line with his grandmother. The station was typical of those on Portland's interurban lines and was painted battleship gray during the Portland Traction days. It was located one stop south of Milwaukie, where River Road joined McLoughlin Boulevard.

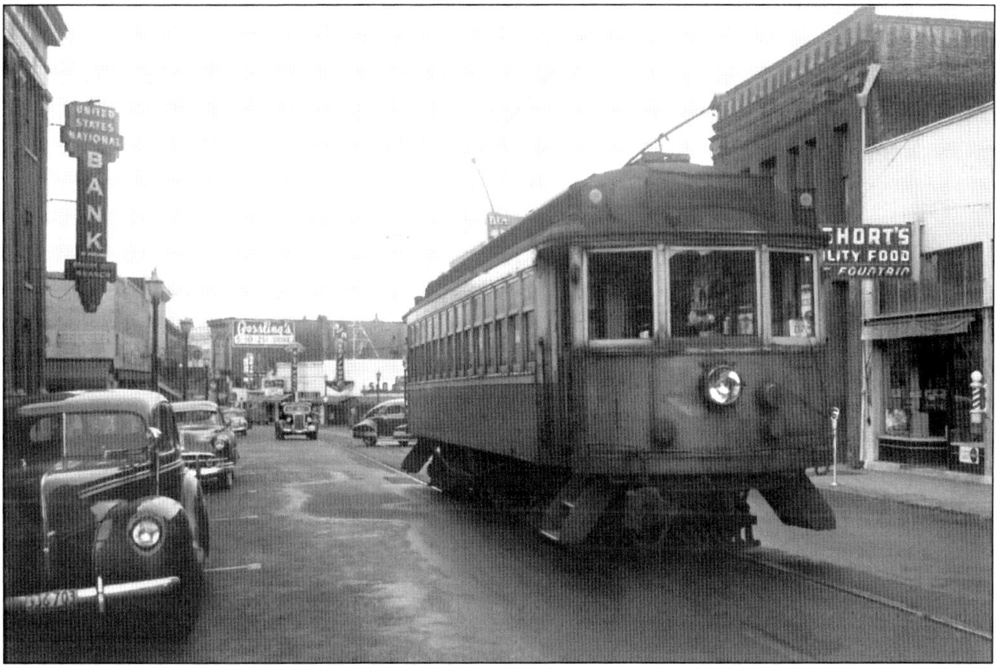

The operator clutches a pad of transfers as he brings PTC car No. 1101 to a halt in front of the US National Bank on Main Street in Oregon City. This was the stop where the author usually got off. Other businesses visible in this 1952 scene include Gossling's Dime Store, Oregon City Auto Parts, S&N Men's Shop, Mr. Pix Cameras, and Short's Fountain.

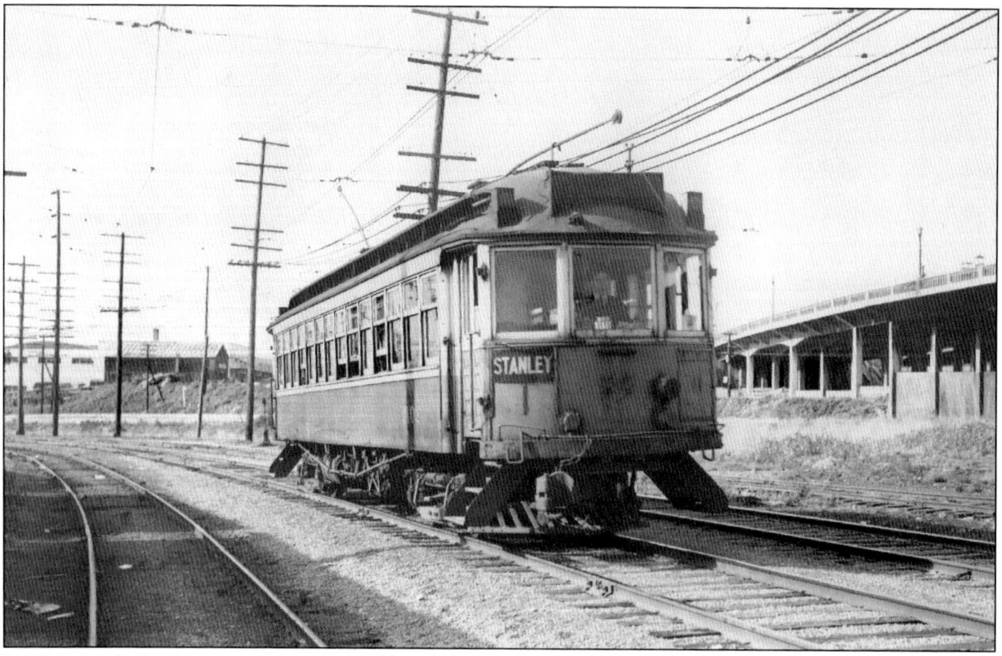

In this c. 1951 photograph, outward bound car No. 1102 is performing once-a-day duty as the local train to Stanley Station on the Bellrose Line. The orange-and-cream interurban would have departed Southwest First and Washington Streets at 5:20 p.m., traveling over to the East Side, where it is seen rolling southward past the Grand Avenue viaduct. No. 1102 was the last car in her series, emerging from the PRL&P shops in 1912.

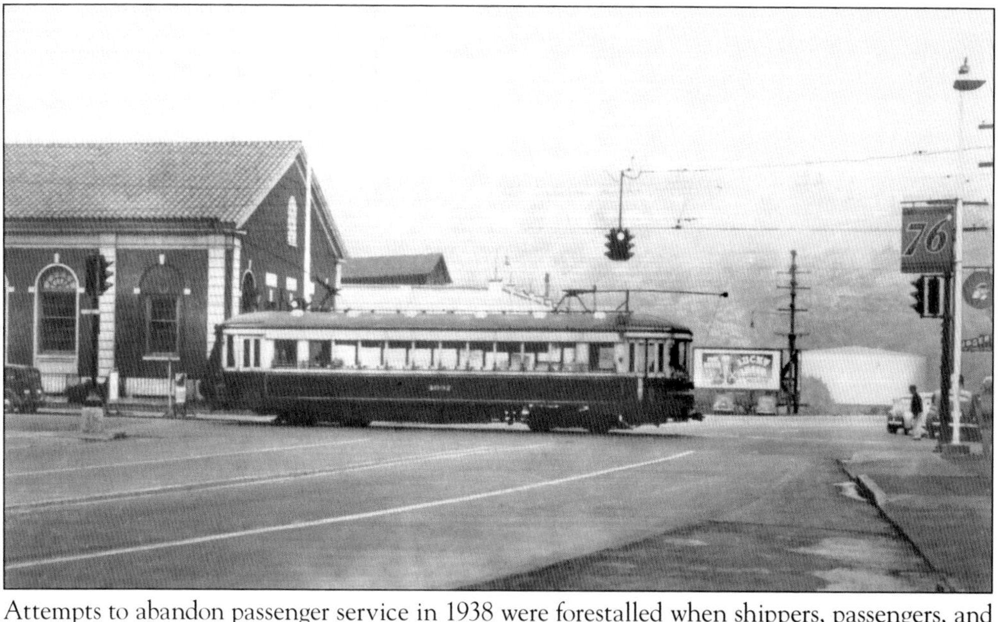

Attempts to abandon passenger service in 1938 were forestalled when shippers, passengers, and employees agreed to adjusted fares, schedules, and reimbursement. A nationwide search for "new" cars began the next year. No. 4002, seen crossing Pacific Highway in Oregon City on a rainy day in 1942, was in the first group to arrive in 1940. The former Indiana Railroad car is painted navy and cream. (Photograph Alfred L. Haij.)

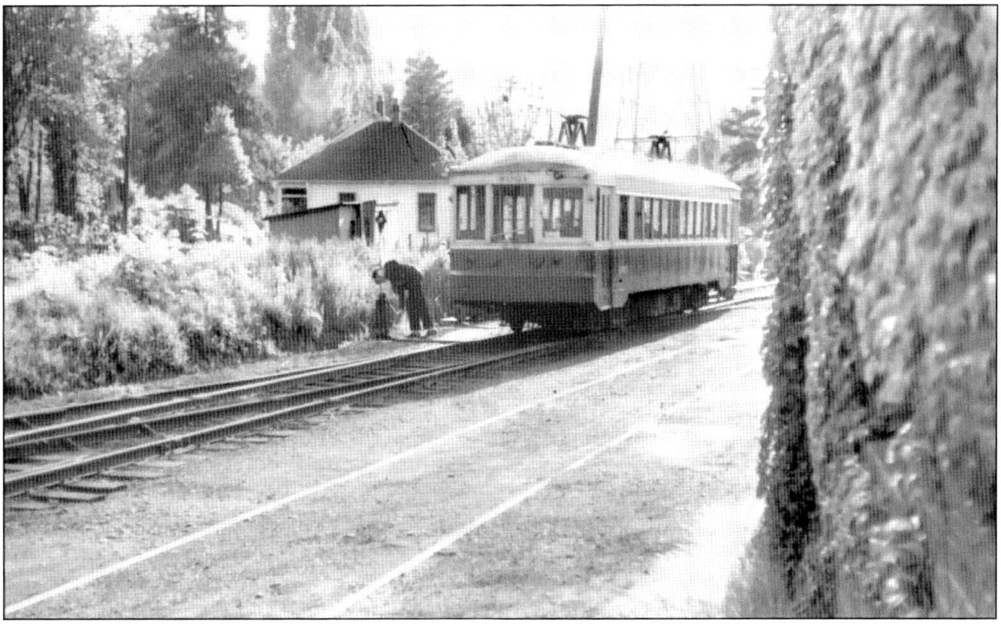

Portland's secondhand cars were nicknamed according to their place of origin, so the six streetcars bought from Indiana in 1940 were "Indianas." Operators, like the one seen here with Indiana No. 4001 at Golf Junction, were responsible for throwing switches and calling the dispatcher for clearance. (This streetcar is preserved at the Western Railway Museum in Suisun, California, where it has been restored in Indiana Railroad colors). (Photograph Roy Bonn.)

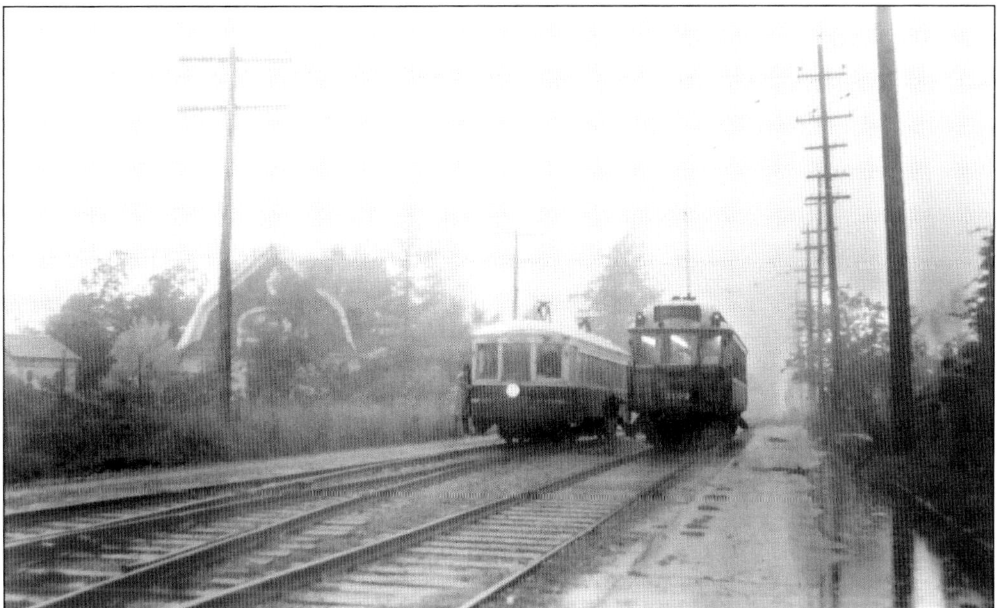

The lights inside old wooden interurban No. 1102 shimmer through a rainy 1940s afternoon as the car meets one of the ex–Indiana Railroad cars at the unique double crossover track in Oak Grove. The Dutch gable hip-roofed house at left is still there today on Southeast Arista Drive along the North Clackamas Parks and Recreation District's six-mile-long Trolley Trail. (Photograph Alfred L. Haij.)

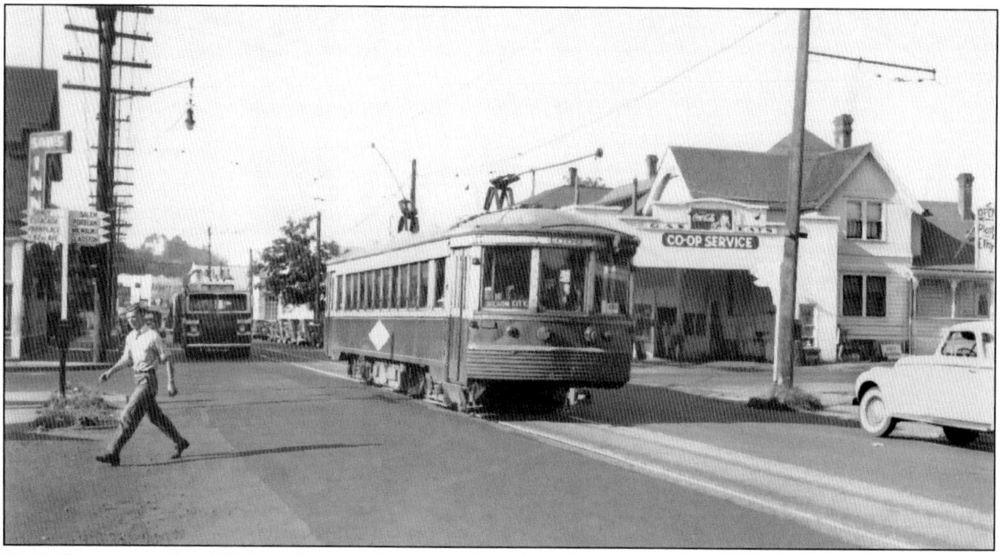

Ex-Indiana car No. 4000 is about to be overtaken by a bus as it hums northward on Main Street at Fourteenth Street in Oregon City. The historic building that housed Sam's Inn, at left, survives today. No. 4000, on the other hand, was not a survivor. The car was retired after a 1949 collision (see photograph below). The Indianas were an ill-fated group—cars No. 4002, No. 4004, and No. 4005 were also wrecked.

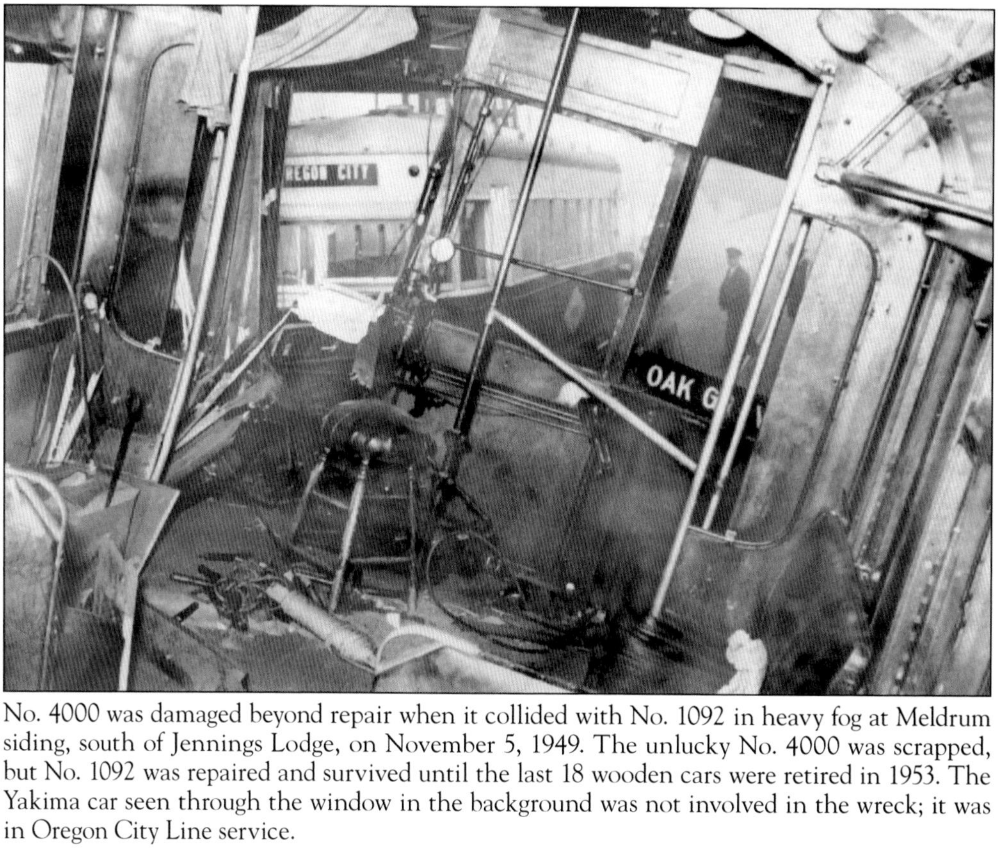

No. 4000 was damaged beyond repair when it collided with No. 1092 in heavy fog at Meldrum siding, south of Jennings Lodge, on November 5, 1949. The unlucky No. 4000 was scrapped, but No. 1092 was repaired and survived until the last 18 wooden cars were retired in 1953. The Yakima car seen through the window in the background was not involved in the wreck; it was in Oregon City Line service.

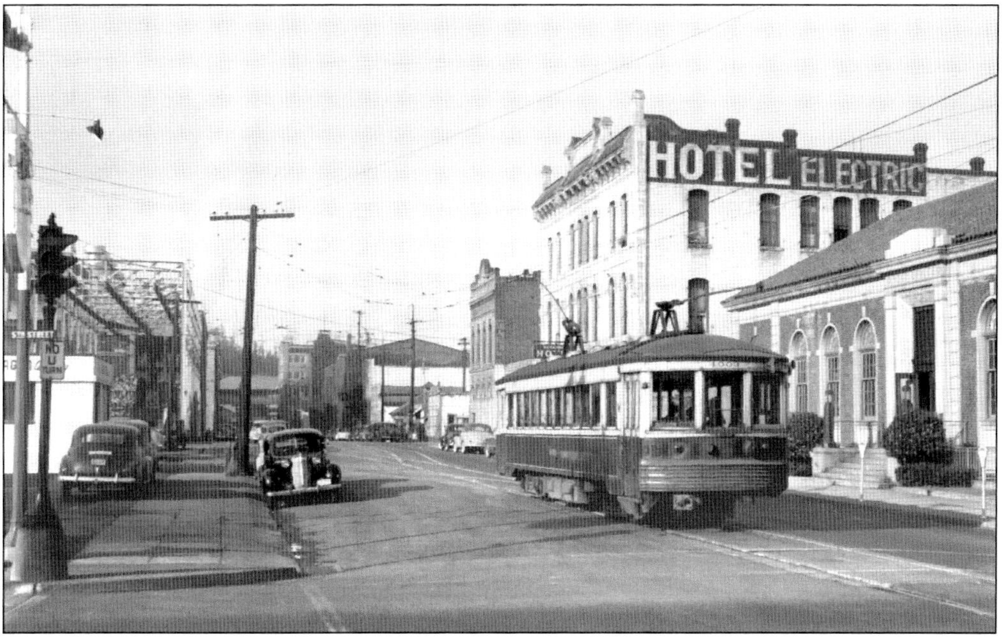

Car No. 4003 reflects the early morning sun at the Oregon City terminus on Main Street between Fourth and Fifth Streets. In 1952, superintendent Edward Vonderahe announced a plan to move the terminus six blocks farther north, to Eleventh Street, after 3 p.m. each day. Most of the buildings seen here are long gone, including (from background center, left to right) the Oregon Woolen Mill, Opera House, Hotel Electric, and the post office.

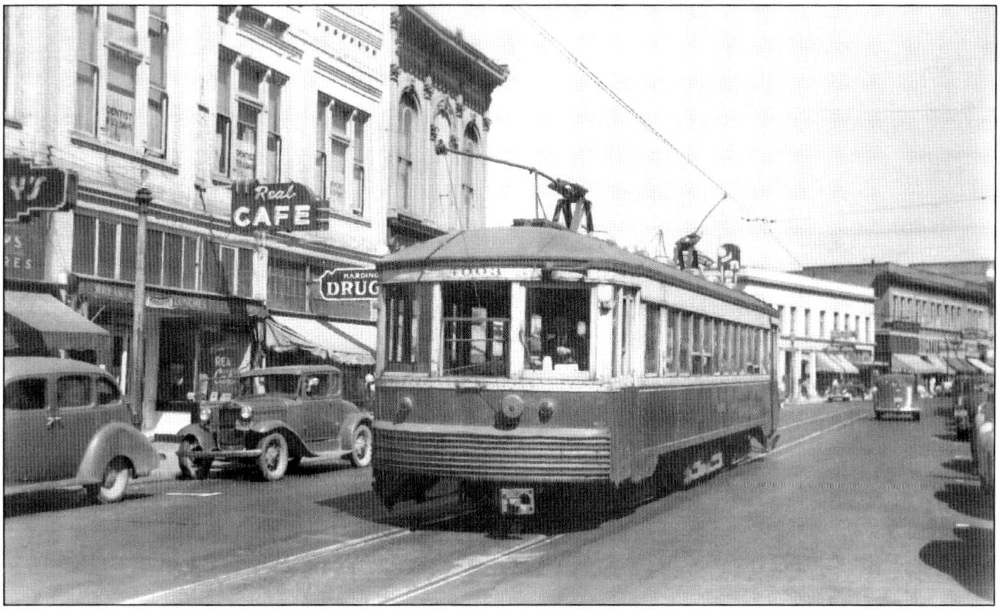

PTC No. 4003 hums down Main Street in Oregon City in 1949. The only real modifications to former Indiana Railroad car No. 205 were the removal of its permanent headlight and the addition of air horns. Following retirement in 1958, it went to Bob Hively's Puget Sound Electric Railway Association site in Snoqualmie, Washington. After Hively's death in 1993, the much-deteriorated car was rescued by the Illinois Railway Museum.

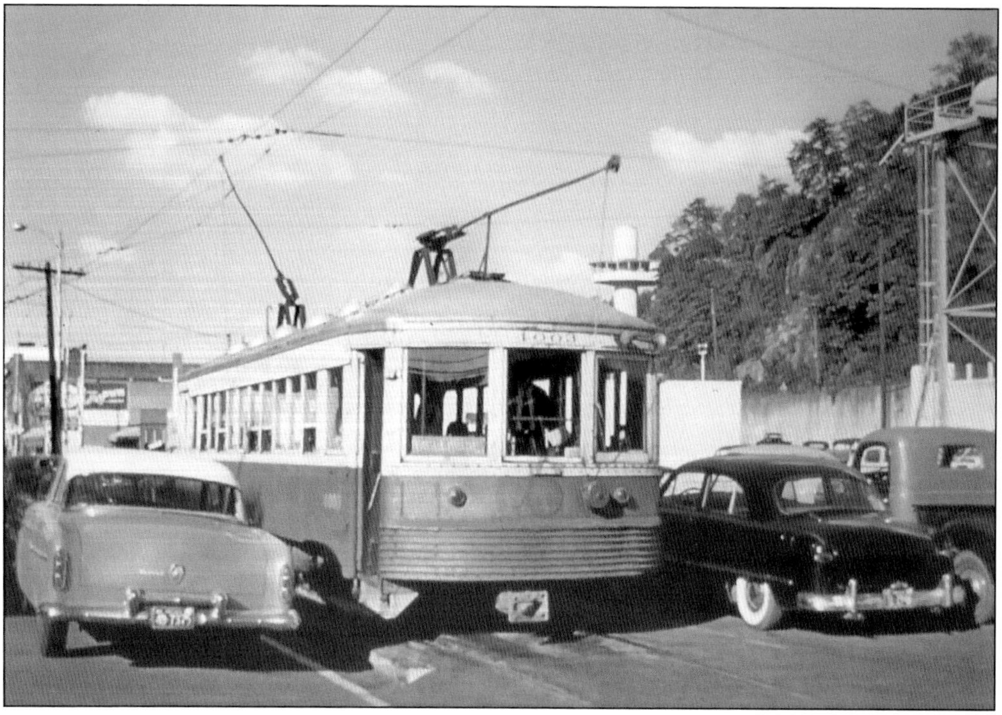

Indiana No. 4003 might be a special, since it is displaying an incorrect destination sign (for Bellrose) as it squeezes between the cars parked near Publisher's Paper Company at Fourth and Main Streets in Oregon City during the last years of service. The historic Oregon City elevator in the background had been rebuilt in 1955 and is now the only municipally operated elevator in the United States. (Photograph Kenn Lantz.)

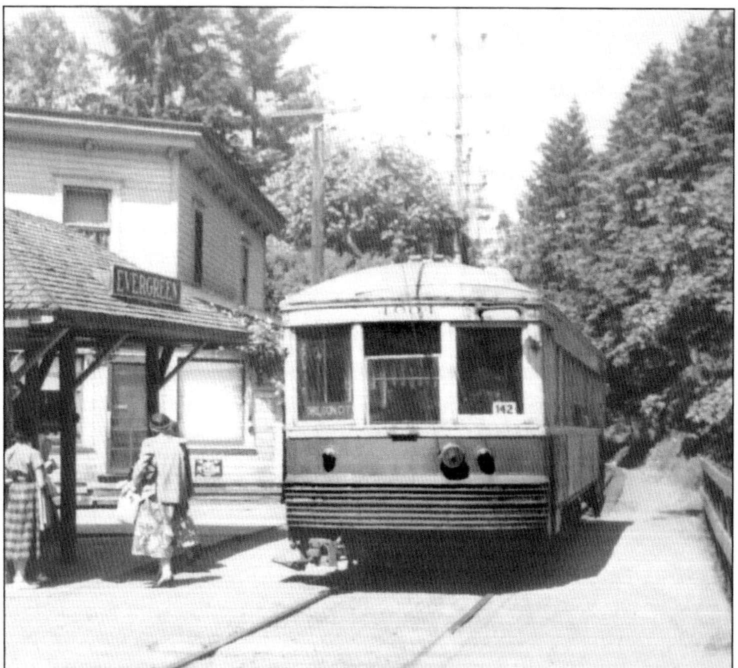

Passengers have just gotten off No. 4004, now painted red and cream, at Evergreen Station. Young riders looked forward to buying penny candy at the store next to the station. To the right, a wooden bridge crossed the gully next to McLoughlin Boulevard. These "high speed" cars were capable of traveling 50 miles per hour and performed all base service on the Oregon City Line for several years. (Photograph Charles E. Hayden.)

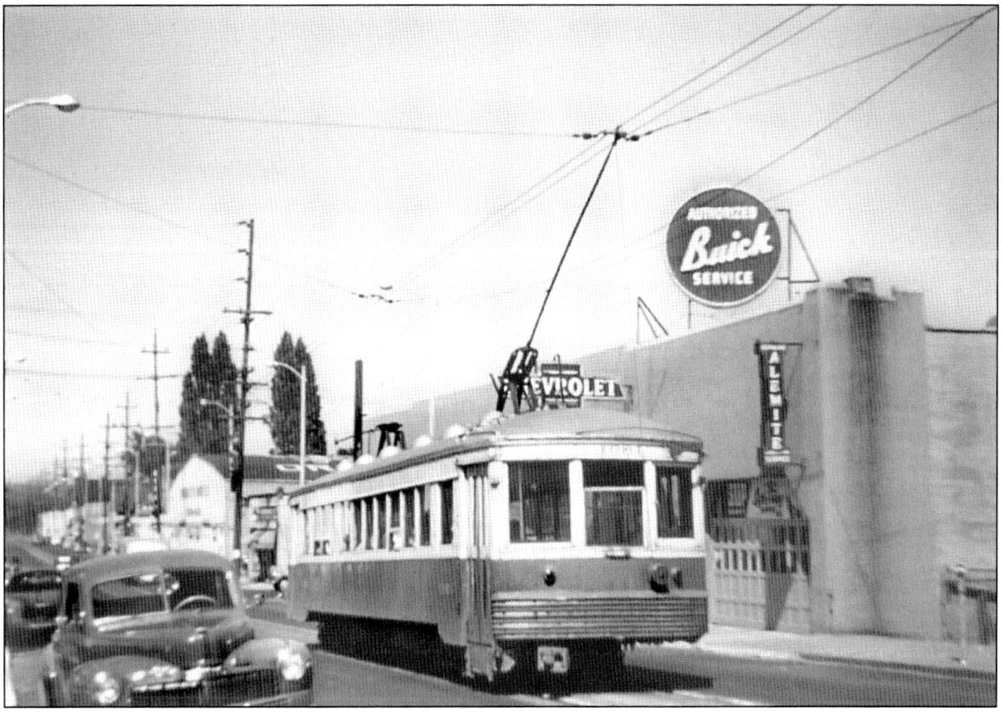

No. 4004 rumbles past the Chevrolet and Buick dealership as it heads for Fourteenth and Main Streets in Oregon City, a stop originally called Green Point. Built for the Illinois Public Service Company by the Kuhlman Car Company of Cleveland, Ohio, this 1927 vintage lightweight metal car spent most of its working life as Illinois Railroad No. 204. (Photograph Kenn Lantz.)

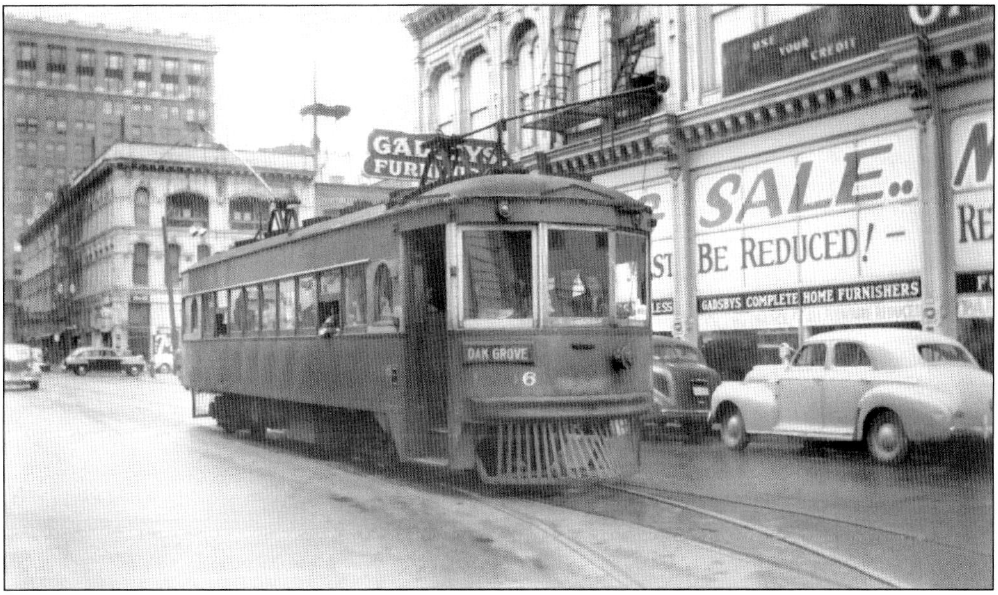

Oak Grove tripper No. 4006, seen here at the Southwest First Avenue and Washington Street terminal, was originally Albany Southern Railroad No. 60 in New York. It had become Fonda, Johnstown, and Gloversville No. 176 when it, and sister No. 177, were purchased by PTC in 1942. These cars were once equipped with third-rail shoes and pantographs, as well as trolley poles.

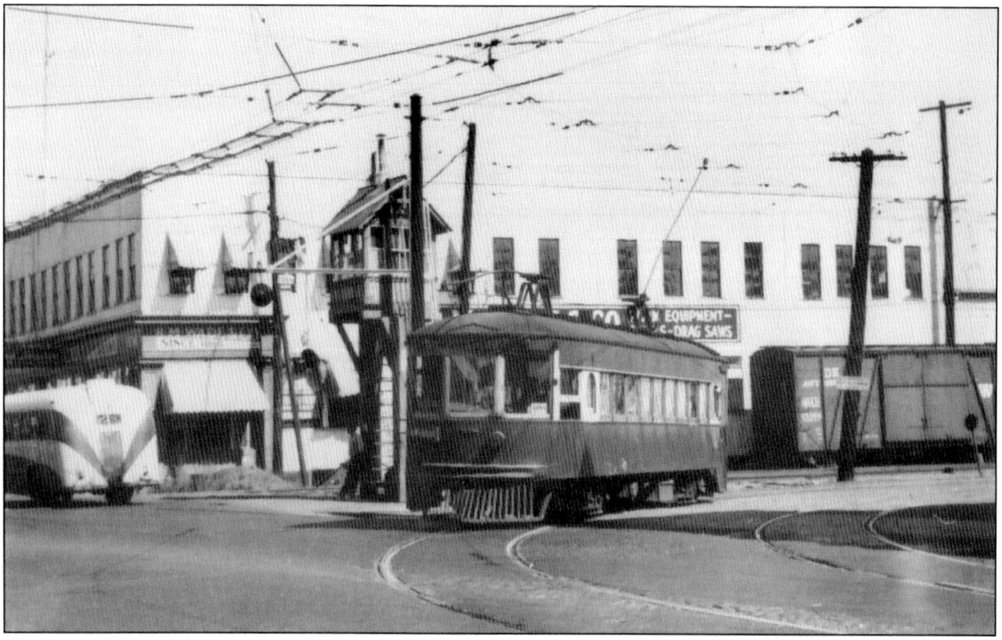

No. 4006 is rounding the corner of Southeast First Avenue and Hawthorne Boulevard in front of the R.M. Wade Company, with the old Southern Pacific Railroad crossing tower at the left. Before retirement as Illinois Railroad No. 176 in 1938, this lightweight suburban car made the last trip between Schenectady and Gloversville, New York. PTC painted these cars orange with cream trim and black highlights.

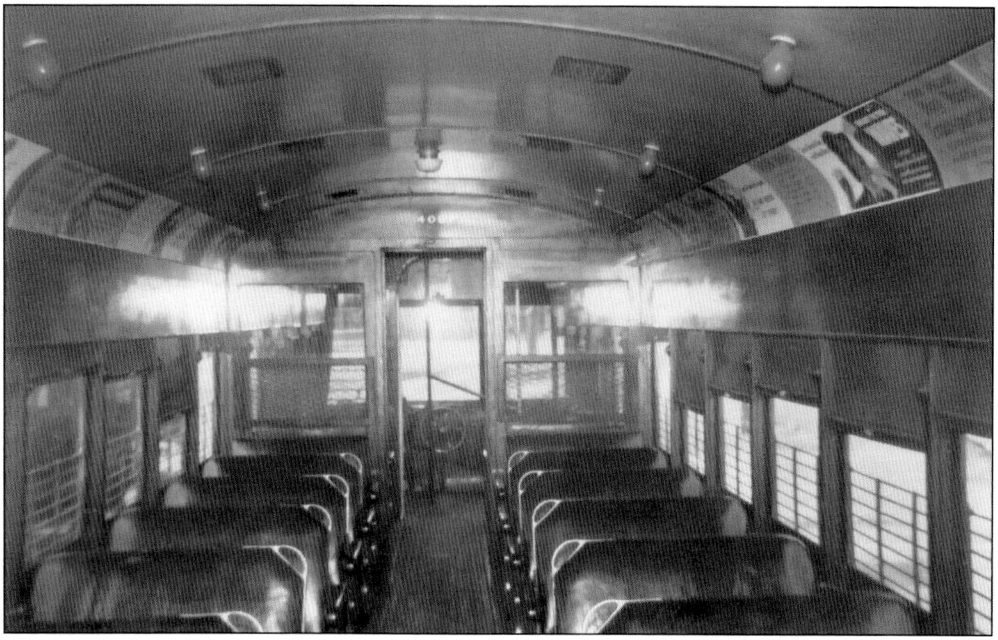

Although PTC found cars No. 4006 and No. 4007 to be fast and reliable, management considered their 44-passenger capacity small and typically assigned them to the lighter traveled Bellrose Line or to tripper duty. This interior view of No. 4007 shows comfortable leather seating. The Fonda, Johnstown, and Gloversville pair were built by the Cincinnati Car Company in 1925.

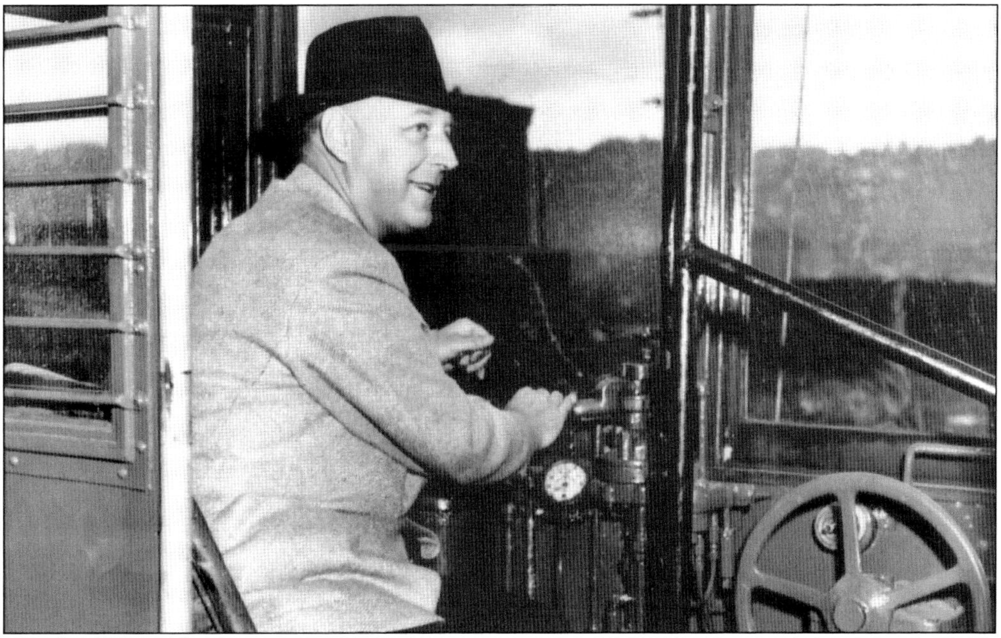

"The Boss," general superintendent Edward E. Vonderahe, poses at the controls of former Fonda, Johnstown, and Gloversville car No. 4007 as it is readied for a fan trip to Gresham on Labor Day 1951. Vonderahe traveled around the country in search of secondhand streetcars like this, for which he never paid more than scrap value. His wife, Xarissa, helped select the cars on these buying trips.

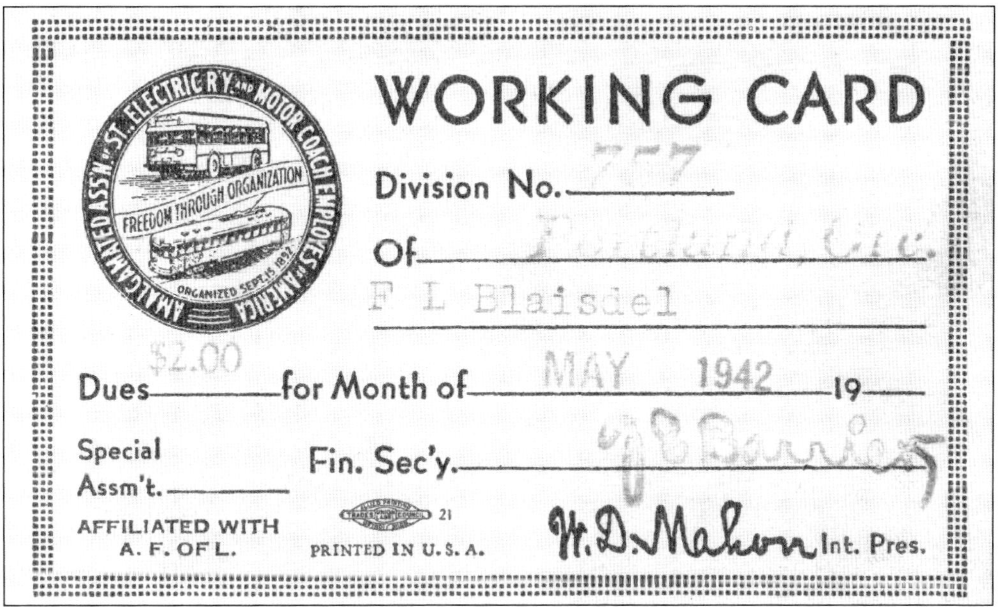

AMALGAMATED ASS'N OF ST. ELECTRIC RY. AND MOTOR COACH EMPLOYES OF AMERICA
FREEDOM THROUGH ORGANIZATION
ORGANIZED SEPT. 15, 1892

WORKING CARD

Division No. 757

Of Portland, Ore.

F L Blaisdel

Dues $2.00 for Month of MAY 1942 19

Special Assm't.

Fin. Sec'y.

AFFILIATED WITH A. F. OF L.

21

PRINTED IN U.S.A.

W. D. Mahon Int. Pres.

This is the May 1942 working card for operator Fred L. Blaisdell (his last name is misspelled on the card), whose photographs appear throughout this book. He was a member of Local 757 of the Amalgamated Association of Street, Electric Railway, and Motor Coach Employees of America. Local 757, now part of the Amalgamated Transit Union, still represents Portland's transit workers.

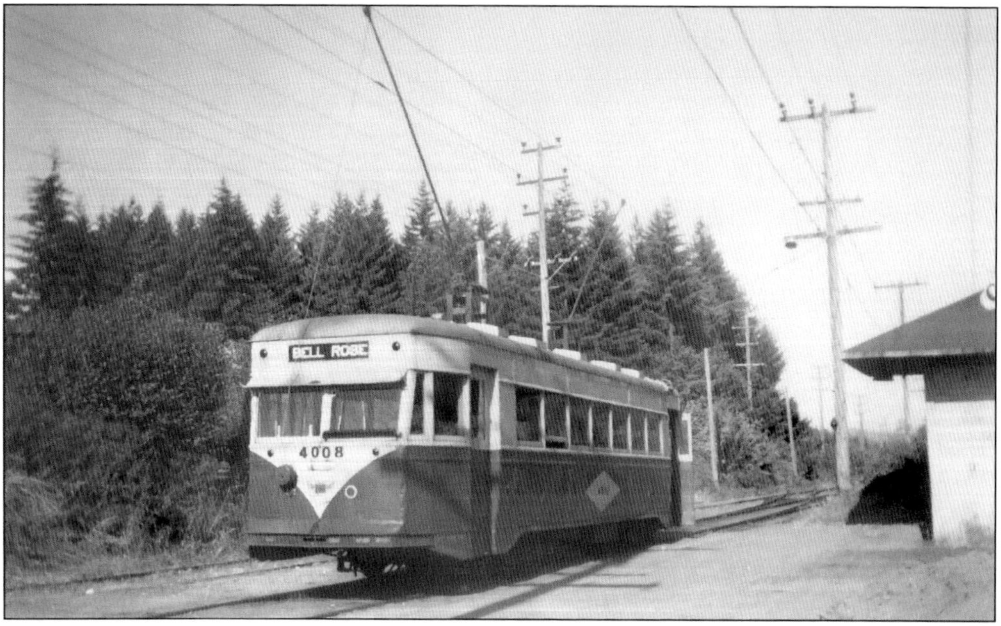

In September 1947, Portland Traction bought cars Nos. 20–22 from Washington's Yakima Valley Transportation Company (YVT). Renumbered 4008, 4009, and 4010, they were built by J.G. Brill subsidiary American Car Company for the YVT in 1930. Although styled somewhat differently, particularly on the ends, these three cars were very similar to Portland's own Brill Master Units. The No. 4008 is seen above at Bellrose Station. (Courtesy Jerry Risberg.)

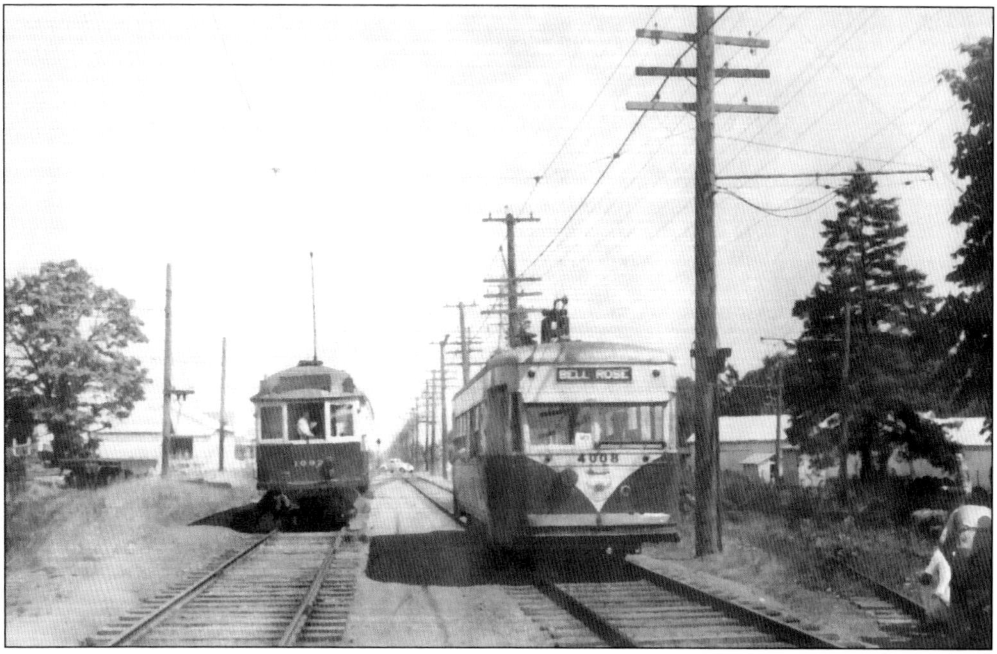

The year is 1949, and veteran wooden interurban No. 1092 has just rolled past No. 4008, one of the three cars nicknamed "Yaks." The presence of the group holding cameras on the siding at right means this Bellrose Line photograph was probably taken during a fan trip. The occasion may well have been the end of service to Gresham. (Courtesy Mark Moore.)

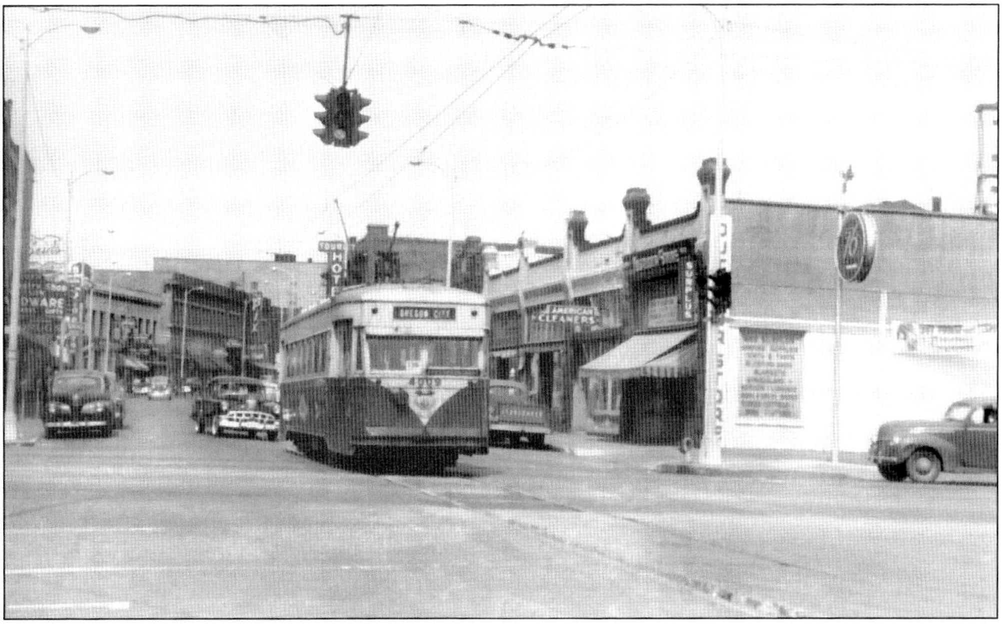

In this c. 1953 photograph, "Yak" No. 4009 is headed for the Oregon City terminus. Businesses in view along Main Street include (from left to right) Nelson Hardware, Harding Drugs, Seid's, Oregon City Auto Parts, Mode O'Day, Mr. Pix Cameras, the Tourist Hotel, American Cleaners, and the Outdoor Store. Compare with the picture looking in the opposite direction on page 101. (Photograph Roy Bonn.)

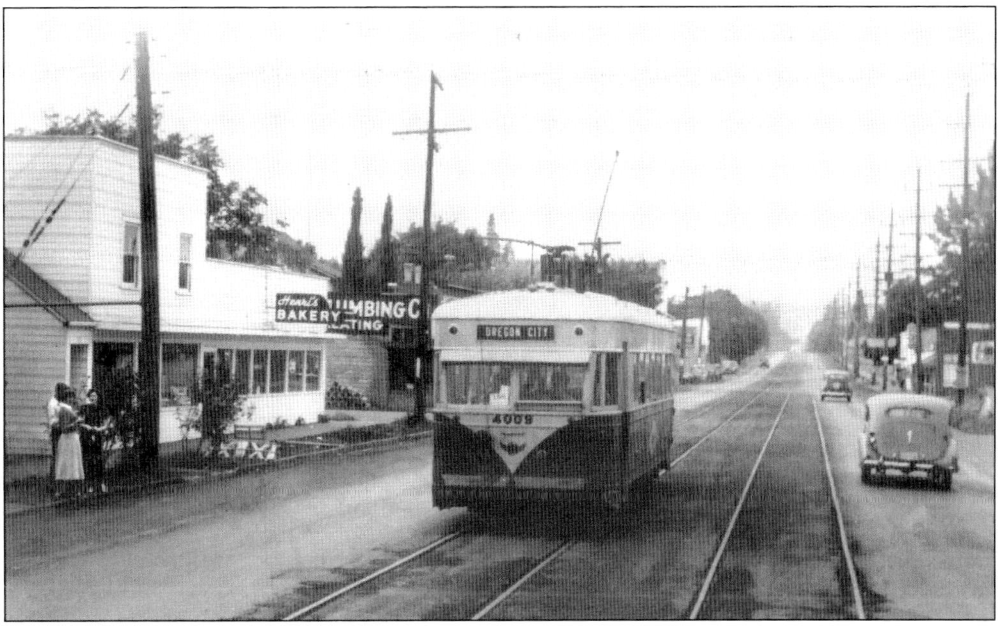

No. 4009 trundles southward past Henri's Bakery on Portland Avenue in Gladstone on August 15, 1948. This car was saved after operations ceased in 1958, going first to Bob Hively's Puget Sound Electric Railway Association in Snoqualmie, Washington. In the late 1980s, it and car No. 4010 were returned to Yakima. The Yakima Electric Railway Museum has restored No. 4009, once again numbered 21, to operating condition.

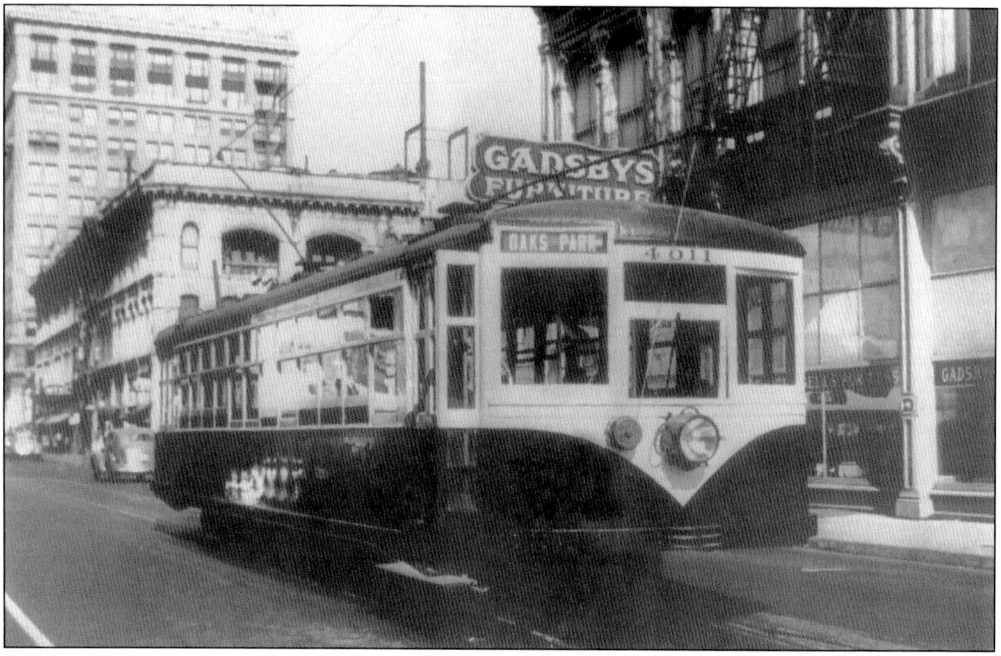

Ex–Key System streetcar No. 987 from Oakland, California, arrived in Portland in 1949. It is seen here at Southwest First Avenue and Washington Street, renumbered 4011 and painted in Portland Traction colors. Changes necessary for this streetcar to operate on the interurban division included adding larger wheels, marker lights, additional seats on each platform, Hunter roll signs, and the removal of built-in headlights.

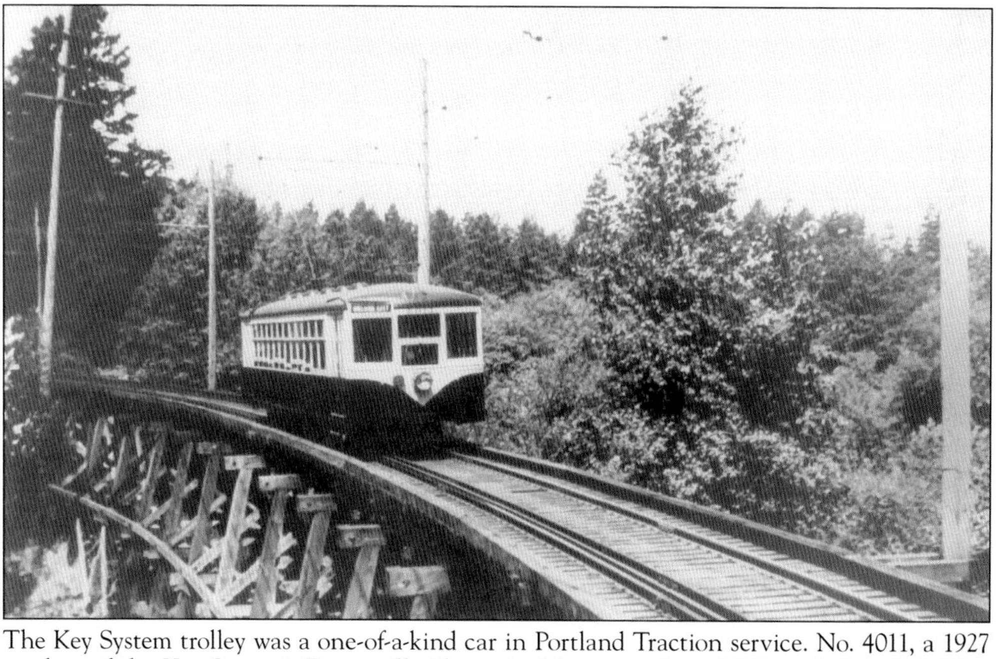

The Key System trolley was a one-of-a-kind car in Portland Traction service. No. 4011, a 1927 product of the Key System's Emeryville Shops, had been numbered 899, and then 987. This photograph on the Milwaukie trestle is thought to have been taken on July 11, 1953, during a Bay Area Electric Railway Association fan trip.

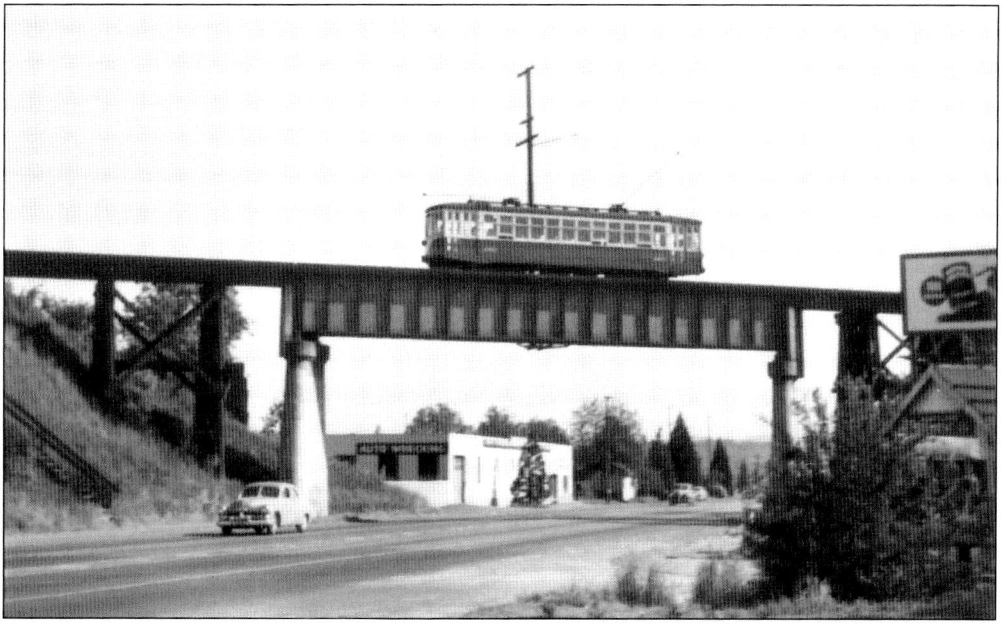

Key System No. 4011 is crossing the bridge over Southeast McLoughlin Boulevard on the Bellrose Line. The streetcar was on loan from the Western Railway Museum from 1949 to 1958. When service ended in Portland, it was returned to the museum, where it now regularly operates. The bridge, removed in 1991, has been replaced by a bike bridge for the Springwater Corridor Trail. (Photograph Charles E. Hayden.)

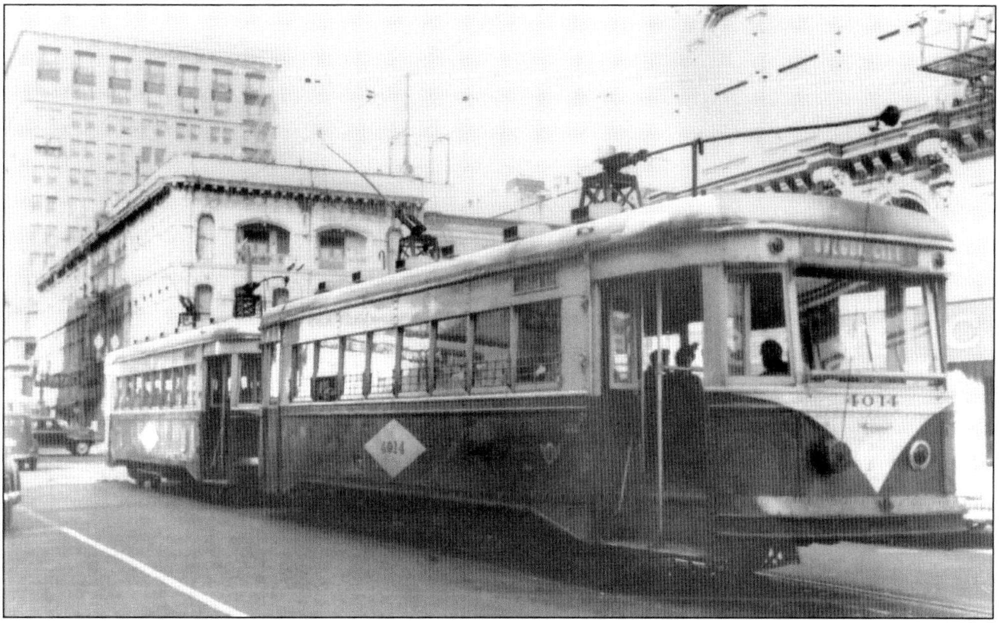

In 1950, two narrow-gauge Portland streetcars were modified for interurban use. Ironically, these 1932 Brill Master Units became the newest cars in the interurban division. Both are seen here in 1953 at Southwest First Avenue and Washington Street. While No. 4012 (ex-813) was successfully refitted with standard-gauge trucks, No. 4014 (ex-800) simply had its axles altered, creating a slow and rough-riding car that was retired by 1954.

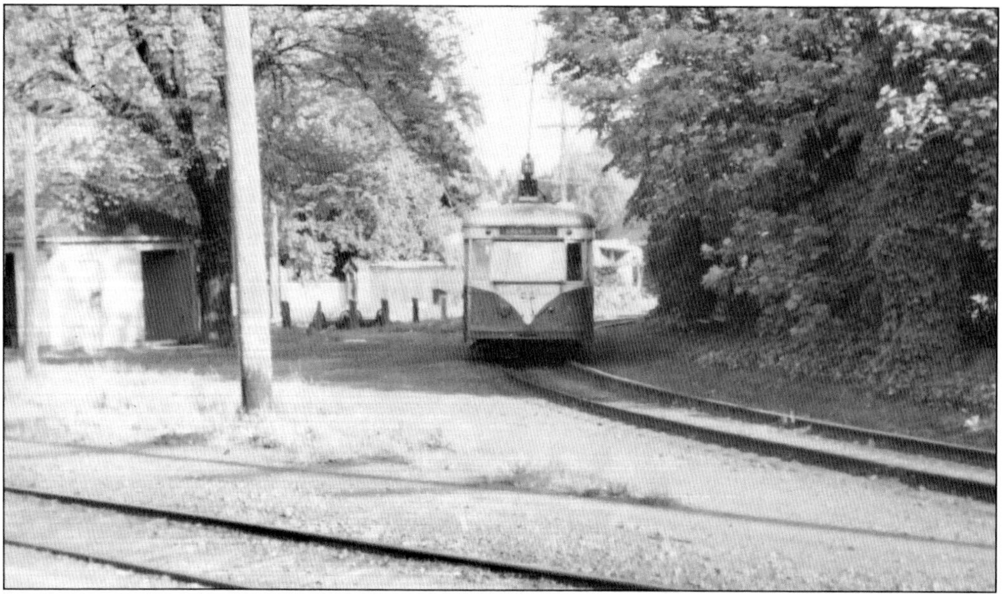

"Broadway" car No. 813, now No. 4012, is seen heading south at Golf Junction during the 1950s. When passenger service on the interurban division ceased in 1958, this car was saved, eventually becoming part of the Oregon Electric Railway Historical Society collection. The fully restored car has seen operation both at Antique Powerland in Brooks, Oregon, and the Willamette Shore Trolley between Portland and Lake Oswego. (Photograph Roy Bonn.)

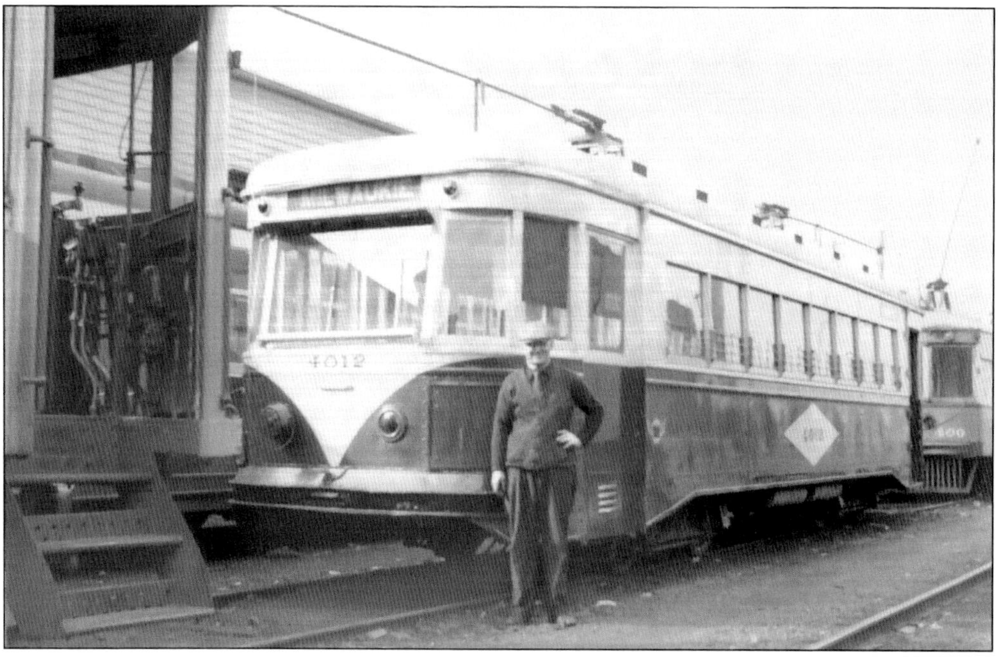

PTC superintendent of equipment Roy E. Reinke was the master mechanic who kept the fleet running even after the rails were cut to the Center Street Shops. He is seen here in the East Portland Yards with "Broadway" No. 4012, which is sandwiched between a 1090 and No. 4007. The No. 4012 was spared the scrapper's torch and has been restored by the Oregon Electric Railway Historical Society in Brooks, Oregon.

PTC INTERURBAN

MODERNIZED EQUIPMENT

Revised Rates

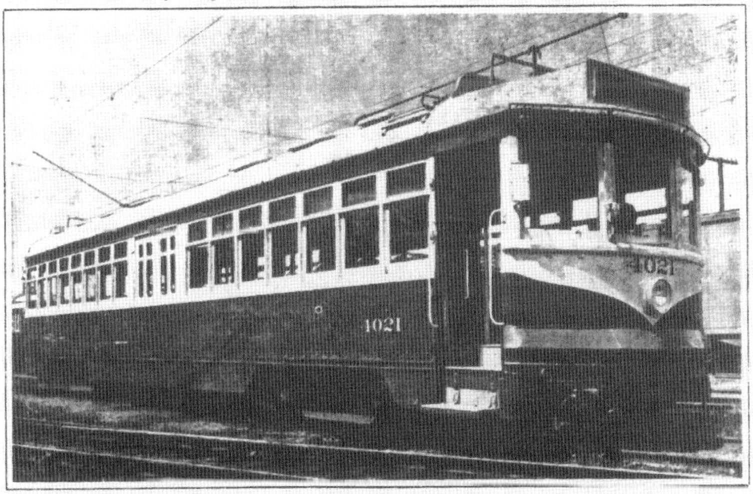

Revised Rates

10 RIDE COMMUTATION

	RATES Cents per coupon	Per Book
Between - Portland and Ardgour to Concord, inc	16	$1.60
Vineyard to Jennings Lodge, inc.	18½	$1.85
Hull Ave. to Gladstone	22	[illegible]
Park Place to Oregon City, inc.	25	$2.50
Brookwild to Lents, inc.	16	$1.60
[illegible]	18½	$1.85
Between-Oregon City and Park Place to Vineyard, inc.	12½	$1.25
Concord to Evergreen, inc	17½	$1.75
Lakewood to Milwaukie, inc.	20	$2.00

FROM PORTLAND TO:	Fare	FROM OREGON CITY TO:	Fare
Golf Jct.	15c*	Park Place	15c
Ardgour	20c	Gladstone	15c
Overlinks	20c	Fern Ridge	15c
Reeves	20c	Glen Echo	15c
Lawrence	[illegible]	Meldrum	[illegible]
Milwaukie	20c	Hull Ave.	15c
Island	20c	Jennings Lodge	15c
Lakewood	20c	Ashdale	15c
Evergreen	20c	Rothe	15c
Silver Springs	20c	Naef	15c
Torbank	20c	Vineyard	15c
Courtney	20c	Concord	20c
St. Theresa	20c	Risley	20c
Oak Grove	20c	Rupert	20c
Rupert	20c	Oak Grove	20c
Risley	20c	St. Theresa	20c
Concord	20c	Courtney	20c
Vineyard	25c	Torbank	20c
Naef	25c	Silver Springs	20c
Rothe	25c	Evergreen	20c
Ashdale	25c	Lakewood	25c
Jennings Lodge	30c	Island	25c
Hull Ave.	30c	Milwaukie	25c
Meldrum	30c	Lawrence	25c
[illegible]	[illegible]	[illegible]	[illegible]
Fern Ridge	30c	Overlinks	25c
Gladstone	30c	Ardgour	25c
Park Place	35c	Golf Jcts.	30c
Oregon City	35c	East Portland	35c
		1st & Wash.	35c

* 15c cash fare or city line transfer.

Modernized equipment has been provided for patrons of the INTERURBAN DIVISION of the Portland Traction Company, as an indication of our good faith and our concern for the people who find this service necessary and convenient.

Because of the declining patronage and the increasing deficit in passenger operation on these lines, the PTC management some months ago requested abandonment of its interurban passenger service.

IN THE PROCESS OF THE HEARINGS BEFORE THE PUC COMMISIONERS, many citizens living and having businesses located along the lines of our operation, appeared and appealed for continuance of passenger service.

A VERY AGGRESSIVE CITIZENS COMMITTE DEVELOPED CONSIDERABLE support for a program that promised a greater use of service and a willingness to accept a substantial fare increase, if the company would improve the equipment and continue service.

WITH THIS ASSURANCE, THE PTC MANAGEMENT PURCHASED eight used 65-passenger interurban cars to replace some of the company's oldest cars. These newly purchased cars are all steel, have comfortable foam rubber seats with mohair upholstry, comfortable and easy riding. These cars have been completely refinished inside and out, and will provide good service for a great many years.

A REVIEW IS MADE OF THESE CIRCUMSTANCES NOW, in the hope that our good friends and patrons may organize themselves as effectively to help us increase the riding, as they have been in support of maintenance of the service at a comparatively very low fare. We have already demonstratd our interest and our good faith and we assure you we shall always be available to discuss plans and programs for service changes and improvements. Now we anxiously and hopefully look forward to a reciprocal cooperation and a sufficient increase in riders to justify the increased investment in the interurban division.

President.

PORTLAND TRACTION COMPANY

In 1953, with the debut of eight refurbished Los Angeles streetcars, Portland Traction Company announced modernized equipment and service on its last two interurban lines. The ex–Pacific Electric cars were final acquisitions made by superintendent Vonderahe, who had begun augmenting the aging Portland fleet with secondhand equipment prior to World War II. When this public relations campaign did not result in increased patronage, PTC resumed efforts to discontinue passenger service.

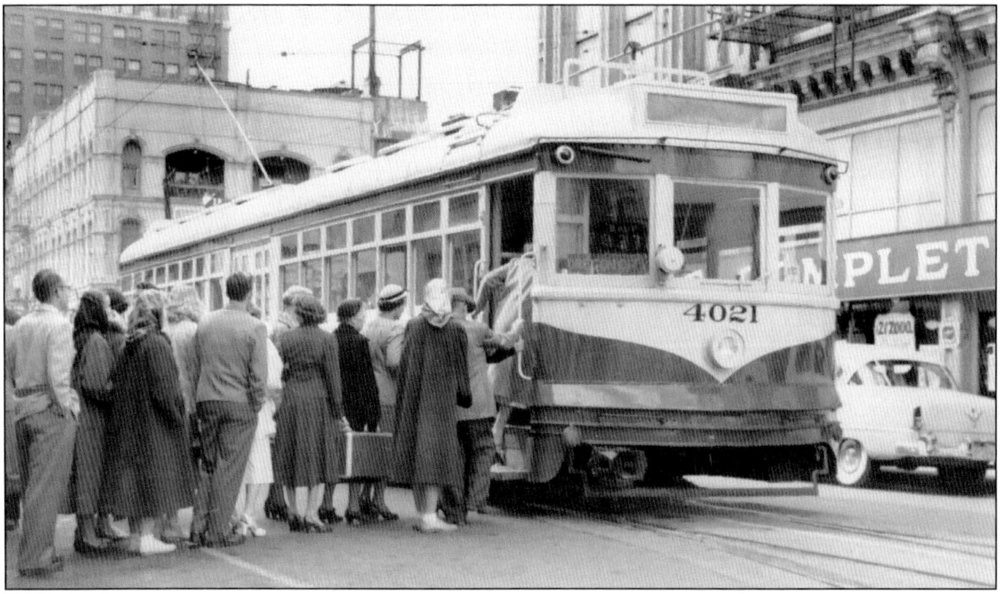

Car 4021 is loading passengers on Southwest First Avenue and Washington Street on June 6, 1953, the first day of operation for the newly acquired Pacific Electric "Hollywood" cars. Although roll signs had not yet been installed, we know that the "Hollywoods" were working the Oregon City run, while the Indianas covered Bellrose service. If only ridership had remained at this level. (Photograph Roy Bonn.)

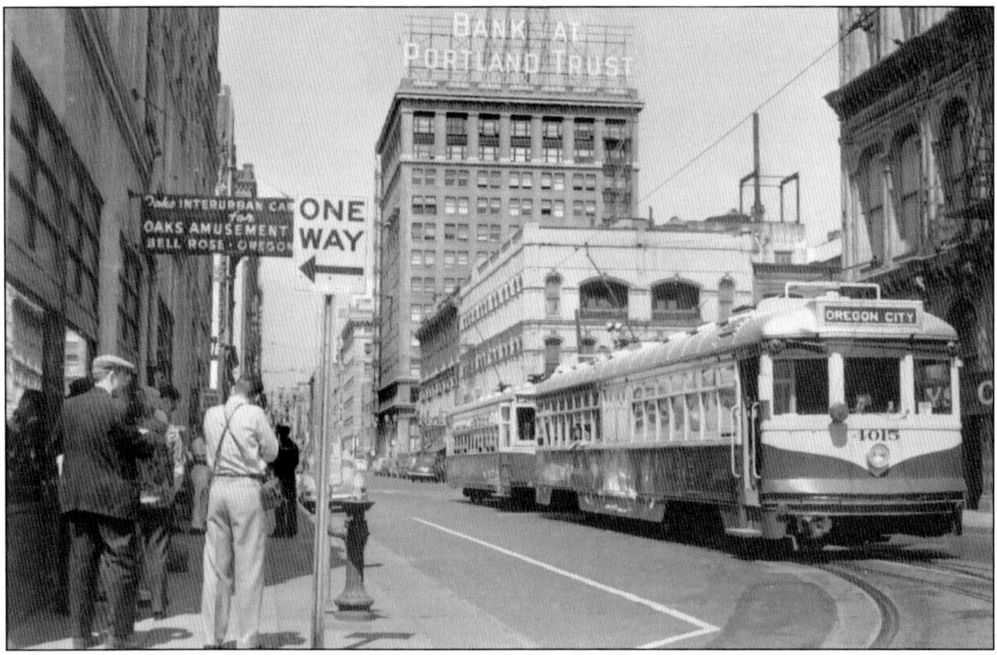

"Hollywood" No. 4015 and Key System No. 4011 wait at the interurban station on the corner of Southwest First Avenue and Washington Street in 1954. Washington Street was one-way westbound, so the interurbans operated against traffic between First and Second Avenues. The neon sign above the station reads, "Take INTERURBAN CARS here for OAKS AMUSEMENT PARK, BELL ROSE, OREGON CITY."

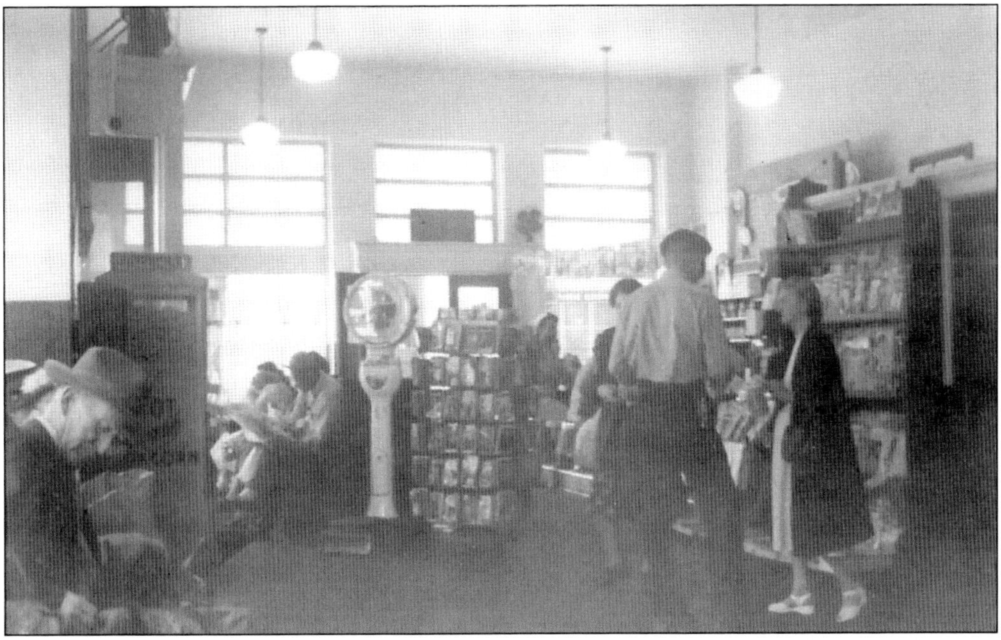

This early 1950s photograph of the interurban depot waiting room at 118 Southwest Washington Street was taken during its final years. The building was demolished in September 1956 to make way for new Morrison Bridge ramps. The station may not have been fancy, but passengers appreciated a chance to buy a magazine, enjoy popcorn, or even get weighed while they waited for the arrival of their streetcar.

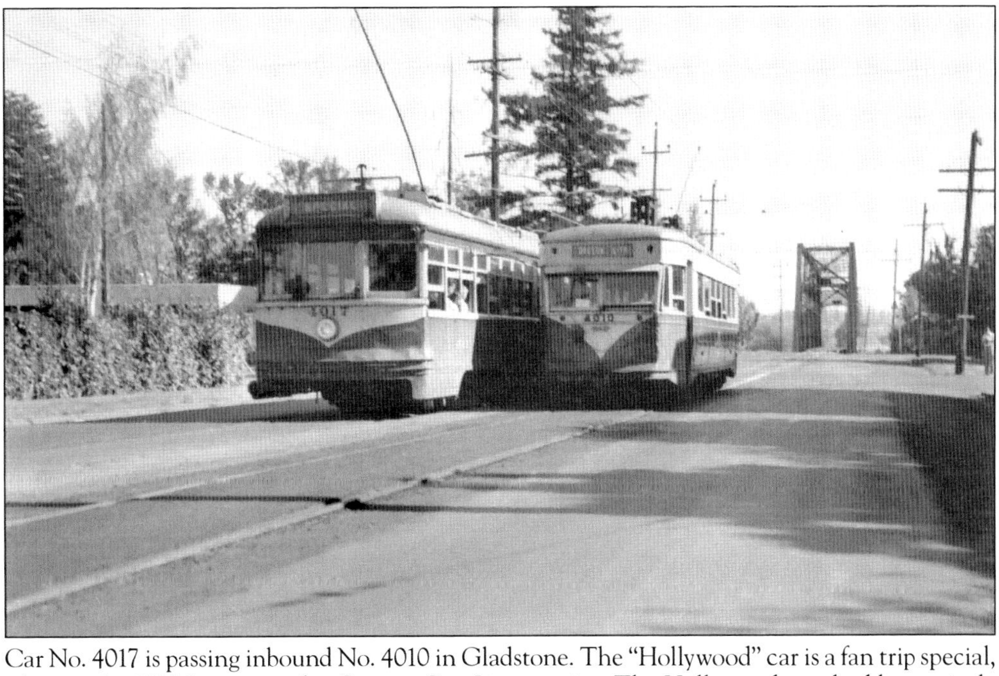

Car No. 4017 is passing inbound No. 4010 in Gladstone. The "Hollywood" car is a fan trip special, whereas the "Yak" is on regular Oregon City Line service. The Hollywood cars had been nicely repainted in PTC livery by Pacific Electric but were not in good mechanical condition and experienced frequent breakdowns. The Clackamas River Bridge is in the background.

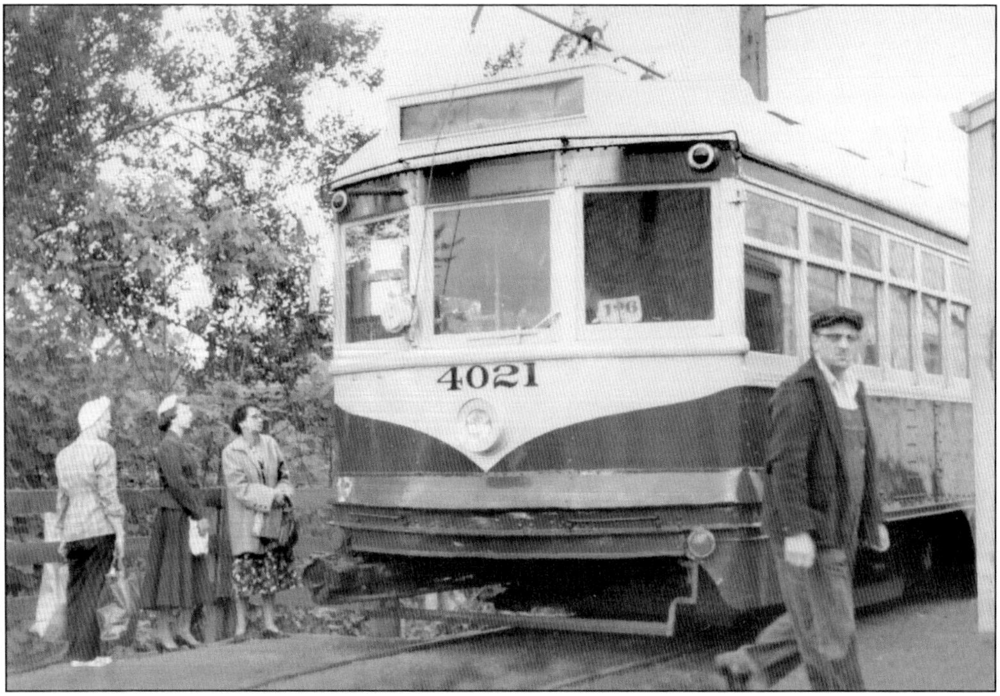

The man at right may be helping with a mechanical problem, or perhaps he was loading something aboard No. 4021, seen here at Milwaukie Station in 1953. In addition to passengers, interurban streetcars had always carried packages, bundles, mail sacks, and boxes. Train No. 126 was an Oregon City local that arrived in Milwaukie at 10:49 a.m. each morning. (Photograph Roy Bonn.)

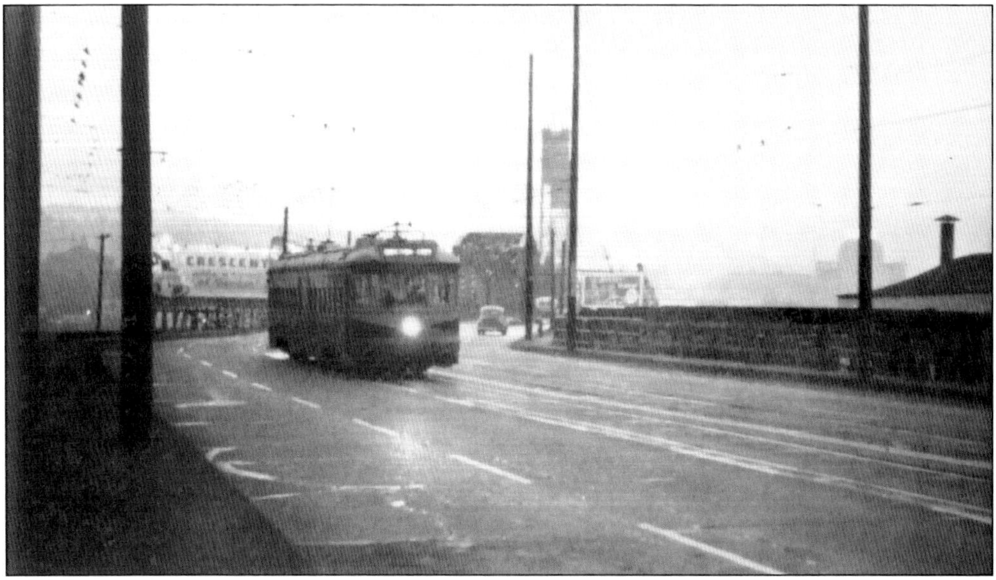

Oregon City Line car No. 4021 is heading into the twilight in more ways than one. It is on the east approach to the Hawthorne Bridge, which would be remodeled without tracks in 1956. When the Portland Traction Company declined to exercise its right to have the new bridge ramps include railroad tracks, it sounded a death knell for Portland's last streetcars. (Photograph Alfred L. Haij.)

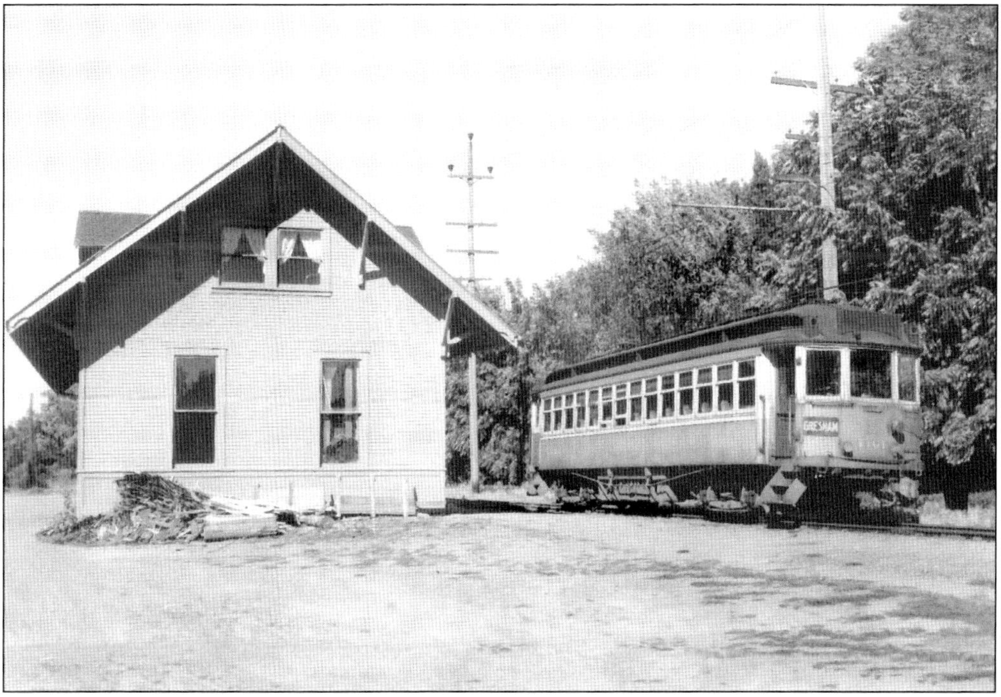

Car No. 1101 rests at Gresham's Mount Hood Station sometime after the 1944 rerouting of service from the Springwater Division Gresham Station. The station was on the south side of the tracks, between Northeast Roberts and Hood Avenues. This view is looking toward the waiting room. Offices were in the middle of the building, a freight house at the other end, and living quarters for the station agent on the second floor.

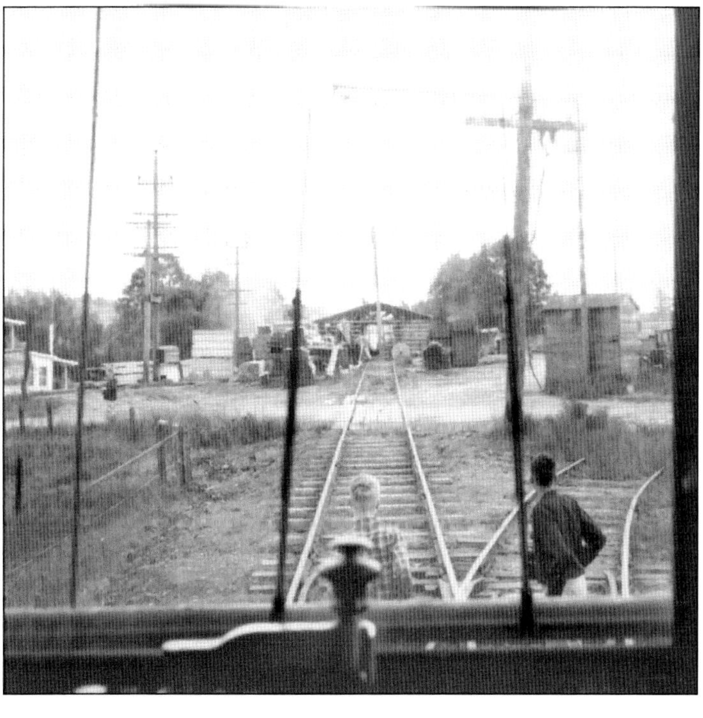

On May 10, 1950, choirboys from St. Peter's Church rode to a place streetcars hadn't visited in 20 years. Their trip was supposed to terminate at the Mount Hood Gresham depot, but when the railfans begged to go farther, No. 1097 proceeded cautiously until the rails ended in the middle of a small sawmill at East Gresham. A GE K-6 controller handle can be seen in the lower center of the photograph.

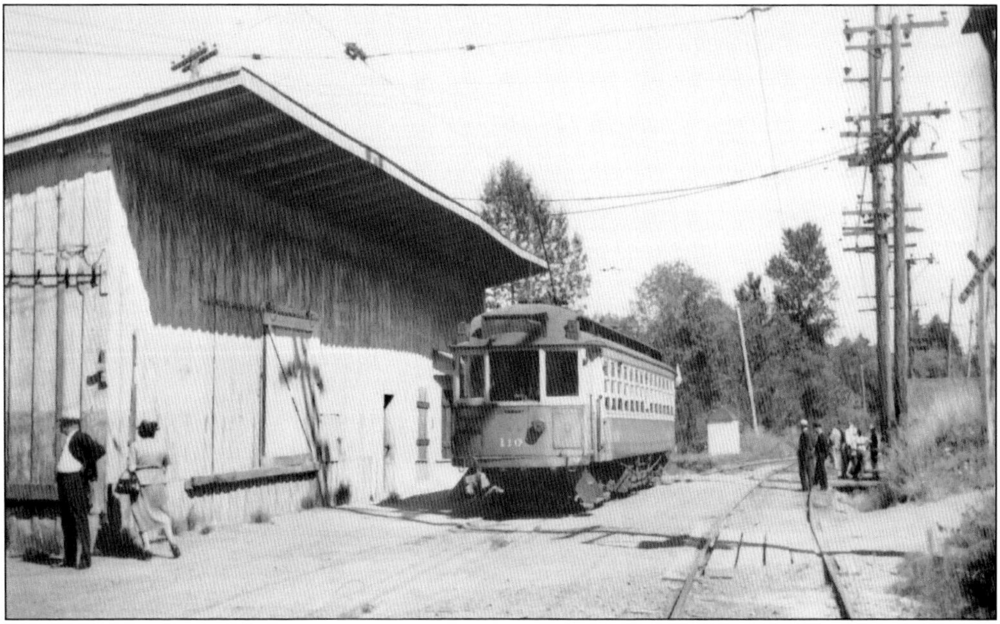

Extra No. 1101 is making a picture stop at the abandoned Springwater Division Gresham Station en route to Boring during an early 1950s fan trip. Known as the OWP depot, this building was divided into three sections: a freight house on the left, a passenger waiting room in the center, and offices on the right. It was located at the foot of South Main Avenue. (Photograph Charles E. Hayden.)

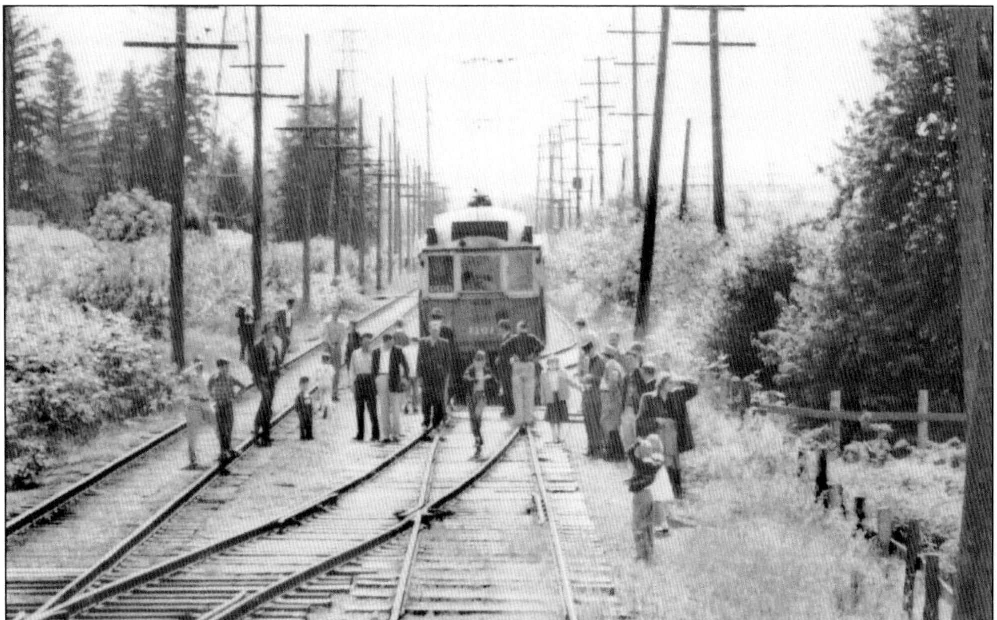

On June 21, 1953, No. 1101 carried members of the Pacific Northwest Electric Railway Association on an excursion to the end of rail in Boring. It was the last trip for a classic wooden interurban and the first time a passenger train had been seen beyond Gresham in many years. Noted railfans in this group include Paul Class, Al Haij, Kent Haley, Charles Hayden, and John Labbe.

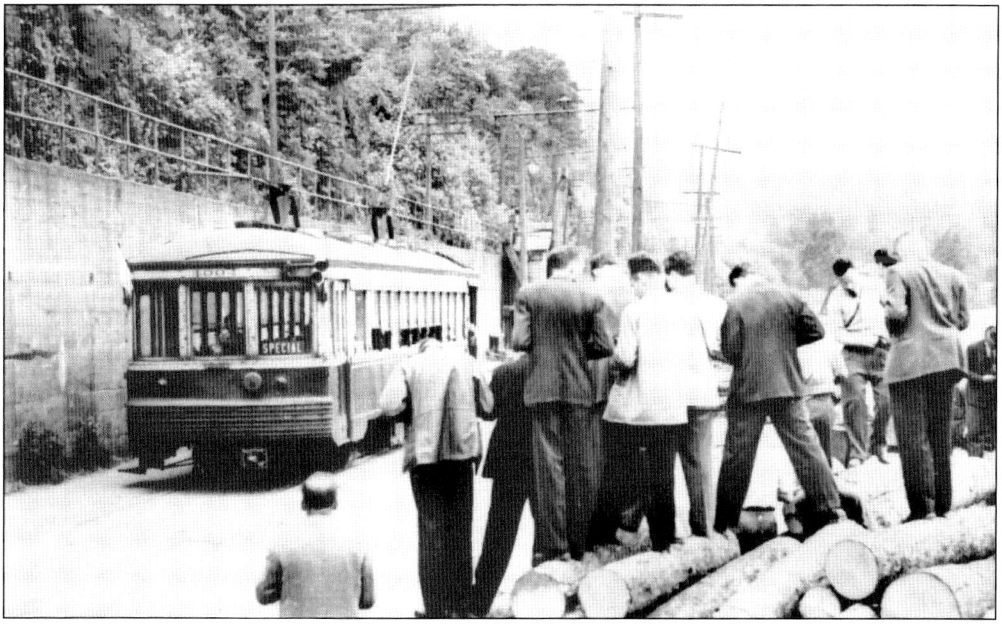

A record was set on May 30, 1947, when Indiana car No. 4004 hosted a Bay Area Electric Railway Association fan trip. It was the first use of the tracks south of Oregon City by a passenger streetcar in 15 years. The stop seen here, one-half mile from downtown Oregon City, served a paper mill. There are at least 11 photographers balancing on those logs.

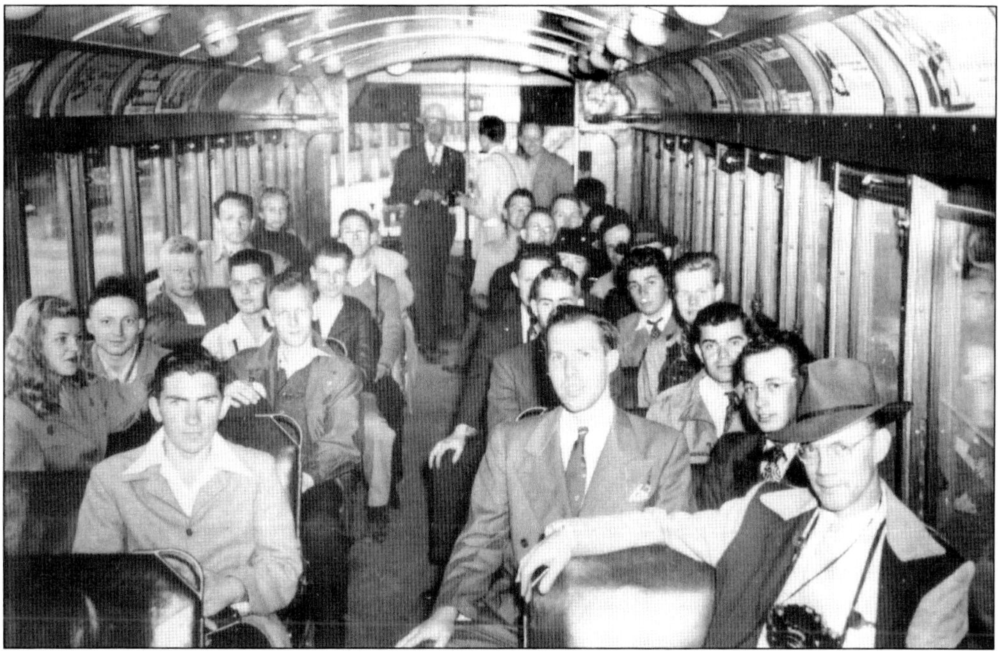

Would you believe 29 men but just one woman? Portland Traction Company assistant general superintendent Phil Adams has joined Bay Area Electric Railway Association traction enthusiasts aboard Indiana car No. 4004 for its 1947 fan trip. He is standing at the rear, wearing a hat. Longtime railfan and photographer Al Haij (in glasses) is sitting on the aisle in the next-to-last row on the right side of the car.

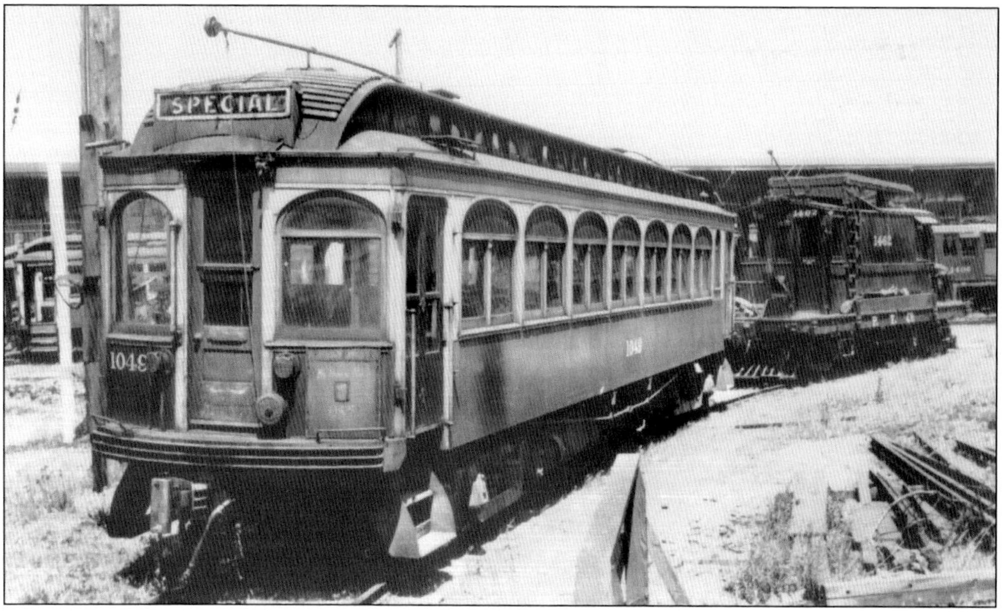

How the mighty have fallen. In 1937, former Mount Hood Railway No. 1125 was converted into wrecker No. 1049, becoming the second car to be assigned that number. But, as can be seen in this photograph taken in East Portland during the Portland Traction Company years, the car was still beautiful. In the background are tower car No. 1462, which was retired in 1940, and steeplecab No. 1406.

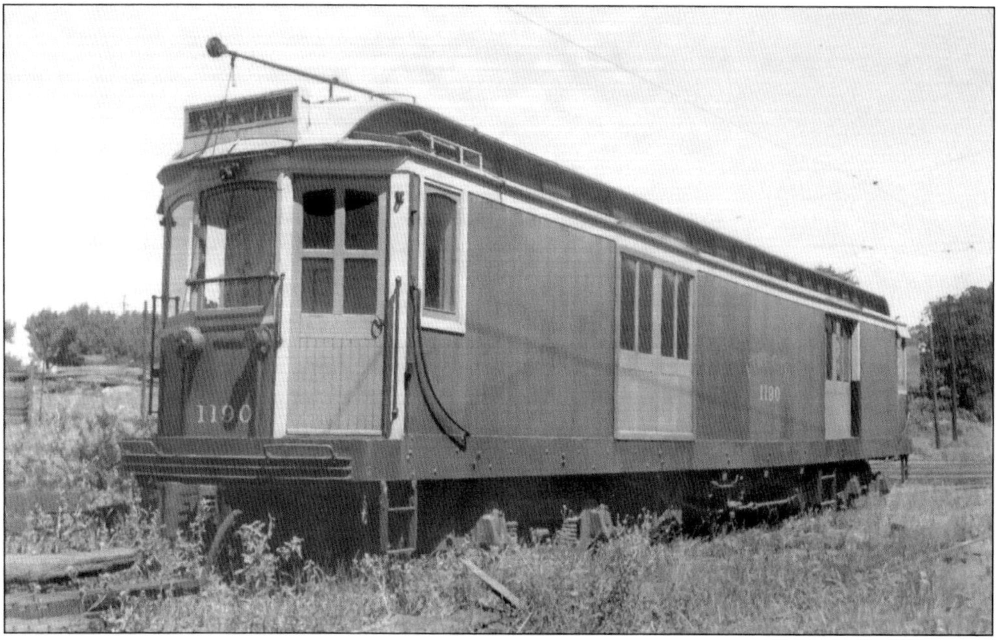

After retirement from passenger service, some interurbans were saved as work cars. In 1937, No. 1190 became a fire car. A large tank was placed inside the one-time Mount Hood Railway mail and express car. Although there were seldom fires to put out, notes kept by PTC superintendent of equipment Earl B. Richardson indicate that the car was also used for spraying weeds along the right-of-way. Final retirement for this car came in 1951.

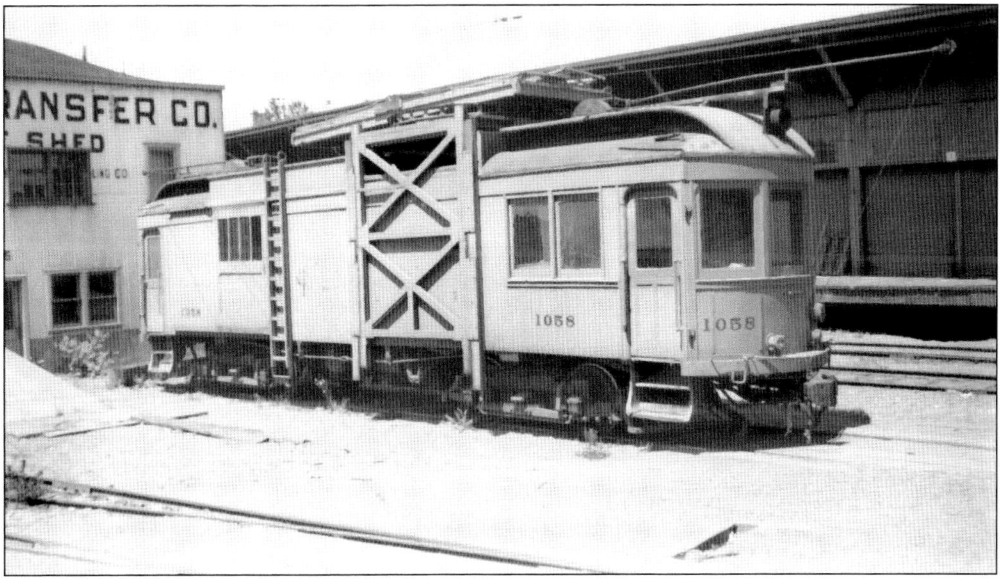

No. 1058 is seen in the East Portland Yard during the final years of PTC operation. The once-attractive interurban had been converted into an overhead line repair car in 1929. Its 22 cross-bench seats were replaced by wire storage bins, and a tower was installed. The 1903 vintage Niles car survived in this new capacity until 1958, when it was bought by Bob Hively in Washington State.

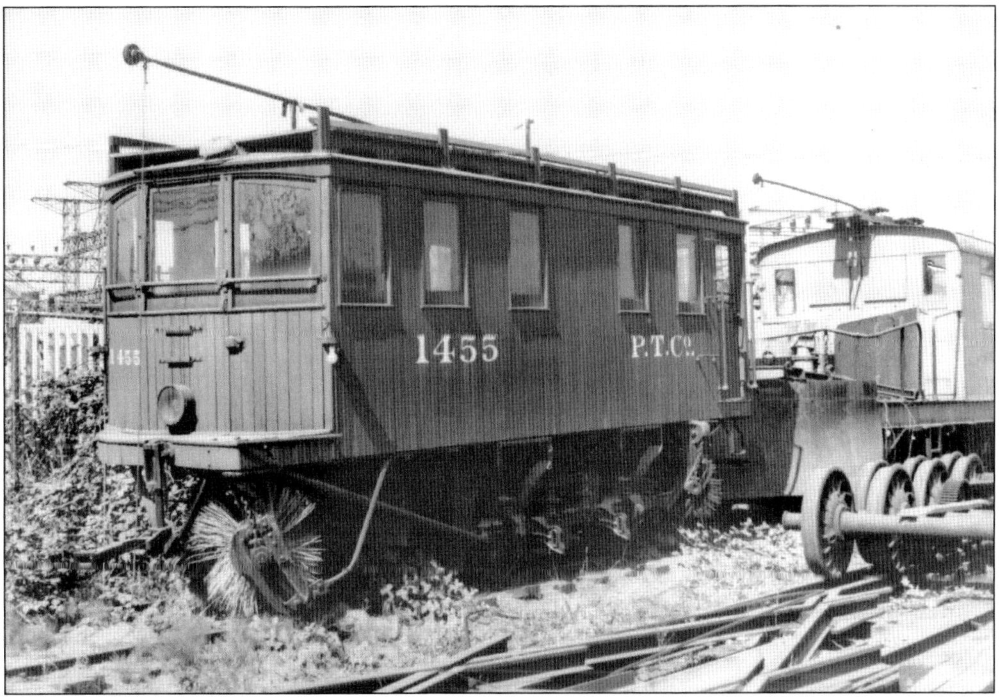

No. 1455 deserves mention as the oldest surviving vehicle from the nation's first interurban railway. It is a snow plow built by McGuire in 1899. After official retirement in 1940, it was stored in the East Portland Yard, shown here, and remained available for service. "The Broom" was last used for snow removal in January 1954 and is now part of the Oregon Electric Railway Historical Society collection in Brooks, Oregon.

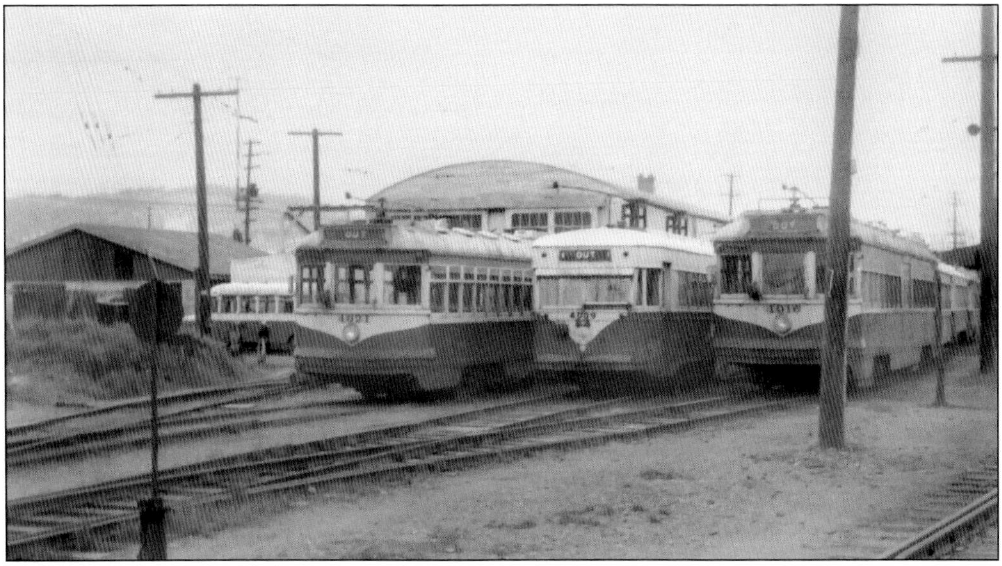

Three strikes and you're out. Shown here from left to right, cars No. 4021, No. 4009, and No. 4016 display roll signs ironically set to "OUT" (meaning out of service) as they languish in front of the East Portland carbarn in 1958 after it was all over. Of the last 15 passenger cars in the PTC yard, eight were saved from the scrapper's torch, including "Yak" No. 4009 seen here. (Photograph Jack Holst.)

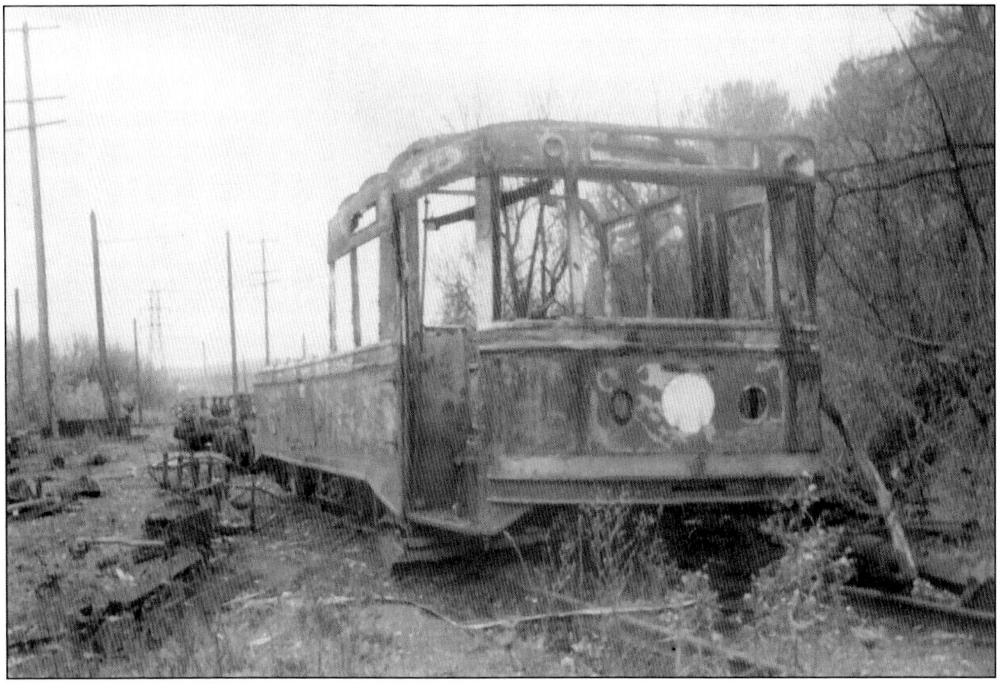

This is the fate that awaited most of Portland's streetcars and interurbans. "Broadway" car No. 4014, whose conversion to standard-gauge for interurban operation had not been successful, is seen here on the rip track in East Portland after having been burned for scrap metal. Fortunately, sister car No. 4012 was saved and can be seen at the Oregon Electric Railway Historical Society's museum in Brooks, Oregon.

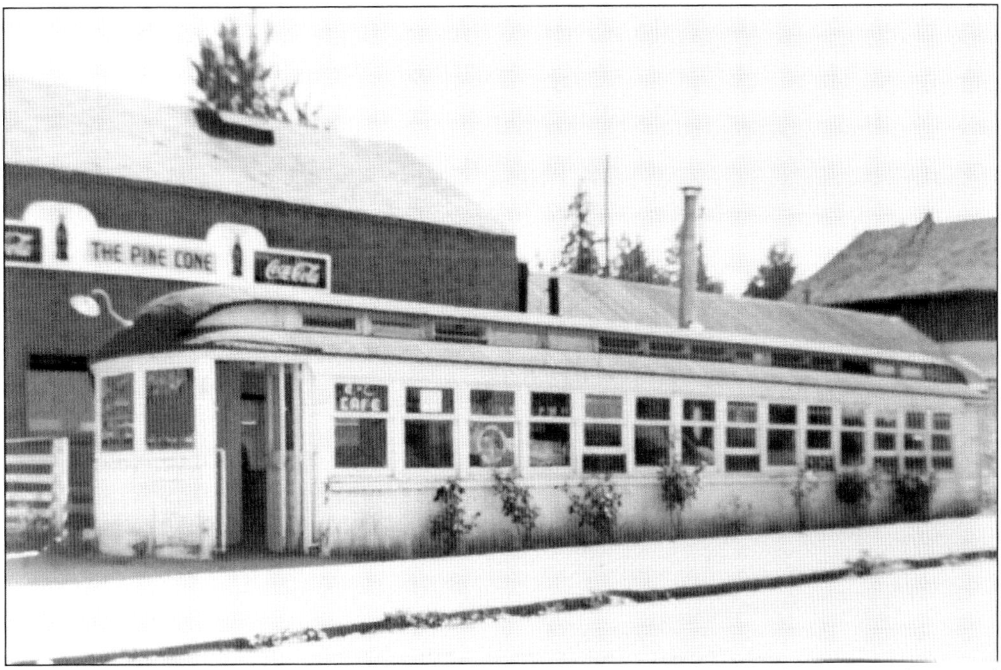

Car No. 1094 became a diner in Estacada. James West took this picture of the A&L Café around 1949. However, when he next visited Estacada, the diner was gone, apparently having been torn down. It was located next to the Pine Cone Tavern. On January 3, 1949, 13-year-old James rode sister car No. 1101 on the last trip to Gresham (see page 99). (Photograph James West.)

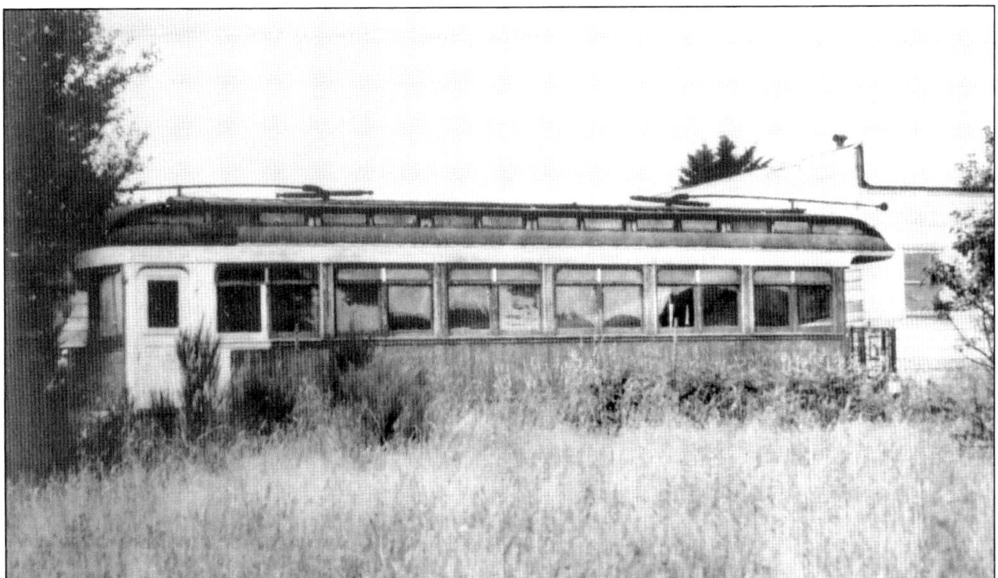
This picture shows car No. 1057 during its days as Edgar Zehrung's ill-fated House of Hobbies on Southeast Eighty-second Avenue. A 1940 fire destroyed the car and the hobby complex. No. 1057 had once been the proud parlor car *Portland*. When the 1903 Niles interurban was retired in 1937, sister car No. 1058 got a new lease on life as a line repair car.

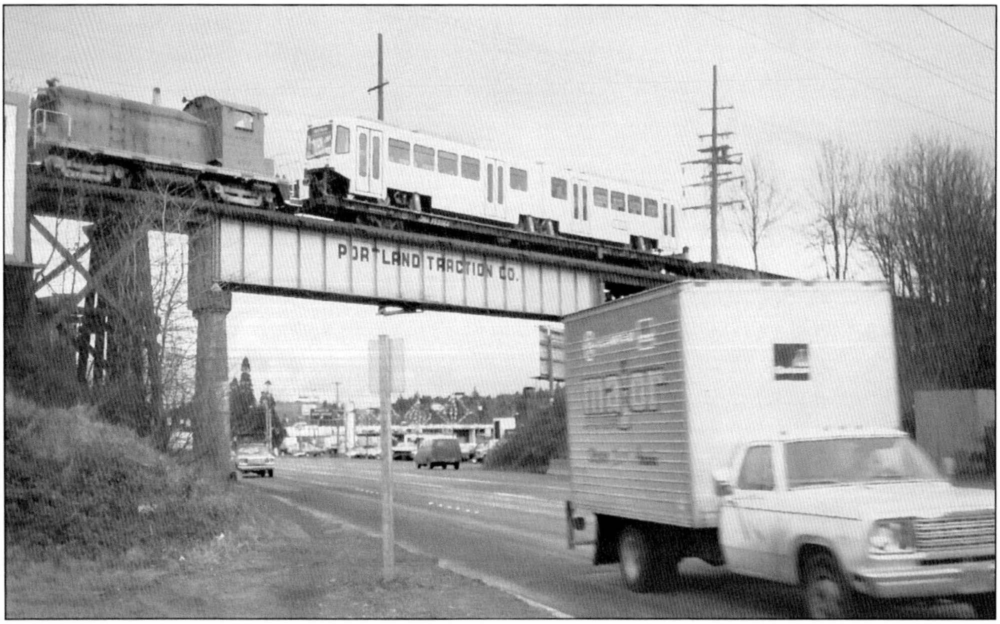

In 1984, Portland's transit agency, Tri-Met, began to take delivery of a new generation of interurbans known as "light-rail vehicles." PTC switcher No. 200 hauls a flatcar carrying new Bombardier LRV 108 across the bridge over McLoughlin Boulevard on February 20, 1985. Fittingly, delivery to the Ruby Junction carbarn was on interurban tracks used until 1949, during the final years of passenger service to Gresham. (Photograph Steve Morgan.)

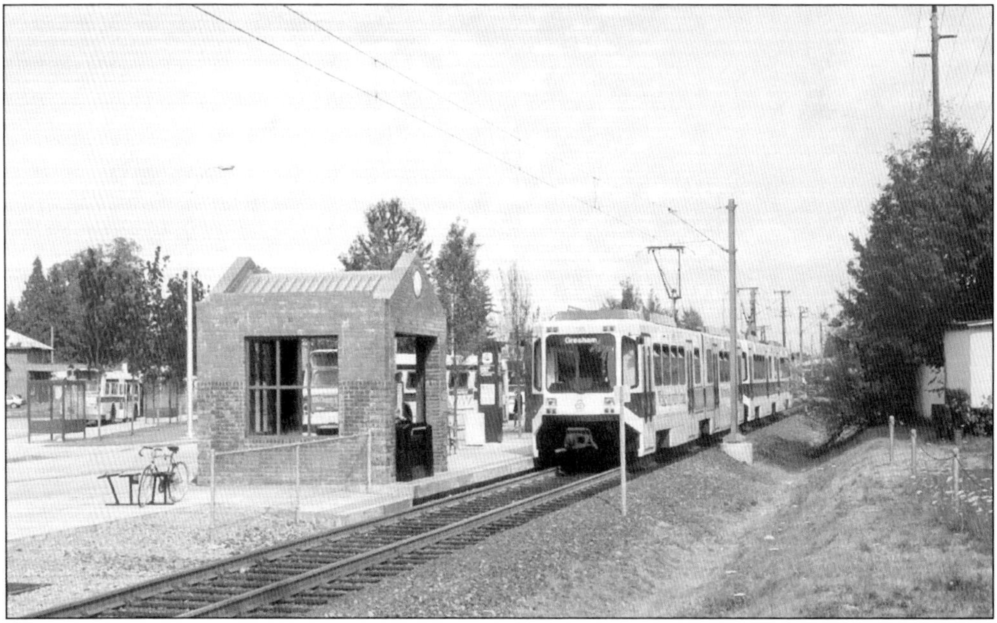

The opening of the first MAX light-rail line in 1986 brought interurban service back to Gresham after a 37-year absence, on the same right-of-way that had been used in the last years of PTC's Gresham service. This 1987 photograph looking east from Hood Avenue shows an eastbound MAX train at Gresham Central Station. PTC's station had been located on the other side of Hood Avenue. (Photograph Steve Morgan.)

INDEX

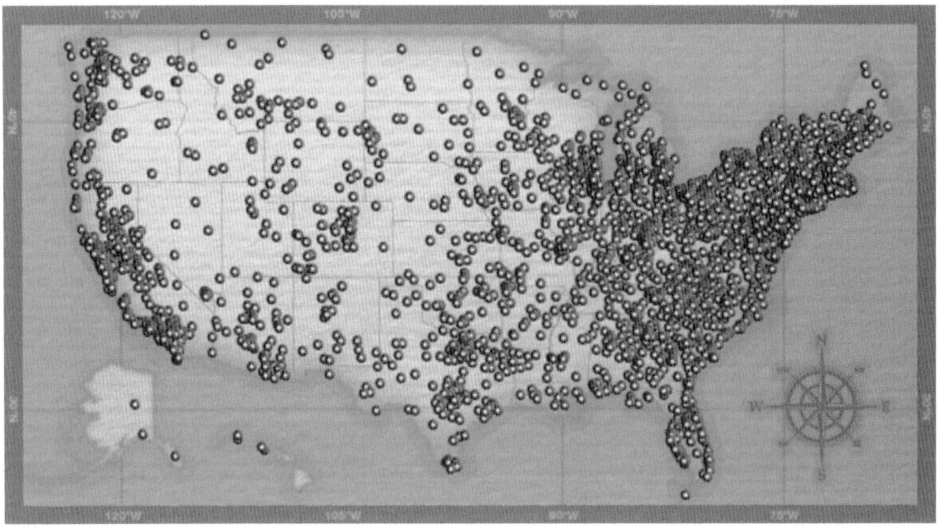